Mothers and Daughters

Mothers and Daughters

*Connection, Empowerment,
and Transformation*

edited by
Andrea O'Reilly
and
Sharon Abbey

ROWMAN & LITTLEFIELD PUBLISHERS, INC.
Lanham • Boulder • New York • Oxford

ROWMAN & LITTLEFIELD PUBLISHERS, INC.

Published in the United States
by Rowman & Littlefield Publishers, Inc.
4720 Boston Way, Lanham, Maryland 20706
http://www.rowmanlittlefield.com

12 Hid's Copse Road, Cumnor Hill, Oxford OX2 9JJ, England

British Library Cataloguing in Publication Information Available

Library of Congress Cataloging-in-Publication Data

Mothers and daughters : connection, empowerment, and transformation / edited
by Andrea O'Reilly and Sharon Abbey.
    p.   cm.
    Includes bibliographical references and index.
    ISBN 0-8476-9486-0 (alk. paper)—ISBN 0-8476-9487-9 (pbk. : alk. paper)
       1. Mothers and daughters.   2. Motherhood.   3. Mothers and daughters in
literature.   I. O'Reilly, Andrea, 1961–   II. Abbey, Sharon.
HQ755.86.M67   2000
306.874'3—dc21   99-045590

Printed in the United States of America

♾ ™ The paper used in this publication meets the minimum requirements of
American National Standard for Information Sciences—Permanence of Paper for
Printed Library Materials, ANSI/NISO Z39.48-1992.

There is an unsung woman
in all of our beginnings
Dark as the womb
Unknown as the other
side of the moon
Unseen as the roots of an ancient tree
and just as basic
She held us before we had words
She nursed us before we knew
our body from hers
Her song stirs us deep
in the cave of our dreams
Lullaby of the first cry
Lullaby of the last sigh
    of our lives
    She is the most loved woman
    She is the most feared woman
and we name her our mother
and we name her our grandmother
and we name her the Great Mother
and we name her ourselves.

            —Naomi Ruth Lowinsky

Contents

Acknowledgments

We would like to thank the many people at the Center for Feminist Research at York University who helped make possible the conference from which this volume was developed, including Brenda Cranny, Jaskiran Dhillon, Cheryl Dobinson, Lara Karaian, Charlene Kish, Lisa Rundle, Lily Gilbert, and Marlene Richman. In particular, we owe the deepest appreciation to Dr. Nancy Mandell, former director of the Center for Feminist Research; her unfailing commitment and support made the conference vision a reality. We also thank the Social Science and Humanities Research Council of Canada for their financial assistance for the conference. We are grateful to Rowman & Littlefield and our editors Rebecca Hoogs, Christine Gatliffe, Janice Braunstein, and Laura Larson for their sustaining belief in this project. Finally, we are deeply indebted to Jennifer Conner, Andrea O'Reilly's research assistant, for her work in preparing the manuscript. Words cannot adequately convey our appreciation for her tireless devotion to this project; through meticulous attention to detail and incisive suggestions she created order from chaos. Special thanks to Jenn, an emerging feminist intellectual, respected colleague, and always a close Daughter-friend.

We also want to acknowledge our families for their encouragement, support, and commitment to our feminist mothering, in both theory and practice. Andrea O'Reilly gives special thanks to Terry Conlin, her common-law spouse of seventeen years; his feminist parenting, in both word and deed, has made mothering enjoyable and writing possible. Most of all, Andrea O'Reilly would like to thank her children Jesse, Erin, and Casey O'Reilly-Conlin; although quite young, they have graciously accepted that books and a computer are a normal part of mothering. Sharon Abbey would like to thank her husband Fred for giving her wings, and her children Hilary and Graham for giving her a reason to fly.

This book is dedicated to our daughters:

To Hilary Jo-Ann: You are a child of the universe and together we will always be part of its great unfolding. Continue to trust your heart and believe in your dreams.

And to Erin and Casey O'Reilly-Conlin, who are my inspiration: Casey and Erin—in love, joy, admiration, and trust—I dedicate this book to you. As you stand at the threshold of womanhood, you model, in your courage and compassion, your wisdom and wit, your confidence and connectedness, both the achievements of feminism and its future possibilities. Our relationship and both of you, Casey and Erin, bear testimony to the power of connection to empower women and transform the world we live in.

PERMISSIONS

For chapter 1, "Mothers at Work" by Elizabeth Bourque Johnson:

Excerpts from *Mama*. Copyright © 1987 by Terry McMillan. Reprinted by permission of Houghton Mifflin Co. All rights reserved.

Excerpts from *The Bingo Palace*. Copyright © 1994 by Louise Erdrich. Reprinted by permission of HarperCollins Inc.

Excerpts from *Love Medicine*. Copyright © 1984 by Louise Erdrich. Reprinted by permission of Henry Holt and Company, Inc.

Excerpts from *The Dollmaker*. Copyright © 1954 by Harriette Simpson Arnow, renewed 1982 by Harriette Simpson Arnow. Reprinted by permission of Simon & Schuster.

Excerpts from *The Joy Luck Club*. Copyright © 1989 by Amy Tan. Reprinted by permission of Putnam Berkley, a division of Penguin Putnam Inc.

For chapter 3, "Never One without the Other" by María-José Gámez-Fuentes:

Excerpts from "Du su ventana a la mí" by Carmen Martín Gaite. Reprinted by permission of Anagrama.

Excerpts from "Primer amor" by Cristina Peri Rossi. Reprinted by permission of Anagrama.

Excerpts from "Al colegio" by Carmen Laforet. Reprinted by permission of and copyright © by the Carmen Balcells Literary Agency.

For chapter 4, "Journeying Back to Mother" by Cath Stowers:

Excerpts from the works of Michèle Roberts by permission of the author.

For chapter 5, "Bitches with Broomsticks" by Susan MacCallum-Whitcomb:

Excerpts from *The Complete Poems of Anne Sexton*. Copyright © 1981 by Linda Gray Sexton and Loring Conant, Jr., executors of the will of Anne

Sexton. Reprinted by permission of Houghton Mifflin Co. All rights reserved.

Excerpts from *Anne Sexton: A Self-Portrait in Letters* edited by Linda Gray Sexton and Lois Ames. Copyright © 1977 by Linda Gray Sexton and Loring Conant, Jr., executors of the will of Anne Sexton. Reprinted by permission of Houghton Mifflin Co. All rights reserved.

The line from "Hunger," from *The Dream of a Common Language: Poems 1974–1977* by Adrienne Rich. Copyright © 1978 by W. W. Norton & Company, Inc. Reprinted by permission of the author and W. W. Norton & Company, Inc.

Excerpt from "Mother/Child" from *The Mother/Child Papers* by Alicia Ostriker. Boston: Beacon Press, 1986. Reprinted by permission of the author.

Anne Stevenson. "Generations" from *Selected Poems, 1956–1986*. New York: Oxford University Press, 1987. Reprinted by permission of Oxford University Press.

Margaret Atwood. "Solstice Poem" from *Two-Headed Poems*. Toronto: Oxford University Press, 1978. Reprinted by permission of Oxford University Press.

For chapter 6, "Rewriting 'Cinderella'" by Jeanne Wiley:

Excerpts from "Ashputtle *or* the Mother's Ghost: Three Versions of One Story" from *Angela Carter: Burning Your Boats—The Collected Short Stories* (New York: Penguin, 1995). Copyright © 1995 by the estate of Angela Carter. Reprinted by permission of the estate of the author c/o Rogers, Coleridge & White Ltd., 20 Powis Mews, London W11 1JN.

For chapter 9, "'I come from a long line of Uppity Irate Black Women'" by Andrea O'Reilly:

Excerpts from "Family Tree" by Kate Rushin from *Double Stitch: Black Women Write about Mothers and Daughters*, Patricia Bell-Scott et al., eds. (New York: HarperPerennial, 1993). Reprinted with permission.

Excerpt from "Hush. Mama's Gotta Go Bye-Bye" by Renita Weems from *Double Stitch: Black Women Write about Mothers and Daughters*, Patricia Bell-Scott et al., eds. (New York: HarperPerennial, 1993). Reprinted by permission of the author.

Mothers and Daughters

Introduction

Andrea O'Reilly and Sharon Abbey

"The cathexis between mother and daughter—essential, distorted, mis-used," wrote Adrienne Rich in 1976, "is the great unwritten story."[1] In the nearly quarter century since the publication of *Of Woman Born*, there has been a virtual groundswell of interest in the mother-daughter rela-tion. As early as 1981, Marianne Hirsch observed in her review of feminist mother and daughter literature that "[since] Rich demonstrated the ab-sence of mother-daughter relationship [in mainstream scholarship] many voices have come to fill this gap, to create speech and meaning where there has been silence and absence."[2] The proliferation of mother and daughter studies continues to this day; dozens upon dozens of books, ar-ticles, and narratives, particularly in the field of pop psychology, have been written on this subject, and mothers and daughters have become the mainstay of daytime talk shows and TV miniseries. However, as the mother and daughter relationship has captured the minds and hearts of journalists and academics alike, few have examined the specific ways in which this relationship is both experienced and represented as a site of empowerment in women's lives and stories.

In response to both Rich's lament twenty-five years earlier and the puz-zling silence around mother/daughter empowerment, the Center for Feminist Research at York University, Toronto, Ontario, hosted the inter-national conference "Mothers and Daughters: Moving into the Next Mil-lennium," in September 1997, attended by more than 150 speakers from around the world. The overwhelming response to the conference demon-strated the compelling need for women to come together and share their experiences, insights, and concerns about mothers and daughters. This volume draws together the collective voices of twenty-one women schol-ars who participated in this first international conference on mothers and daughters. With this collection we hope to expand and enrich, honor and

1

highlight, this new and burgeoning field of feminist inquiry by examining the theme of mother-daughter connection, empowerment, and transformation.

The loss of the daughter to the mother, the mother to the daughter, is the "essential female tragedy," writes Rich. "We acknowledge Lear (father-daughter split), Hamlet (son and mother), and Oedipus (son and mother) as great embodiments of the human tragedy, but there is no presently enduring recognition of mother-daughter passion and rupture."[3] Rich goes on to acknowledge that the mother-daughter bond was historically once recognized and celebrated in the ancient Elyeusis rites of Demeter and Persephone. This book may be read as a modern rendition of this ancient myth in that it foregrounds mother-daughter connection and examines how such identification empowers mothers and daughters alike and gives rise to the transformation of patriarchal culture. The volume is divided into four sections that represent the central topics or stages in this connection-empowerment-transformation trajectory. From various standpoints, literature, film, narrative, theory, as well as psychoanalysis, philosophy and psychology, the contributors explore how maternal stories, the motherline, gynocentric mothering, and feminist socialization foster and sustain mother-daughter connectedness that make possible personal empowerment and cultural transformation.

The mother and daughter relationship has been a salient issue in feminist scholarship since at least the late 1970s; only recently however has the intention of this literature been to investigate the linkages among mother-daughter connection, female power, and social change. In the 1970s, mother-daughter connectedness was seldom a topic of inquiry; when it was examined, more often than not it was interpreted as occasioning gender difference, male dominance, and the continued devaluation of women.[4] Over the last decade the mother-daughter relationship has gained prominence in maternal scholarship, and increasingly feminists, both lay and academic, have linked female power to mother-daughter relationality. The recent interest in mothers and daughters stems, in part, from the growing realization among feminists that our adolescent daughters are in trouble. Groundbreaking studies, such as *Meeting at the Crossroads* by Lyn Mikel Brown and Carol Gilligan, and best-sellers such as *Reviving Ophelia: Saving the Selves of Adolescent Girls* by Mary Pipher, *Celebrating Girls: Nurturing and Empowering Our Daughters* by Virginia Beane Rutter, attest to the loss of the female selfhood in adolescence: they argue as well that a close and vital mother-daughter connection is essential for female adolescent empowerment. Mothers, writes Pipher, must "strengthen girls, guide and protect them";[5] Rutter emphasizes, in turn, that mothers need to nurture girls' self-esteem by affirming and celebrating the feminine in everyday practice and ritual, to allow girls to claim power and gain self-worth in and through their female identity. Strong mother-daughter connection, these writers conclude, is what makes possible a strong female self. The concern among feminists then becomes how best to secure and sustain this connection.

This book continues and expands this ongoing feminist conversation about connection and empowerment. It does so in several ways. First, it revisits this theme from the perspective of adult women as well as adolescent girls; mothers, as well as daughters, are empowered through connection. Second, the connection-empowerment-transformation trajectory is mapped along various life paths to include differences of race, ethnicity, sexuality, age, class, religion, and nationality. Themes of disconnection as well as connection are also explored; as contributors imagine and investigate ways to foster mother-daughter bonding, they also identify and interrogate those cultural forces that seek to fracture this relationship. Literature and life, theory and practice are examined to give depth and breadth to this inquiry. Finally, the essays, both together and alone, confirm the centrality of mother-daughter connection to women's empowerment, not only because such enhances self-esteem, as the writers on adolescent girls have observed, but also because quite simply it unites women and identifies patriarchal culture and not each other as the "dragon to be slain."

Organizing the chapters of the book proved to be a difficult task because of the complex intertwining of the topics and issues raised. In the end, after many revisions, we decided on a thematic arrangement. The first section, "Mothers Telling Their Stories," foregrounds the centrality of maternal stories for women's empowerment, for both mother and daughter; "Dismantling Patriarchal Motherhood," the second section, emphasizes the importance of mothers defining for themselves their maternal experiences. The essays in the third part, "Empowering Daughters," seek to imagine and implement a truly feminist mode of raising empowered girls; while the final section, "Connecting/Disrupting the Motherline," locates the mother-daughter relation in the motherline and examines cultural forces that both sustain and sever herstorical identification.

MOTHERS TELLING THEIR STORIES

The transformation of mothering to effect change both inside and outside the home has been a concern of feminist theory and praxis over the last two decades; in addition, this aim informs most feminist thinking on the empowerment of girls. For daughters to be empowered through identification with mothers, mothers themselves must model strength and connection; they must, in other words, practice relational and resistant mothering. However, in patriarchal culture resistant mothering and mother-daughter relationality are, needless to say, regarded as subversive practices and hence condemned, curtailed, and censored. Speaking about African-American playwright Angelina Weld Grimke's play *Rachel*, but applicable generally to lived mother-daughter relationships, Elizabeth Brown-Guillory writes, "Mothers must tell their daughters the truth about the obstacles in the world which they will probably face and instruct them to survive with strength and dignity;[. . .] mothers must model for their daughters the various ways to reach inside to find courage to overcome race and gender barriers."[6] Given the patriarchal sanction against mother-daughter connection and feminist mothering, this modeling may be difficult to convey or decode. Therefore, as we struggle to model firsthand resistance and relationality, we must also represent them in narrative.

In *Writing a Woman's Life*, Carolyn Heilbrun observes:

> Lives do not serve as models, only stories do that. And it is a hard thing to make up stories to live by. We can only retell and live by stories we have heard. Stories have formed us all: they are what we must use to make new fictions and new stories.[7]

In earlier times the ancient lore of female talk was told around the village well or at the quilting bee; today "old wives' tales," or motherwit, is shared in written narratives. However, as Rich observed in 1976, there is a dearth of such stories. "We know more about the air we breath, the seas we travel," writes Rich, "than about the nature and meaning of motherhood."[8] "Motherhood," Marni Jackson explains in *The Mother Zone*, "is an unexplored frontier of thought and emotion that we've tried to tame with rules, myth and knowledge. But the geography remains unmapped."[9] "Motherhood may have become an issue," Jackson emphasizes, "but it's not yet a narrative."[10] Perhaps the maternal is, as Marianne Hirsch speculates in *Mother/Daughter Plot*, unnarratable: "Could it be," she asks, "that maternal discourse can exist . . . only on the condition that it remain fragmentary, incomplete and mediated through the perspective of the daughter-writer?"[11] "It is hard to speak precisely about mothering," as Sara Ruddick observes in *Maternal Thinking*. "Overwhelmed with greeting card sentiment we have no realistic language in which to capture the ordinary/extraordinary pleasures and pains of maternal work."[12] Maternal voices, Ruddick continues:

> have been drowned by professional theory, ideologies of motherhood, sexist arrogance, and childhood fantasy. Voices that have been distorted and cen-

sored can only be developing voices. Alternatively silenced and edging toward speech, mothers' voices are not voices of mothers as they are, but as they are becoming.[13]

Feminist writers and theorists today, while recognizing how difficult it is to speak that which has been censored, distorted, and silenced, seek to make the maternal story narratable.

Recent feminist preoccupation with maternal narrative results from the presupposition among writers on girls' empowerment that girls need to hear their mothers' stories in order to forge a strong mother-daughter bond. Elizabeth deBold, Marie Wilson, and Idelisse Malave in *Mother Daughter Revolution* suggest that the loss of female selfhood may be resisted, or at the very least negotiated, when the mother connects with the daughter through story. The mother, in recalling and sharing with her daughter her own narrative of adolescence, gives to her daughter strategies of struggle and hence constructs an alternative script of coming into womanhood. Spoken or written maternal narratives can model the resistance and relationality that may not be readily apparent or available in our lived lives. "Learning how to be daughters [however]," as Ruddick cautions, "includes learning how to expect and respect maternal thinking. And this means really listening when mothers speak."[14] For mothers as well, maternal narratives, both their own and those of contemporary or historical women, can enact the resistance mothers envision and seek to achieve. Stories, to paraphrase Heilbrun, are models to live by. Narration is also in itself a transgressive act; "speaking," as Ruddick explains, "changes the speaker."[15] African-American essayist and poet Audre Lorde once said, "We must name the nameless so that it can be thought."[16] Indeed, through narration mothers may name, claim, and transform their lived realities; and bequeath to daughters—and other mothers—a vision of emancipatory connectedness and care.

This vision is conveyed in the various narratives examined in part I. Based on Sara Ruddick's framework of maternal practice, Elizabeth Johnson, in the first essay of this section, examines literary texts that figure mothers as subjects of the narrative. Reading across a spectrum of North American subcultures of race, class, and ethnicity, the chapter locates commonalities and differences in maternal practice in order to identify and contextualize mothering in various conditions, while resisting an essential or universal definition. Reading the fiction from the perspective of Ruddick's three demands of mothering—preservation, nurturance, training—Johnson observes that mothers speaking as mothers is far more prevalent in marginalized cultures than it is in white middle-class society. She speculates, on the one hand, that the stories of privileged mothers may not be as noteworthy or as interesting as the stories of mothers who struggle for basic survival. On the other had, this tendency may also result from the belief among white middle-class mothers that their lives should remain private. When they do write, white middle-class mothers focus on the struggle for identity within the institution of motherhood rather than on their work with children. The novels studied by Johnson, in narrating the work that mothers do from the perspective of the mothers, convey the maternal stories that are essential for empowerment.

The second chapter, "Restorying Jewish Mothers," by Janet Burstein examines how contemporary Jewish women recall, revision, and transform maternal constrictions of earlier decades to gain possession of their maternal stories so that they may be empowered by them. She emphasizes the importance of maternal stories for daughters and describes these stories as maternal gifts that capture for daughters the strategies that their mothers used for living and surviving. She points out that while the male narrative is based on guilt and rupture that necessitates killing the father, the female narrative is founded on continuing dialogue in which daughters become writers through identification with mothers. As Burstein explores how maternal connection for Jewish daughters enables them to conceive and convey themselves as subjects and writers, María-José Gámez-Fuentes, grounding her study in the work of French feminist thought, investigates how daughters form identity through reciprocal identification with their mothers—what Kristeva terms "permanent alteration," "never the one without the other," in contemporary Spanish women's writing. In opposition to the "official" discourse of motherhood that silences mothers and severs mother-daughter connection, the short stories examined by Fuentes in chapter 3 foreground the maternal voice and interweave the subjectivities of mother and daughter. As the one daughter poignantly concludes in the short story "First Love," "Not only have I grown up enough to reach her [my mother], but, sometimes, I am the mother and she is the daughter. This has been our particular way of changing men's law."

Cath Stowers, likewise, in "Journeying Back to Mother: Pilgrimages of Maternal Redemption in the Fiction of Michèle Roberts," explores how Roberts's fiction voices mothers' stories and offers alternative narrative structures to those of Oedipality. Examined also by Stowers is the way in which Roberts's novels fictionally represent the shifts in feminist thinking on motherhood, signified by rejection and return. Stowers concludes that, while Roberts's earlier works "otherized" the mother, as did feminism at the beginning of the second wave, her later works function as maternal narratives in their exploration of the meaning of the maternal body, acknowledgment of maternal experience, and finally in the portrayal of mother-daughter anger, themes that Marianne Hirsch argues signify maternal writing. As with the women writers examined by Johnson,

Burstein, and Gámez-Fuentes, Stowers in chapter 4 envisions maternal re-demption, reparation, and resistance.

DISMANTLING PATRIARCHAL MOTHERHOOD

In *Of Woman Born,* Adrienne Rich makes a clear distinction between two meanings of motherhood: "the potential relationship of any woman to her powers of reproduction and to children, and the institution, which aims at ensuring that that potential—and all women—shall remain under male control."[17] In this book we use the terms *motherhood* to refer to the institution of motherhood that is male-defined and -polarized and *mothering* to refer to experiences of mothering that are female-defined and -centered. According to Rich, the reality of patriarchal motherhood contradicts the possibility of gynocentric mothering, limits female potentiality, and alienates women from their own bodies. As a result, throughout history and across cultures most women mother according to the prescribed institution of motherhood; that is, women's mothering practices and identities are defined and controlled by the larger patriarchal society in which they live. Mothers don't make the rules, Rich emphasizes—they simply enforce them. Sara Ruddick adds that mothers "relinquish authority to others, [and] lose confidence in their own values."[18] Consequently, mothers who identify with the institution of motherhood and fail to question it often raise daughters to conform to these same patriarchal structures.

Feminists recognize that such mother-daughter socialization often results in practices of mother blame, devaluation of motherhood, fear of maternal power, daughter centricity, and untimely disconnections. As a result, daughters may feel a sense of resentment toward the powerlessness, compromise, and inauthenticity they see in their mothers. Rich calls this split between mothers and daughters matrophobia—the fear of becoming one's mother. Paula Caplan argues that this type of mother blame is rampant in contemporary culture. In fact, the institution of motherhood encourages daughters to feel this way.

However, in spite of such societal scripts and imposed patriarchal values, some mothers and daughters have developed strategies of resistance and a politic of empowerment. This section of the book examines some of the strategies used to transcend stereotypes, including the use of alternative fictional characterizations of the mother figure, historical caricatures, and cultural images, as well as autobiographical accounts of diverse intersections of race, class, gender, and sexuality.

Beginning with "Bitches with Broomsticks: The Bad Mother in American Maternity Poetry," Susan MacCallum-Whitcomb focuses on the post–

World War II period when the psychological discourse of the good mother was established. During this era, mothers were condemned for failing to live up to an unrealistic set of ideal standards. MacCallum-Whitcomb draws parallels between these maternal criticisms and the persecution of women during the witch hunts two centuries earlier, pointing out that many women writers of that time used the persona of the witch in their work. Through the imagery of the witch, these poets attempt to disrupt the assumptions of the institution of motherhood. According to the poet and theorist Alicia Ostriker, the image of the good mother in our culture is "selfless, cheerful and deodorized."[19] In contrast, by introducing the complex figure of the witch-mother, these poets transcend stereotypes and also confront the darker side of mothering—fear, anger, violence, alienation, and erotic pleasure—emphasizing her potential to be both death dealing and life affirming. MacCallum-Whitcomb concludes that the authentic vision of motherhood these writers offer is both welcome and necessary.

In the next chapter, "Rewriting 'Cinderella': Envisioning the Empowering Mother-Daughter Romance," Jeanne Wiley uses a traditional folktale to critique the silencing, mutilation, and subjugation of maternal agency in the socialization of children. She recounts the story of mothers who are either cruel and repressive in relation to daughters (stepmothers) or mystified and instrumental in service to their daughters' subject formation and conscription into patriarchal society (fairy godmothers). Through her analysis of the writing of Angela Carter and Marianne Hirsch, this essay explores an alternative to these disempowering mother figures and intersubjective relationships in order to assess and articulate the image of an enabling and reciprocal mother-daughter dyad that is potentially transformative. Wiley emphasizes the need to carefully scrutinize the stories we tell to our children.

Andrea Doucet and Gillian Dunne move the debate about essentialism and the social construction of motherhood from literary critiques to real-life experiences in the next chapter, "Heterosexual and Lesbian Mothers Challenging 'Feminine' and 'Masculine' Concepts of Mothering." Drawing on their qualitative research and their interpretation of mothers' lives, these authors explore the diverse intersections of gender and sexuality as expressed by women who attempt either to equitably share child rearing with their male partners or to mother with other women in order to dismantle patriarchal motherhood. Doucet and Dunne conclude that mothers hold on to the overall care and responsibility for young children as a form of resistance against the still-hegemonic masculine discourse of separation, disconnection, and autonomy. They recognize both economic independence as well as emotional interdependence in their attempt to balance work and home life.

This section of the book concludes with Ivy Schweitzer's chapter, "The Mammy and the Mummy: Cultural Imaginary and Interracial Coalition." In this essay, Schweitzer argues that historically, motherhood has been an arena for cross-race and cross-class solidarity. To this end, she studies the two pervasive caricatures of black and white women that come down from the period of slavery in America: the black mammy and her privileged counterpart, the white mummy. Because these cultural images are so intermeshed and interdependent, Schweitzer argues that we must dismantle both symbolic constructs simultaneously.

Schweitzer points out that the importance of this double deconstruction is illustrated in the enigmatic first chapter of Alice Walker's novel *Meridian* and in Adrienne Rich's accounts of her black nanny in *Of Woman Born*. Schweitzer argues that the manufactured image of the mammy as desexualized, loyal, and loving actually reveals more about the sexual tension within the white culture that invented her than it does about historical reality. Such stereotypes also serve to substantiate the equally corrosive myth of the white woman's frailty, purity, and dependent nature. Schweitzer concludes that, in the end, the historical separation of women based on race and class also serves to separate all women from themselves.

EMPOWERING DAUGHTERS

"What do we mean by the nurture of our daughters?" asks Rich. "What is it we wish we had, or could have, as daughters; could give, as mothers?"[20]

> Deeply and primarily we need trust and tenderness—surely this will always be true of every human being. But women growing up in a world so hostile to us need a very profound kind of loving in order to learn to love ourselves. But this loving is not simply the old institutionalized, sacrificial "mother love" which men have demanded; we want courageous mothering. The most notable fact that culture imprints on women is the sense of our limits. The most important thing one woman can do for another is to illuminate and expand the sense of actual possibilities. For a mother, this means more than contending with reductive images of females in children's books. It means that the mother herself is trying to expand the limits of her life. *To refuse to be a victim;* and then to go on from there.[21]

The empowerment of daughters thus depends on the deconstruction of patriarchal motherhood discussed in the previous section. Writing of lesbian mothering in *Politics of the Heart,* Baba Cooper describes "radical mothers [as] involving children in disloyalty to the culture that the mother is expected to transmit at the expense of woman-bonding and female empowerment."[22] Mother-daughter empowerment depends on mothers living, in the words of Mary Kay Blakely, as "'outlaws from the institution of motherhood' as Adrienne Rich described those who drift—or flee—from traditional roles and expectations."[23] This gynocentric mothering nurtures the power of the mother's female self and that of her daughter. Whether it be termed courageous mothering, as Rich described it, or radical mothering as defined by Cooper, this practice of mothering calls for the empowerment of daughters and mothers and recognizes that the former is only possible with the latter. As Judith Arcana concludes: "If we want girls to grow into free women, brave and strong, we must be those women ourselves."[24] What the mother models for her daughters is therefore not necessarily success but struggle: an everyday lived resistance to the world that seeks to claim and control mothers and their daughters, a Demeter who rages, revenges, and reclaims the loss of her daughter to patriarchy.

Mother-daughter connection, as examined in part I, is at the heart of emancipatory care and, like radical mothering, is essential for empowering daughters, particularly in adolescence. Adolescent girls' well-being, according to Carol Gilligan and Mary Pipher among others, hinges on their connection with their mothers. However, Western culture in general, and normative psychological theory in particular, mandate separation from parents in adolescence to enable the merging adult to achieve an autonomous sense of self. Recent feminist writers on adolescent girls' empowerment, most notably Elizabeth deBold, Marie Wilson, and Idelisse Malave in *Mother-Daughter Revolution,* call into question this sacred cow of developmental theory—the equivalency of separation and autonomy—and argue that it constitutes a betrayal of both mothers and daughters. They explain:

> Separation and autonomous are not equivalent: a person need not separate from mothers emotionally to be autonomous. Under the domain of experts, mothers are urged to create a separation and disconnection from daughters that their daughters do not want. Early childhood and adolescence are the two stages of life where separation has been decreed as imperative to the independence and autonomy of children. To mother "right," women disconnect from their daughters and begin to see them as society will. Rather than strengthen girls, this breach of trust leaves girls weakened and adrift.[25]

What is most disturbing about this pattern of separation and betrayal is its timing. "In childhood," they write, "girls have confidence in what they know, think and feel."[26] With the onset of adolescence, girls between the ages of nine and twelve come up against what they call the wall. "The wall is our patriarchal culture that values women less than men. . . . To get through the wall, girls have to give up parts of themselves to be safe and accepted within society."[27] Daughters are thus abandoned by their mothers when they need them the most. Central to *Mother-Daughter Revolution* is the belief that mothers can aid daughters in their resistance to the wall. The key to the mother's resistance is the reclamation of her own girl self:

> If mothers decide to join with daughters who are coming of age as women, mothers first must reclaim what they themselves have lost. Reclaiming is the first step in women's joining girls' resistance to their own dis-integration. Reclaiming is simply a process of discovering, describing and reappropriating the memories and feelings of our preadolescent selves.[28]

This reclamation empowers the mother and enables her to aid the daughter in her resistance. Emancipatory mothering and relationality are explored in the first three chapters of this section. Drawing on contemporary African-American feminist theory, O'Reilly, in the first essay of this section, details a specific philosophy and practice of mothering that is distinctly different from the dominant Anglo-American discourse on mothering. She goes on to explore how this Afrocentric model of mothering empowers women and creates a concept of motherhood that is empowering to the daughters of these women. African-American daughters, contends O'Reilly, achieve agency, authority, and authenticity through connection with their mothers, and this is because motherhood itself operates as a site of power for mothers in African-American culture. Deborah Orr in "Mothers as Moral Educators: Teaching Language and Nurturing Souls" argues that the work of Carol Gilligan in moral philosophy and Wittgenstein in the philosophy of language move us toward a restoration of the mother to her rightful place as moral educator in the lives of her children. Mothers, according to Orr, socialize their children to be moral subjects largely though the language games they engage in with their children when they are young. From these practices, children develop what Orr terms a soul that becomes the model for their later-developed moral ethos, defined by Orr as "the spiritual erotic of generative love." "The power and the ethical import of mothering," writes Orr, "lie in the ability of actual mothers to nurture complete human souls and to teach both their daughters and sons to insist on the expression of their full humanity."

As Orr examines the transformative impulse of "moral" mothering, Barbara Turnage, in her chapter "The Global Self-Esteem of an African-American Adolescent Female and Her Relationship with Her Mother," explores the radicalizing power of mother-daughter connection for adolescent African-American girls. Turnage's research examines the interrelationships among the daughter's global self-esteem, ethnic identity, appearance evaluation, and trust of her mother. Turnage concludes that girls' relationships with their mothers have a direct bearing on their global self-esteem. Modeling and presenting empowering images of black womanhood, instilling a love for African-American-oriented features, and demonstrating the capacity to cope with adversity, African-American mothers prepare their daughters to enter society with a positive self-esteem. The significance of this research, Turnage emphasizes, cannot be overstated: "These girls, as they grow into Black womanhood, grow with the knowledge that they can accomplish their goals, that they are worthy of love and respect." Certainly a lesson to live by.

Education is another central theme in the feminist literature on the empowerment of daughters. Girls' education has become the topic of the 1990s; study after study has shown conclusively and alarmingly that, to paraphrase the title of Myra and David Sadker's book on the subject matter, education is failing at fairness; schools are cheating girls.[29] Sadkers' book, *School Girls* by Peggy Orenstein, and *The Difference* by Judith Mann, all published in 1994, confirm what most of us, and particularly what girls, already knew: there is a glaring gender bias in education. "From grade school through graduate school," write Myra and David Sadker, "female students are more likely to be invisible members of the classrooms. Teachers interact with males more frequently, ask them better questions, and give them more precise and helpful feedback."[30] The American Association of University Women national survey, discussed in *School Girls,* demonstrated, in Orenstein's words, that "for a girl, the passage into adolescence is marked by a loss of confidence in herself and her abilities, especially in math and science. It is marked by a scathingly critical attitude toward her body and a blossoming sense of personal inadequacy."[31] Overall female self-esteem in adolescence consistently ranked below that of boys'; however, the study found that far more African-American girls maintained their overall self-esteem in adolescence, retaining a stronger sense of both personal and familial worth. The reasons for this are investigated in Turnage's essay in this section.

Charting, challenging, and correcting this gender bias in education remains a priority among feminists. Moreover, feminists continue to be committed to female learning; as women lobby for increased educational opportunities for girls and women, they link empowerment to education. Significantly, Sherrie Inness opens her introduction to *Millennium Girls* with the disturbing statistic that only 68 percent of the world's girls have made it to fifth grade."[32] "Choice and economic independence are the foundations of women power," writes Mann, "hence they are the first crucial lessons in teaching our daughters girlpower."[33] And it is education, more often than not, that make choice and economic independence possible. This argument is made by Sue Marie Wright in "Educated Mothers as a Tool for Change: Possibilities and Constraints," the fourth chapter in this section. Based on a literature review of women's education and social conditions in eighteen nations, this essay explores the effects of culture and economic development on women's access to education, women's use of education as a resource, and the process of accelerated social change in terms of women's equality. Formal schooling, Wright contends, promotes equality and autonomy for most women, particularly as it is generationally reproduced in the socialization of daughters. However, in some of the more egalitarian, "non-Western" cultures—West African, Native American—education, Wright argues, works against female autonomy because, as part of Western colonization, it undercuts women's traditional economic role. Given this, Wright concludes that "women must be involved in development, especially education, in ways that ensure their economic and ideological autonomy."

Education—equal, accessible, and female defined—mother-daughter connectedness, and emancipatory mothering are recognized as essential for women's empowerment, for both mother and daughter. Integral to these objectives is a commitment to feminism. Feminism scripts and stages the empowerment explored in this section. Put simply, feminism makes possible the education and emancipatory mothering required for such empowerment. Less straightforward and less studied, however, is the relationship between feminism and mother-daughter connection. This inquiry informs and gives rise to a whole series of questions about the relationship between feminism and the mother-daughter relationship: What impact does feminism have on the mother-daughter relationship? How is feminism "passed down" generationally? How do daughters respond to their mothers' feminism and position themselves in relation to "The Movement"? What is the relationship between feminism and mothering? Finally, how does the mother-daughter relation—being a mother, having a daughter—reconfigure feminism? As the daughters of second-wave feminist mothers grow into adulthood, feminism has become increasingly concerned with such issues. Recent works such as *Daughters of Feminists* (1993) by Rose Glickman, *Feminist Mothering* (1990) by Tuula Gordon, and *The Conversation Begins: Mothers and Daughters Talk about Living Feminism* (1996) by Christina Looper Baker and Christine Baker Kline each, in its own way, examine the impact of feminism on the mother-daughter relationship. However, what is less examined by these authors is the relationship between feminism and mother-daughter connectedness; does feminism foster or forestall the mother-daughter relationality deemed essential for personal empowerment and social change? This question is explored in the two essays that conclude this section.

Christina Baker in "Telling Our Stories: Feminist Mothers and Daughters," the fifth chapter in this section, discusses the author's findings in her book *The Conversation Begins*. The book probes one of the most intimate and complicated relationships of a woman's life. Baker asked feminist pioneers of the second wave and their grown daughters to talk about their relationships as they attempt to live their feminism. In this chapter Baker examines the generational "passing down" of the feminist legacy and the "cost of combining motherhood with a career." Baker maintains that daughters overwhelmingly embraced their feminist inheritance. However, the second question proved to be far more complicated. Mothers and daughters alike expressed how difficult it was to combine motherhood with their feminist career. As Arlie Hochschild points out, "Feminism is infinitely easier when you take motherhood out but then it speaks to fewer women."[34] In "Biting the Hand That Feeds You: Feminism as the 'Bad Mother,'" the final essay of this section, Astrid Henry examines the writings of what is being termed "the third wave." This chapter explores how the mother-daughter relationship has become a central trope in depicting the generational structure between second and third waves of U.S. feminism, based as it is on an age difference that is equivalent of one generation. The authors examined include Rene Denefield, Kate Rophie, Rebecca Walker, and Naomi Wolf. Henry argues that young women today see feminism, in her words, as their "birthright," something that is inherited as opposed to created, as it was with the older generation of feminists. While these women identify with their own flesh and blood mothers and regard them as "good" mothers, the movement of feminism itself is seen negatively and comes to represent the "bad" mother in the writings of these women. The need to distance themselves from mother feminism is understood and experienced as the process of individuation mandated by psychological theory. To become autonomous, these women believe they must make a "clean break" from the feminism of their mothers. The separation from the mother stipulated by psychoanalytic theory in this instance is enacted as a repudiation of second-wave feminism, suggesting that the "Movement" may function as an expendable stand-in for the "Mother." Be that as it may, these women sever the motherline to gain autonomy, while for most of the daughters, fictional or real, examined in this volume, connection to the motherline is what secures and sustains empowerment.

CONNECTING/DISRUPTING THE MOTHERLINE

This section begins with Jungian analyst Naomi Lowinsky's description of the primal experience of giving birth as the universal connection of the origin of all human life to the woman's body. Grounding her research in her own personal experience as a mother, Lowinsky positions her younger self in her children and her older self in her mother. Although the concept is elusive and hard to explain, she uses the term *motherline* to refer to the sacred experience of the embodied feminine mysteries when mother and daughter stand out of time in a moment of unspoken recognition as the life vessel. She also points out that these feminine mysteries are not honored in our culture and clash with societal views of mastery over nature. As such, mothers and daughters continually struggle with their bodily, generational, and emotional differences. Lowinsky argues that motherline stories will also encourage women to embrace a more healthy autonomous view of mothering than that used by the patriarchy, which restricts the sphere of women's experiences to little more than reproduction. By reclaiming our motherline stories, Lowinsky also believes women will heal the wounds of separation as we weave the body and psyche across the generations into one fabric again.

As a clinical psychologist and mother, Paula Caplan begins her essay with her own personal observations of how mothers are always held responsible for everyone else's problems. In her chapter, "Don't Blame Mother: Then and Now," she describes aspects of girls' and women's socialization that create or exacerbate problems between mothers and daughters as well as strategies used to repair these rifts. As Caplan explains, there are bad-mother myths that are used as evidence against mothers while their significant work and actions go unnoticed. There are also good-mother myths that set impossible standards to live up to. She argues that these myths, which are often mutually exclusive, are used to create scapegoat groups by the people in power. Caplan advises readers to expose these myths for what they are, using excerpts from a play script she has written as a way to disentangle the motherline and bring about such a confrontation.

In the next chapter, "Motherline Connections across Cultures and Generations," Sharon Abbey and Charlotte Harris question how prepared they are to pass on motherline stories to their daughters. Once again, these authors turn to their lived experiences growing up in their respective middle-class white and black communities to examine their own legacy of social constructions across four generations of women in their families. By reclaiming their maternal stories, Abbey and Harris came to realize that there is more diversity among generations of women than among their cultures. Each foremother, for example, made a dramatic change in the life she was raised to value—by leaving her homeland, by resisting religious and reproductive scripts, by acquiring an emancipatory education, or by breaking codes of silence and submissiveness. To pass on thoughtful and well-considered motherline stories to their daughters, Abbey and Harris now recognize that they must first look inward and deconstruct their own dominant ideologies and hegemonic discourses. Furthermore, they conclude that our assumptions about the values and insights we hand down to our daughters may, in fact, not be what we actually do pass on or should pass on. The motherline is an unfolding and emerging story that, in the end, each of us can only hope to tell a small part of from a very limited viewpoint.

In her essay, "Constantly Negotiating: Between My Mother and My Daughter," Joonok Huh also uses personal motherline stories of her Asian mother and Asian-American daughter to examine her own identity as a first-generation Korean immigrant. She argues that her immigrant status as well as her mother-daughter relationship has intensified the nature of personal and political discourses and conflicting expectations. Deciding not to replicate her own mother's traditional self-sacrificing role, Huh came to America to study and to become an independent woman. During a visit from Korea, Huh's mother revealed her own unfulfilled dreams as well as critical stories about Huh's westernized grandmother. Years later, during her first pregnancy, Huh feared the loss of her own acquired independence as well as the clash of cultural pressures and prejudices for her unborn daughter. However, as her daughter grows up, Huh realizes that the unfolding relationship between a mother and daughter caught between traditions continues as she watches her daughter now struggle with and deny her marginalization and foreign heritage. Huh concludes that reflecting on the motherline defines a new kind of middleness that accounts for both limitations as well as empowerment.

The final essay, "Revisioning the Maternal Body: Loving in Difference in Ngozi Onwurah's Film *The Body Beautiful*," also confronts identity constructions between two generations of women. Using an autobiographical account, Andrea Liss addresses aging, illness, disfigurement, and revisioning the maternal gaze. To make her point about loving in difference, she juxtaposes her own intersubjectivities with the film's theme of self-sacrifice, psychic desire, and maternal realities. This chapter brings together significant elements of the motherline addressed throughout the book as women attempt to reclaim a healthy and autonomous view of mothering from our own lived perspectives somewhere in the middle.

Adrienne Rich writes in her chapter on motherhood and daughterhood in *Of Woman Born*, "until a strong line of love, confirmation, and example stretches from mother to daughter, from woman to woman across generations, women will still be wandering in the wilderness."[35] She concludes her chapter with the observation that

> at the edge of adolescence . . . [w]omen are made taboo to women not just sexually, but as comrades, cocreators, conspiritors. In breaking this taboo,

we are reuniting with our mothers; in reuniting with our mothers, we are breaking this taboo.[36]

This collection, written almost a quarter century after Rich wrote these words, affirms the power of tabooed mother-daughter intimacy that delivers them from the patriarchal wilderness. From various standpoints, the contributors to this volume explore how women may secure and sustain connection and how they may resist the cultural forces that threaten to sever this connection. This volume, in charting and modeling relations of mother-daughter connectedness, blueprints, to borrow the title from Elizabeth deBold et al.'s book, a mother-daughter revolution so that we, as daughters and mothers, may in life and literature, in theory and practice, in public and private, secure connection to bring about personal empowerment and cultural transformation. Mothers and daughters together can, as deBold and her coauthors conclude, "claim the power of connection, community and choice, and this power might bring down [patriarchy]."[37]

NOTES

1. Adrienne Rich, *Of Woman Born: Motherhood as Experience and Institution* (New York: Norton, 1976), 235.
2. Marianne Hirsch, *Mother/Daughter Plot: Narrative, Psychoanalysis, Feminism* (Bloomington: Indiana University Press, 1989), 211.
3. Rich, *Of Woman Born*, 237.
4. Nancy Chodorow, author of the now classic *Reproduction of Mothering: Psychoanalysis and the Sociology of Gender* (Berkeley: University of California Press, 1978), contends that female mothering constructs gendered identities that are both differentiated and hierarchical. The pre-Oedipal mother-daughter attachment, she argues, is more prolonged and intense than the mother-son relationship. Because the daughter and the mother are the same gender, the mother perceives and treats her daughter as identical and continuous with herself. The sameness and continuity of the pre-Oedipal mother-daughter symbiosis engenders a feminine psychic structure that is less individuated and differentiated. The daughter's sense of self is relational; she experiences herself as connected to others. The relational sense of self that women inherit from their mothers and bring to their own mothering, Chodorow goes on to argue, exacerbates female self-effacement and frustrates women's achievement of an authentic autonomous identity. Relationality, Chodorow concludes, is problematic for women because it hinders autonomy, psychological and otherwise, and since mother-daughter identification is the cause of this relationality in women, it is, in her words, "bad for mother [daughter] alike" (217).
5. Mary Pipher, *Reviving Ophelia: Saving the Selves of Adolescent Girls* (New York: Grosset/Putnam, 1994), 13.

6. Elizabeth Brown-Guillory, ed., *Women of Color: Mother-Daughter Relationships in Twentieth Century Literature* (Austin: University of Texas Press, 1996), 191.

7. Carolyn Heilbrun, *Writing a Woman's Life* (New York: Ballantine, 1988), 32.

8. Rich, *Of Woman Born*, 11.

9. Marni Jackson, *The Mother Zone: Love, Sex, Laundry in the Modern Family* (Toronto: Macfarlane, Walter & Ross, 1992), 9.

10. Jackson, *The Mother Zone*, 3.

11. Hirsch, *Mother/Daughter Plot*, 185.

12. Sara Ruddick, *Maternal Thinking: Toward a Politic of Peace* (New York: Ballantine, 1989).

13. Ruddick, *Maternal Thinking*, 40.

14. Ruddick, *Maternal Thinking*, 39.

15. Ruddick, *Maternal Thinking*, 40.

16. Audre Lorde, "Poetry Is Not a Luxury," in *Sister Outsider: Essays and Speeches* (New York: Quality Paperback Club, Triangle Classics, 1993), 37.

17. Rich, *Of Woman Born*, 13.

18. Ruddick, *Maternal Thinking*, 111–12.

19. Alicia Ostriker, *Stealing the Language: The Emergence of Women's Poetry in America* (Boston: Beacon, 1986), 179.

20. Rich, *Of Woman Born*, 246.

21. Rich, *Of Woman Born*, 246.

22. Baba Cooper, "The Radical Potential in Lesbian Mothering of Daughters," in *Politics of the Heart: A Lesbian Parenting Anthology*, ed. Sandara Pollack and Jeanne Vaughn (Ithaca, N.Y.: Firebrand, 1987), 238.

23. Mary Kay Blakely, *American Mom: Motherhood, Politics, and Humble Pie* (Chapel Hill, N.C.: Algonquin, 1994), 3.

24. Judith Arcana, *Our Mothers' Daughters* (Berkeley, CA: Shameless Hussy Press, 1979), 33.

25. Elizabeth deBold, Marie Wilson, and Ideisee Malave, *Mother-Daughter Revolution: From Good Girls to Great Women* (New York: Bantam, 1994), 36.

26. deBold et al., *Mother-Daughter Revolution*, 11.

27. deBold et al., *Mother-Daughter Revolution*, 12.

28. deBold et al., *Mother-Daughter Revolution*, 101.

29. Myra and David Sadker, *Failing at Fairness: How Our Schools Cheat Girls* (New York: Simon & Schuster, 1994).

30. Sadker, *Failing at Fairness*, 1.

31. Peggy Orenstein, *School Girls: Young Women, Self-esteem, and the Confidence Gap* (New York: Doubleday, 1994), xvi.

32. Sherrie Innes, ed., *Millennium Girls: Today's Girls around the World* (New York: Rowman & Littlefield, 1998), 1.

33. Judy Mann, *The Difference: Growing Up Female in America* (New York: Time Warner Books, 1994), 261.

34. As quoted in Christina Looper Baker and Christine Baker Kline, *The Conversation Begins: Mothers and Daughters Talk about Living Feminism* (New York: Bantam, 1996), xv.

35. Rich, *Of Woman Born*, 246.

36. Rich, *Of Woman Born*, 255.

37. deBold et al., *Mother-Daughter Revolution*, 38.

Part I

Mothers Telling Their Stories

1

Mothers at Work: Representations of Maternal Practice in Literature

Elizabeth Bourque Johnson

In the opening scene of Harriette Arnow's 1954 novel *The Dollmaker*, Gertie is carrying her three-year-old son on a mule down a country road toward town. The child is struggling to breathe, sick with an illness that is occluding his throat. Realizing the boy will asphyxiate before she can get him to the doctor, she lays him on a flat rock, his head tipped backward to expose the soft place below the larynx.

> The long bright knife [drew] swiftly away from the swollen neck, leaving behind it a thin line that for an instant seemed no cut at all . . . until the blood seeped out. . . . A red filmed bubble streaked with pus grew on the red dripping wound, rose higher, burst; the child struggled, gave a hoarse, inhuman whistling cry. The woman wiped the knife blade on her shoe top. . . . She gently but quickly wiped the blood and pus from the gaping hole, whispering to the child as it struggled . . . brought out a hairpin, wiped it on the handkerchief, inserted the bent end in the cut, and then slowly, watching the hole carefully, drew her hand from under the child's neck, all the while holding the hole open with the hairpin.[1]

Rare in American literature are such detailed descriptions of a mother at work, doing whatever her job requires, especially when it is not of such a heroic nature. Mothers are often shown as daughters, sons, and as others see them, and as forces to be resisted. As figures from whom these protagonists are declaring independence, they are often one-dimensional and oppressive. The child's point of view does not make available the other side of the story: what the job of raising the child was like.

Mothering *is* a job, a kind of work. The word *mother* may also indicate a relationship or a title or a way of caring, but primarily a mother is a worker, a person who takes responsibility for the care and development of a child. She may be the repressive mother in Freud, the Imaginary pre-language mother of Lacan, the good-enough mother of Winnicott, or the Lady Capulet–like enforcer of patriarchy that Adrienne Rich has named, but in these child-centered conceptions of her we see little of the real person doing her work. The discourse of feminist theorizing about motherhood elides an explication of the subject actively doing mothering. The concept of mother and the institution of motherhood take primacy over the person. Much poststructuralist theorizing seems to be inadequate as well because of its emphasis on endless deferral of meaning and on denial of the authority of the subject. Claiming the need for an alternative theorizing that can support a feminist politics, Linda Alcoff asks, "What can we demand in the name of women [read mothers] if 'women' [mothers] do not exist? . . . How can we demand legal abortions, adequate child care?"[2] Alcoff suggests that studying maternal subjectivity is an important step, and I would add that it should include an examination of the work in which the subject engages that contributes to the construction of subjectivity.

To demystify the mother figure, then, it is important to shift the point of view from the concept to the practice and to contextualize the practice in the various conditions in which it operates. To do so, I propose to examine literary texts in which a mother figure is the central consciousness, the subject, not an object; to observe these subjects at their work; and to observe how they think about what they do as they continually construct, evaluate, and reconstruct their work. Reading across a spectrum of North American subcultures of race, class, and ethnicity, I locate commonalities and differences in maternal practice without suggesting a universal definition of mothers. Arising from these readings is a picture of maternal practice as a recursive pattern of action and evaluation, a pattern that suggests a dynamic, challenging occupation as varied in its manifestations as the many settings in which it is practiced.

In her important work *Maternal Thinking*, Sara Ruddick legitimates the idea of mothering as a work by defining it, in the language of philosophy, as a practice constituted by aims held in common by those who engage in it. Maternal practice, she asserts, "begins in a response to the reality of a biological child in a particular social world. To be a 'mother' is to take upon oneself the responsibility of child care, making its work a regular and substantial part of one's working life."[3] I would add that a commitment to long-term responsibility for a specific child distinguishes maternal practice from other kinds of nurturing work. Day care workers, for example, engage in nurturing activities that are aspects of mothering work, but their responsibility ends at pickup time. Taking responsibility is an act of choice, whether carefully considered or not, whether openly expressed or not. Many biological mothers assume that the responsibility automatically accompanies parturition, and they accept it even if they do not desire it. Many mothers are overwhelmed by it and must choose to continue or to turn away. In any case, it is choice, not instinct, that keeps a mother on the job.

Ruddick is careful to suggest that a "biological child" does not have to be one's own birth child and that a birthmother is not the only or even the best person to mother the child. She allows for the work of mothering to be undertaken by any person who chooses it. Indeed, in defining a mother as one who "takes upon oneself" that responsibility, she opens the field much more widely than her critics admit in their fear that nurturing might be reductively defined as essentially and only a feminine quality, which could then be used to oppress women into maternal work and no other. Nor is mothering work the sole province of women. Men can mother, and in families where parenting work is shared, fathers routinely engage in child care tasks. Much of the time, however, the primary awareness of a child's needs and the primary responsibility of managing the services required to meet those needs resides in the mind of the woman in the sharing pair. Although mothering is constructed in patriarchy to replicate itself from mother to daughter as a learned system of behaviors, as Nancy Chodorow has formulated, the texts examined here do not substantiate a claim that there is anything in the psychic or bodily makeup of either women or men that requires one to mother and the other not to.[4] Bodies respond physically and emotionally to various hormonal stimuli, but human beings are also cognitive and resilient. What I do recognize, from both my experience and my reading, is that most maternal work is performed by women. Most of the mothers I examine here are women, and I rely most often on feminine pronouns. If maternal practice is to be extended to other than birth givers, an understanding of what performative and self-reflexive activities are observed to constitute the practice may be useful. Although many authors here are also mothers, an equation between author and persona cannot be assumed. Literature, though it may represent life, is not itself the life of the author but life as the mind can imagine it, allowing literature to enlarge human perception of itself.

The aims of maternal practice in Ruddick's schema are preservation, nurturance, and training. The most basic of these is *preservation*, the physical care that infants and small children need to stay alive. Providing food, clothing, shelter, and health care fall into this category. Gertie's emergency tracheotomy is an extraordinary example of preservation; more common are her activities of putting mittens on her children, cooking their supper, getting the heater going in the winter. Preservation implies keeping steady what is within one's immediate control.

Preservation soon extends to protection against outside forces: oncom-

ing traffic, malevolent strangers, sharp objects. A hallmark of protection
is the alertness of the mother's senses that allows her to know where her
children are. Gertie repeatedly displays what Ruddick calls the "scruti-
nizing gaze,"[5] her head lifted, her eyes sweeping the hills of the Kentucky
farm or the Detroit alley out her kitchen window. Her action is more of a
quick look or an ear cocked for sound, however, than the contemplation
suggested by scrutiny. Her "glance," the word used in the text, does not
interrupt her other work or conversation. Even when the children are not
present, Gertie is alert to where they should be and to the moment when
they should return, checking a clock, listening for their voices outside.
When one voice is missing, she can tell and goes to look for the child. It
is tempting to equate maternal alertness with an animal's alertness on an
open plain, but that action is instinctual and the implication essentializ-
ing. Rather, maternal alertness is a learned behavior in response to a
child's demonstrated need for protection.

Gertie's children need protection from many things. The time is World
War II; the family has followed the father from Kentucky to Detroit for a
job in a factory. Everything is new, from the train trip to the rows of government projects where they will live. Compared with their rural home
where family and friends formed a community, the city seems rough and
unfriendly. The alley teems with children toughened by urban experience
to know how to negotiate territory, to find their way to school, and to
avoid the danger of the nearby rail yards. Gertie walks the young ones to
school and keeps them in their apartment when a fight is brewing in the
alley. She is painfully alert because she cannot always distinguish what is
dangerous from what is merely strange. What were safe parameters in
Kentucky do not apply here, yet holding the children back prevents them
from making the adjustments they must in the new place. On the first day
of school, she sees her son Enoch tripped and taunted by a bully. She
starts to rush to him "but hid again behind the storm door . . . watched
him brush the black snow from his clothing . . . wanted to ask if they had
hurt him much, but did not. Enoch would rather have her belief that he
could take care of himself than her sympathy."[6] Here Gertie has reevalu-
ated her impulse to protect and comfort. Even in Kentucky she would
have had to make adjustments, but in the new environment she must
evaluate her methods even more.

What makes mothering a dynamic practice is the need to respond to
changing situations. Children grow; to grow with them, mothers must
be able to analyze what works and what doesn't, a critical component of
maternal practice that is less obvious than glancing or feeding but is no
less integral to the ongoing work. In stories in which the mother is the
protagonist, the reader can participate in her self-reflexivity.

Comfort is one aspect of *nurturance*, Ruddick's second aim for maternal practice. A good deal of nurturance is supervisory, monitoring children's activities and needs. Monitoring also includes what Ruddick calls "administration," arranging for school, homework, teacher conferences, and health care, all of which Gertie does. In addition, it means assessing the child's development and emotional growth; it also means knowing when to encourage, as Gertie does with her son Reuben in his trials at school.

> She put her hand on his head. He shook it off. "Git away." . . .
> "Lots a your teachers at school likes you, an you liked Sunday school."
> He made her no answer . . . she sat on the edge of the bed and tried to smooth his hair.[7]

Of the many stories of mothers at work I have read, Arnow's is the most detailed in describing the small gestures of maternal preservation, protection, care, comfort, and guidance, continuously interweaving Gertie's daily actions with her thoughts, feelings, and adjustments as the story progresses. Reading it, I *see* what a mother does all day—and why.

Perhaps a mother's most complicated and important task is the *preparation* of children to take over the work of preserving and caring for themselves. It is a task tinged with irony: A mother has no sooner mastered the skills of maternal practice when she must send the grown children out on their own, a letting-go process that can be a wound, a relief, an accomplishment, or some combination of these. Activities of preparation include teaching, modeling, guiding, and mentoring in various overt and covert modes. In Kentucky, where Gertie understands the society and its mores, she sits her children on the edge of the bed in their Sunday clothes and teaches them Bible stories; each child has a verse to learn by heart and understand. She enters into conversations with her youngest daughter Cassie and Cassie's imaginary friend Callie Lou in order to learn what the child is thinking and feeling. She assigns to each child the chores manageable at his or her age, chores that teach them skills and responsibility. Ruddick claims that mothers must *train* children for their places in society; that term feels militaristic in tone and places the needs of society in the central focus. It seems more appropriate to say that mothers attempt to *prepare* their children for a societal niche in which they will be able to take adequate care of themselves. One mother may insist that the child follow her guidelines exactly; another, depending on her understanding of possibilities, may be able to imagine paths to meaningful work and relationships different from her own and to encourage her children toward those goals. Intentionally or not, mothers do transmit both values and possibilities, including those about the future. In Detroit where she does not understand the urban working-class culture, Gertie does not know how to steer her children through the new experiences around her. The

children want money for movies and store-bought clothes. Gertie has little money, knows little about movies or about other things they want to
do. Her daughter can bargain better with the vegetable peddler than Gertie can and begins to earn her own money by baby-sitting, a practice new
to Gertie, who in Kentucky had always taken her children everywhere or
had members of her extended family nearby to mind a child if necessary.
Unable to contend with the present, she cannot envision any future for
herself or for them except to return to Kentucky.

Present and future can be even more complex for racial ethnic mothers,
who, in addition to the basic aims of maternal practice, must contend
with tasks specific to their position in the dominant culture. In response
to feminist theorizing about motherhood that focuses on white women's
search for autonomy and identity within the patriarchal family, Patricia
Hill Collins asserts that the tasks for women of color are different. Racial
ethnic women, she says, must struggle for survival, power, and identity
for themselves and for their children.[8] Their very survival is not assured.
Infant mortality rates are high, living conditions often dangerous. A stable income is not assured, and mothers usually have to work to support
the family, even when a father is present. Separated from her children for
hours, she cannot always protect and guide them herself and must enlist
the aid of other members of the community. Collins points to a strong
tradition of child care shared by both "bloodmothers" and "othermothers" in the black community, a tradition that has developed from the frag-
mentation of slavery and the need for poor women to work outside the
home.[9] Shared mothering contributes not just to economic survival but to
the strengthening of communal identity and a diffusing of the insularity
common in the patriarchal nuclear family.

Preservation in a black community involves not just physical care but
protection from the effects of racism. Facing poverty and discrimination,
Mildred, a black mother in Terry McMillan's *Mama*, tries many avenues
to guide her five children to some security in the world. Her first protective act is to divorce her abusive husband, but without his income she
cannot keep the family housed and fed. Mildred gets a factory job but
loses it, having had to stay home too often with sick children. She cleans
white people's houses. She is quick-tongued with her children, scolding
and commanding. Yet, McMillan tells us, "Motherhood was everything
to Mildred. . . . It made her feel like she had actually done something
meaningful."[10] The actual work of guiding and caring for them she finds
more difficult. The oldest girl, Freda, does much of the cooking and the
supervising of her siblings. What Mildred does is teach them tenacity and
push them to be self-sufficient.

> Y'all ain't never gon' have to worry about eating, that's for damn sure. It may
> not be steak . . . but you won't go hungry . . . y'all is going to college . . . All

y'all got good sense, and I'ma make sure you stretch it to the fullest. . . .
Decency. A good husband. Some healthy babies. Peace of mind. Them is the
thangs you try to get out of life. . . . Niggahs . . . thank they can get something
for nothing and that that God they keep praying to. . .[will] save 'em. . . .
What it takes is real hard work. . . . One thang is true, and this is the tricky
part. White folks own every damn thang. . . . They don't like to see niggahs
getting ahead . . . least you can do is learn how to get around some shit like
that . . . learn to thank for yourself . . . you just as good as the next person.[11]

Through all the ups and downs she and her children experience, and they
are many, Mildred repeats this manifesto and lives it.

Mildred does not, however, reflect on her methods of mothering, and
her mode does not change. She often acts without considering the consequences, albeit she is facing stressful circumstances in which the family's
survival is threatened, and she can rarely be comforting and tender with
her children. What Mildred can do is give them her ability to survive, to
believe in herself, and to believe in them. Against the stereotype of the
welfare mom, they see how hard she works, how inventive she is. All her
children eventually survive, not because she could nurture and mentor
them but because she models survival herself. At the end she tells them,
"Y'all done it all by yourselves."[12] And that's what she taught them they
could do.

Mildred is a strong woman able to survive whatever the white community presents. She is an image of what Barbara Christian calls "the myth
of the black matriarch."[13] Because of her survival skills, the matriarch can
be viewed by white culture as a positive figure. However, the matriarch
is also a figure that contests the patriarchal nuclear family structure. Mildred goes through several husbands and male companions. Each brings
economic and sexual relief but no help with parenting. None stays, and
in each case it is Mildred who initiates their departure. Read through the
lens of the Moynihan Report of 1965, Mildred could fit the stereotype of
the emasculating female; on the other hand, she refuses to keep a man
who does not contribute to her central work, the raising of children. The
Moynihan Report, taking the patriarchal nuclear family as the norm, de-
cries this figure whose "dominance," although forced on her by the racism and sexism of white society, "is assigned the responsibility of the 'pa-
thologies' in the black community,"[14] specifically the black family's
dependence on welfare. Mildred has had to "go on the state" a few times
when laid off from white-owned factories, but she is nothing like the
image of the lazy welfare mother often vilified in the political press. She
rebounds from job to job and actively pushes her children to better themselves. Critiquing this stereotype, McMillan does what Christian identifies as the response of contemporary black women novelists, "creating

their own definition of woman within the scope of their particular milieu."[15]

Struggles for power and identity in a culture of racial domination involve women's control of their minds and bodies, including access to birth control and abortion and resistance to forced sterilization. The choice to have and keep children goes against public policies that attempt to "manipulate the fertility of women dependent on public assistance."[16] In addition, their minds and their children's are manipulated by the larger culture that devalues their heritage in mass media and in schools, where until recently blacks and Native Americans learned none of their histories except in slave and savage images. Many Native American children were removed from the tribal community and sent to government or religious boarding schools where their hair was cut, their clothing changed to uniforms, and their language never spoken. And yet their own cultures are some of their greatest sources of power. Reclaiming those cultural connections takes such time and energy that other mothering practices, especially of an administrative nature, must wait. For racial ethnic mothers, problems of identity center less on the individual psyche and more on racial identity. Raised themselves in the dominant white culture that devalues and would erase them, they have to teach children how to "survive in a culture that would oppress them . . . [but not] at the expense of self-esteem."[17] Reclaiming heritage may be central to teaching their children who they are and what resources they have, but it will likely put them in conflict with white patriarchal institutions.

Conflict between the conquering culture and the conquered informs much of Native American literature. Louise Erdrich's novels, *Love Medicine*, *Tracks*, and *The Bingo Palace*, foreground many mother figures whose subjectivity and maternal practice are shaped by the complex tasks confronting them.[18] These Chippewa and mixed-blood figures protect and guide their tribe's children as other mothers do, but their particular task is to transmit to them the threads of Native American culture that have been systematically broken by the dominant system. Although devalued by that system, these mothers have the advantage of a tradition which has empowered women as policymakers. According to Paula Gunn Allen, tribes were frequently gynocratic in governance, rather than patriarchal: "To address a person as 'mother' is to pay the highest ritual respect."[19] Hertha Wong points to the indigenous woman's central role in "the continuance of tribal tradition, both through childbearing and through transmission of cultural values in stories."[20]

Erdrich's novels reflect the cultural value of communal mothering. Drawing from a worldview that emphasizes the interconnectedness of the earth and all creatures, Native American tribal community members cooperate to share the tasks and responsibilities of mothering. Marie Lazarre Kashpaw has babies everywhere, not just biological children but others, including her niece June and, later, June's son Lipsha. When nine-year-old June is brought to her weak and needy, Marie resists, already having so many children in her care. Yet she cleans the lice from June's hair with kerosene, washes and treats the sores on her skin, and remakes some used clothing for her. In these preservative acts, Marie is also preserving one of their own for the tribe.

Marie must protect June, whom the children are about to hang in a game of horse thief. June, whose mother abused her and allowed her to be raped, was complicit in the hanging, saying sadly, "You ruined it," then screaming "bitch" at Marie. Marie, stunned and confused, washes the girl's mouth out with soap, as much an act of teaching as of punishment. Then Marie looked into June's "sorrowful black eyes . . . There was a sadness I couldn't touch there."[21] It is a moment of self-reflection and evaluation. Only once would June let Marie get close to her: "I held her and I stroked her hair and hummed in her ear. . . . Then sleep took her for real. The strain went out of her."[22] Marie wants to comfort and nurture June, but June will not allow it, and Marie understands why: "It was a mother she couldn't trust after what happened in the woods."[23] Marie would like to be a guide for June as well, but June is closed off. Soon, June goes to live in the woods with Uncle Eli. The task of mentoring is left to this man, who teaches her to hunt, carve, and whistle. Neither he nor Marie, however, is ultimately able to teach June to preserve herself.

Another man in these novels acts as a mother. In *Tracks*, Nanapush nurses Fleur after her parents die of influenza, and then he assumes responsibility for her, the key distinction between nurturing and mothering. Later he nurses Fleur's daughter Lulu as well, when her feet are frozen. Fleur eventually has to send Lulu to the government boarding school because she has no money and because she feels helpless to prepare the girl—or herself—to negotiate white society. When Lulu returns from the boarding school, she refuses to live with her mother, who she felt had abandoned her. Nanapush again takes the mothering responsibility. It is he as a narrator of *Tracks* who tells her Fleur's story in order to reclaim for Lulu her tribal identity, and Lulu eventually takes his name for her last name.

Communal mothering does not dilute attachment to biological children. Lulu has eight sons by different fathers, and although she mothers them much more loosely than the intense Marie, she is no less committed to protection, nurture, and guidance. When her house catches fire, she rescues Lyman, her youngest, by lifting him out a bedroom window and falling out after him. Later, when the man who was his unacknowledged father dies, she consoles him as much as he will allow: "I wanted to hold my son on my lap and let him cry . . . a mother knows when her boy is holding in a painful silence. But we . . . never said another word."[24]

Lulu mentors Lipsha, divulging the identity of his parents, telling him their story so that he will know where he belongs—which is to her. Her son Gerry is his father, and June is his mother, although she abandoned him at birth. In *The Bingo Palace,* Lulu, an old woman now, uses her maternal power to try to restore Lipsha to the tribe. At the same time she is trying to save Gerry, who has been jailed for his participation in the American Indian Movement. Learning that Gerry has escaped, Lulu mails to Lipsha, anonymously, the "Wanted" poster of Gerry. Lipsha responds, and in a complex series of events he locates Gerry and tries to help him. Meanwhile, in a scene of powerful maternal practice and cultural resistance, Lulu waits in the senior center for the federal marshals. That they expect Gerry to come to her is tacit acknowledgment that mothering does not end, that the need to protect remains.

> And she was prepared . . . attired in her full regalia. . . . She carried her fan of pure white eagle tailfeathers. Four of them, upright, in her hand of a sexy grandmother. . . .
>
> Let's say they found a knife . . . some direct proof her son had been to see her. Or let's say they didn't find a thing, but that motherhood itself was more than enough.
>
> "Of course, of course he was here. He came home. . . . Where else would he go?" . . .
>
> They finally take her in . . . but with a kind of ceremony that does not confuse a single one of us, for she has planned it . . . so many popping lights of cameras, whining shutters. . . .
>
> Down the frosted squares of the sidewalk, Lulu Lamartine dances the old-lady traditional . . . with a tucked-in wildness. . . . At the door to the official vehicle, just before they whisk her inside, she raises her fan. Noises stop, cameras roll. Out of her mouth comes the old-lady trill, the victory yell that runs up our necks. . . . [W]e can't help but join her.[25]

The "we" who join her is the unnamed collective voice of tribal history that opens and closes this novel. The voice acknowledges the inscription of tribal identity and power in Lulu's maternal, ritual act.

For Chinese-American mothers also, negotiating identity is a significant task. Neither captive slaves nor conquered indigenous peoples, Chinese Americans represent the immigrant experience of having come to America in the belief that life could be better here. They come by choice, with goals, and often with a strong impulse to assimilate or at least conform. They encourage their children to learn American ways to secure their advancement, at the same time trying to retain for them what they value in their Chinese heritage. The four mothers in Amy Tan's novel *The Joy Luck Club,* who form a communal and competitive system of supportive "aunts," are working- and middle-class women who do not daily face the threat of poverty.[26] They emphasize discipline, obedience, and achievement and are unfailing in the necessary administrative work. Piano practice begins at four p.m. Lindo arranges increasingly competitive chess matches for seven-year-old Waverly. The mothers believe they are preparing their daughters to claim a comfortable place in American society, but when the girls go on to professions and material prosperity, their mothers realize that they have retained less of the uniquely Chinese values that they intended to teach, and they fear that the children are losing their cultural heritage. Lindo says:

> She learned [American circumstances], but I couldn't teach her about Chinese character. How to obey parents and listen to your mother's mind. How not to show your own thoughts, to put your feelings behind your face so you can take advantage of hidden opportunities. Why easy things are not worth pursuing. How to know your own worth and polish it, never flashing it around like a cheap ring. Why Chinese thinking is best.[27]

These mothers have exerted more direct control over their children than have the other racial ethnic mothers represented here, but with grown, assimilated children control is no longer possible, and the mothers, no longer disciplinarians, must adapt their maternal practice to become mentors. At this point they, like Erdrich's Native American mothers, turn to storytelling. They have kept hidden their own stories of conflicts and tragedies in their lives in China, so that what the girls think they know of China, like the Twenty-Six Malignant Gates that symbolize motherly fears, seems all superstition. According to Marina Heung, when mothers keep silent about their lives and wisdom, that silence seems to hide great terrors; their demand that their daughters keep the same silences "binds daughters and mothers in a cycle of self-perpetuating denial."[28] Telling one's story is seen as an assault on the duty and loyalty that a woman owes to her family. Evaluating their maternal practice and the need for change, the mothers realize that they must tell their daughters the stories of their own agency if they want to empower them. Ying-Ying, who has been portrayed as weak and silent, sees her daughter Lena immobile in a painful marriage.

> So this is what I will do. I will gather together my past and look. I will see a thing that has already happened. The pain that cut my spirit loose. I will hold that pain in my hand until it becomes hard and shiny, more clear. And then my fierceness can come back, my golden side, my black side. I will use this sharp pain to penetrate my daughter's tough skin and cut her tiger spirit loose. She will fight me, because this is the nature of two tigers. But I will win and give her my spirit, because this is the way a mother loves her daughter.[29]

Telling her story cuts Ying-Ying's tiger spirit loose again and empowers her as well. Only then can she encourage Lena to leave her harmful marriage. In this way, she and the other storytelling mothers can restore a sense of "Chinese character" to their daughters, "rewriting stories of oppression and victimization into parables of self-affirmation."[30]

The constitutive aims of maternal practice having been achieved to one degree or another, mothers of adult children must negotiate the boundaries of holding on and letting go. They have preserved, nurtured, and prepared their children to assume a place in society and to take care of themselves. But the job is not over. Mothers continue to be alert to their children's situations, even when they are absent and out of contact, as seen in Margaret Laurence's *The Diviners*. Pique, who contested her mother throughout adolescence and has left, refuses to let her mother know where she is or what she is doing, but Morag worries about her nonetheless.[31] When Pique shows up, always without preamble, Morag takes her in with no second thought, for as long as she will stay, despite the disruption in her own life. Adult children come back with new concerns. Mothers must become mentors, knowing when to offer solutions and when to say, "Hmmm." For some mothers, letting go of the product of their life's work may be a frightening prospect, as it is for McMillan's Mildred, who alternates between anger and pride as her children strike out on their own. Asked what she will do when all five are gone, Mildred goes to bed with a headache and falls asleep remembering the times when the young Freda would slip into bed with her. Her children come and go with partners and babies whenever their fortunes are low, and Mildred takes care of them all, albeit with plenty of scolding and loud advice. When the youngest marries, the "thought of all her kids belonging to someone else made her feel like she was breaking into a million pieces."[32]

Like it or not, for everyone's good Mildred has to let go. The turn comes with one more child's request for money, a huge sum she cannot come up with. "I'm about sick of you and everybody else around here asking me to do this and do that, like I'm some kind of goddam miracle worker."[33] Eventually the children get themselves stabilized, and Mildred announces that she will go to school to qualify for a day care license, work that will help her recapture the engagement with children that has informed her life.

Preservation, nurturance, preparation—aims of all mothers. Survival, power, identity—the added tasks of racial ethnic mothers. A white mother like Gertie, removed from her familiar environment, experiences a cross-cultural dislocation with some of the same challenges. Some of her children adapt quickly to the ways of the city, leaving her puzzled about how to teach and guide them. Some of them don't make it. In the novel's horrifying climax, little Cassie is run over by a reversing train as, oblivious, she sits singing on the railroad tracks. Gertie could neither save her nor educate her to the danger.

For most white mothers, variations of maternal practice have much to do with the intersection of economics, class, and race. Being racially white places them in a privileged position but economics affect how they can raise their children. Being poor confronts them with survival tasks similar to those of poor mothers of other races.

Stories of middle-class mothers are fewer and focus on mothering infrequently. One that does is Gail Godwin's *A Mother and Two Daughters*, a novel that offers as well a look at mothering adult children.[34] Nell is a middle-class white mother of two grown daughters very different in personality and lifestyle. Smooth Lydia has a family and irritable Cate a career. Nell's work consists of an ongoing evaluation of each daughter's strengths and weaknesses, partly to guide them but largely to understand them and her own role in their development. She does try to help them get along a little better, being careful to judge what she says to one or the other and urging each to be more tolerant. Nell in her sixties is at a time when she might think her mothering work is over. The effort is tiring and much less engaging than when they were young. She would like to be finished by now, and yet loyalty and their needs keep her involved.

Godwin's novel is unusual in its focus on mothering practice in a secure white nuclear family. When white middle-class mothers are the subjects, it is usually in the context of a crisis or tragedy, as in *Disturbances in the Field* by Lynne Sharon Schwartz in which a child dies, and Sue Miller's *The Good Mother*, in which a divorced mother fights for custody.[35] I could speculate either that the ordinary mothering life of a middle-class woman in stable economic circumstances does not make an interesting read or that this class of women does not write about themselves. The latter argument would be buttressed by the impulse to be proper that Nell expresses about Cate; it is not "nice" to say negative things about family life or children, and any story would likely have some negatives in it. There is also an expectation of privacy in the patriarchal family, of which the middle class is largely composed. What happens in the nuclear patriarchal family stays there, excluding even the extended family from knowledge of what is occurring. Those two forces combine into a powerful silencing gesture. Another possibility is that when women in patriarchal families write, they write about their own struggles for identity in the institution of motherhood rather than about their work with children. Adrienne Rich published the powerful analysis of *Of Woman Born: Motherhood as Experience and Institution*; she did *not* publish, if she wrote them, poems about doing the work of mothering.[36]

Another interesting point is that there is little in the novels here that calls up Freudian notions of the mother. Not even recent feminist psychoanalytic theorizing seems to fit. I speculate two things here. One is that the feminist family romance according to Freud represents a Eurocentric middle-class theory not universally applicable to other classes and races. Another is that Freudian theory is centered on the psychic experience of a little boy developing an individuated stance in his world. When the center shifts to an adult woman doing the work of mothering, the model no longer fits. She is no longer a shadowy figure whose intentionality we do not understand and to which we react in fear. She *is* the subject, the consciousness we inhabit. From this point of view, we see her subjectivity and agency in constructing her practice. We see her thinking and working in a dynamic, challenging occupation, in various conditions of race, class, gender, and social organization, and in a full range of psychological and intellectual modes.

NOTES

1. Harriette Arnow, *The Dollmaker* (Lexington: University Press of Kentucky, 1954), 12.
2. Linda Alcoff, "Cultural Feminism versus Post-Structuralism: The Identity Crisis in Feminist Theory," *Signs: Journal of Women in Culture and Society* 13, no. 3 (1988): 420.
3. Sara Ruddick, *Maternal Thinking: Toward a Politics of Peace* (Boston: Beacon, 1989), 17.
4. Nancy Chodorow, *The Reproduction of Mothering: Psychoanalysis and the Sociology of Gender* (Berkeley: University of California Press, 1978).
5. Ruddick, *Maternal Thinking,* 72.
6. Arnow, *Dollmaker,* 171.
7. Arnow, *Dollmaker,* 308.
8. Patricia Hill Collins, "Shifting the Center: Race, Class, and Feminist Theorizing about Motherhood," in *Mothering: Ideology, Experience, and Agency,* ed. Evelyn Nakano Glenn et al. (New York: Routledge, 1994), 49.
9. Patricia Hill Collins, *Black Feminist Thought: Knowledge, Consciousness, and the Politics of Empowerment* (Boston: Unwin Hyman, 1990), 119.
10. Terry McMillan, *Mama* (New York: Pocket Books, 1987), 13.
11. McMillan, *Mama,* 27–28.
12. McMillan, *Mama,* 258.
13. Barbara Christian, *Black Women Novelists: The Development of a Tradition, 1892–1976* (Westport, Conn.: Greenwood, 1980), 78.
14. Christian, *Novelists,* 78.
15. Christian, *Novelists,* 78.
16. Collins, "Shifting," 53.
17. Collins, "Shifting," 57.

18. Louise Erdrich, *The Bingo Palace* (New York: HarperCollins, 1994); *Love Medicine* (New York: Bantam, 1984); *Tracks* (New York: Harper & Row, 1988).

19. Paula Gunn Allen, *The Sacred Hoop: Recovering the Feminine in American Indian Traditions* (Boston: Beacon, 1992), 16.

20. Hertha Wong, "Adoptive Mothers and Thrown-Away Children in the Novels of Louise Erdrich," in *Narrating Mothers: Theorizing Maternal Subjectivities*, ed. Brenda Daly and Maureen T. Reddy (Knoxville: University of Tennessee Press, 1991), 174.

21. Erdrich, *Love Medicine*, 67–68.

22. Erdrich, *Love Medicine*, 71.

23. Erdrich, *Love Medicine*, 70.

24. Erdrich, *Love Medicine*, 233.

25. Erdrich, *The Bingo Palace*, 261–65.

26. Amy Tan, *The Joy Luck Club* (New York: Putnam, 1989).

27. Tan, *The Joy Luck Club*, 254.

28. Marina Heung, "Daughter-Text/Mother-Text: Matrilineage in Amy Tan's *Joy Luck Club*," *Feminist Studies* 19, no. 3 (Fall 1993): 606.

29. Tan, *Joy Luck Club*, 252.

30. Heung, "Daughter-Text/Mother-Text," 607.

31. Margaret Laurence, *The Diviners* (New York: Knopf, 1974).

32. McMillan, *Mama*, 190.

33. McMillan, *Mama*, 210.

34. Gail Godwin, *A Mother and Two Daughters* (New York: Avon, 1982).

35. Lynne Sharon Schwartz, *Disturbances in the Field* (New York: Harper & Row, 1983); Sue Miller, *The Good Mother* (New York: Harper & Row, 1986).

36. Adrienne Rich, *Of Woman Born: Motherhood as Experience and Institution* (New York: Norton, 1976).

2

Restorying Jewish Mothers

Janet Burstein

Because we know from our earliest memories the power and pleasure of "once upon a time," making stories comes second nature to us all. When we try to explain to ourselves the puzzling behavior of a child or friend, when we struggle to connect the bewilderment of this moment to a future we desire, or to a past that we regret, we make a story. And the story gives shape to material that would otherwise be disturbingly fluid, elusive, resistant to the mind's grasp. The stories we tell one another also construct a shared world—especially for children. But for adults as well the world becomes knowable largely through the stories that represent it and justify its peculiarities. Thus, for individuals and for the cultures that shape and contain them, stories perform multiple functions as they engage and maybe even delight the mind.

For Jews, as Victoria Aarons has pointed out, the cultural burden of stories is particularly salient; Jewish storytelling has long been a means of both "bearing witness to the events of the past and of defining the fluid specifics of Jewish identity."[1] Thus, in the work of Philip Roth, Delmore Schwartz, and Jerome Weidman, for example, Aarons describes the efforts of protagonists trying to find their places within Jewish culture and also trying to define themselves through the agency of the story. The dual questions asked by Roth's Ozzie Freedman in "The Conversion of the Jews" reveal this double quest for both personal and ethnic identity; first he asks: "Is it me? Is it me ME ME ME! It has to be me—but is it!" Finally, he asks "Is it us? . . . Is it us?" Roth's later protagonist in *The Counterlife* will insist that both questions can be answered only through storying— creating narratives that both realize and reveal the self as part of its culture.

In general, these dual objectives of storying seem valid for both male and female American-Jewish writers. But, when they speak about parents and children, male and female narratives diverge from one another. In fact, if we hold women's storying of filial relationships against Harold Bloom's paradigm for such relationships, the gender-related differences become quite clear even to a nonessentialist reader. A long time ago, Bloom called attention to a phenomenon he called "the anxiety of influence" that complicates the connection between male writers and their precursors—a phenomenon that still seems to shadow the filial relationships that men's stories often tell. Bloom understood what he called "the melancholy of the creative mind's desperate insistence upon priority";[2] as "the hungry generations go on treading one another down," he wrote, male writers "misread" the stories of their precursors in order to "beget" themselves.[3] In art as in life, what Freud called the family romance and its inescapable Oedipal conflict dictate, Bloom argues, that strong sons will fight their precursors through "caricature," "distortion," and "perverse, willful revisionism."[4] They fight because the power of the precursor is so great that it dooms each new generation of men— "whether poets or not"[5] to the anxious expectation of "being flooded" by it:[6] "The precursors flood us, and our imaginations can die by drowning in them." But, he warns, "no imaginative life is possible if such inundation is wholly evaded."[7] Thus, the "strong imagination comes to its painful birth" not by evasion but "through savagery and misrepresentation" of the stories it inherits.[8]

This aggressive scenario is sometimes visible in the work of American-Jewish male writers. Herbert Gold's 1961 story "The Heart of the Artichoke" provides a classic example. Gold's narrator sees—too late—the archetypal nature of the battle with his father that followed his refusal to adopt for his own life the plot of his father's story. In retrospect he will realize that when his father stood, menacing, over his rebellious adolescent son, his father's "swaying body knew it loved me as his father had loved him, the woman carrying her child on a belly or breast, the man taking his son only at the eye or the fist."[9] But in the moment, this narrator knows only that he must fight his father to guarantee his own power.

According to Bloom and his precursor Sigmund Freud, these two male creatures fight because fighting is the given of relationships between male precursors and their descendants. According to Nietzsche, Bloom explains, "every talent must unfold itself in fighting."[10] And sure enough, the fight itself, in Gold's story, accomplishes the unfolding of the child into the man he became: as they wrestle, Gold's narrator remembers that his father "hugged . . . my ribs, forcing them up—cracking! pushing my hair out, lengthening my bones, driving my voice deep. Savagely he told me his life, wringing my childhood from me. . . . We embraced like this."[11] Like the embrace of Jacob and the angel as they wrestle in Genesis, this fierce contest unites the contenders only by aggression, but their brief union engenders a new adult identity that will grow mainly by conflict and separation.

One important problem with this mode of male filial bonding, a problem that shows up in many of the male-authored stories that Aarons has studied, is that it produces other long-range consequences as well. For fathers, as Aarons notes, the consequence is "failed expectations." For sons, the filial story becomes what Aarons calls a "saga of guilt" that begets a profound nostalgia for what has been rejected. Thus, Aarons observes in stories by male writers a continuing fascination with the "source of the [son's] estrangement" from his father. In these stories "the past becomes increasingly seductive."[12] For male narrators and/or protagonists, the paternal story begins to hold a meaning that becomes luminous only after it has been rejected, precious only after it has been lost.

Some contemporary critics have assumed this filial dynamic to be so pervasive that they believe it to be characteristic of current American-Jewish literature as a whole. Norman Finkelstein, for example, has argued that because of the agonistic relation of strong writers to their precursors, like that of strong sons to their fathers, Jewish writers work in the mode of nostalgia. "To be modern," he says, "is to experience rupture; to be Postmodern is to reflect upon the experience of rupture, and in doing so repeat and further that experience."[13] Contemporary Jewish writers "honor the past through rupture,"[14] he insists, and then carry it forward in nostalgic recollection.

But rupture and nostalgia don't seem to pervade filial stories written since the late 1960s by American-Jewish women. Like male writers, women also revise and transform parental stories. Like male narrators, women often tell of conflict with their parents, but the emphasis in their stories usually falls on engagement rather than rupture. Perhaps the most powerful example of filial engagement that contains, but is unruptured by conflict is Vivian Gornick's memoir *Fierce Attachments*.[15] Like Gold's narrator, Gornick's must reject—as a pattern for her own life—the story her parent's life has written. In Gornick's work, the plot of the mother's life is the romance of domestic love. Gornick's narrator rejects that plot, but she grasps at the same time a maternal gift that lies beneath it. The source of this gift is the kitchen window where the listening child first hears her mother turning the calls and cries of neighbor women into stories. This window opens onto an alley in the Bronx where "there were no trees, or bushes, or grasses of any kind." Nevertheless, Gornick remembers it as a "place of clear light and sweet air, suffused, somehow, with a perpetual smell of summery green."[16] Here, she believes, not in the bedroom or the nursery, not at the stove or the sewing machine, is the Jewish mother's garden. Here the child learns to appreciate the interest of women's voices, to feel contempt for the work of cooking and cleaning, and to prize above all things the narrative skill that distinguishes her mother from other women. Mama's "running commentary on the life outside the window was my first taste of the fruits of intelligence," her daughter remembers; like the fairy-tale sorcerer who can spin straw into gold, Mama transforms what is base into something precious: she "knew how to convert gossip into knowledge."[17]

The preciousness of this shared gift will carry Gornick beyond the kitchen window into her life as a professional writer. More valuable to her than the paradigm of domestic romance her mother has wanted to transmit, the pleasure of storying that she has learned from her mother surpasses all other pleasures: "Not an 'I love you' in the world could touch it,"[18] she says.

Her relationship to her mother will also include moments of terrible ferocity. But even when she describes physical conflict, language transforms it into a mode of connection—not severance. For example, when Mama Gornick chases her smart-talking college-girl daughter through the apartment and fails to stop at the hastily locked bathroom door, she drives "her fist thru the glass, *reaching for me*" (my emphasis), Gornick says. "I thought that afternoon, one of us is going to die of this attachment."[19] It survives, however, not only this episode but many periodic flashes of competitiveness for control of their joint story. Thus, this memoir creates an image of two women sustaining with great difficulty—in war and peace—a complicated intimacy as they walk the city streets, arguing, bitterly fighting, or simply talking together. At the end, laying down a dishtowel as though it were Prospero's wand, Mama Gornick asks, "Why don't you go already? Why don't you walk away from my life? I'm not stopping you." But Gornick remains "half in and half out" of her mother's house.[20]

These women fight not to vanquish one another but to carry forward the tricky dialogue in which both can remain engaged. It is this model of intermittent conflict and continuing dialogue—not rupture, guilt, and nostalgia—that seems to engage many American-Jewish women writers since the sixties. E. M. Broner's *Ghost Stories*, for example, develops this model.[21] Even after death, the narrator's mother in these stories remains both visible and audible to her daughter. Her reflection appears in the mirror when her daughter combs the wavy hair she inherits from her mother. They argue still about their haircuts. As the daughter observes the weekly ritual of Kaddish for eleven months of formal mourning, her mother sits beside her in the synagogue, criticizing, commanding, interpreting, remembering, continuing the often cranky dialogue in which they both remain engaged. Like Gornick, this narrator shapes her own life and commitments in ways her mother does not always understand or approve. But she seeks as well the sense of blessing that her mother's approval still carries: "If I am her good girl," she asks herself, "will I hear whispered blessings ruffling my hair, my life?"[22] She confronts in their continuing dialogue their mutual disappointments in one another.[23] They fight, like Gornick and her mother, about interpretations of their shared past.[24] But, like Gornick, she hears her mother's story and records it faithfully, without misreading, even though she cannot, would not, relive it. She can't always use her mother's "old words." But this narrator writes them down.[25] And she doesn't transform them; she reminds herself when she gets impatient with her mother's digressive narrative style: "It's my mother's story and she will not be rushed."[26] Conserving that story even as she writes her own, this narrator, like Gornick, escapes the double trap of guilt on one hand and nostalgic longing for a rejected parental past on the other. Rejection, estrangement, and supplantation are not the issues for these women, as Broner's narrator's last words to her mother make very clear: "I don't want you to go from me, Mama. Even if you give everything away. . . . I don't want you to go away. Stay. I'll listen closely to your whispers."[27] Listening closely, staying instead of rejecting, this writing daughter who both resembles and differs from her mother, whose feminist commitments revise the domestic imperatives of her mother's life, restories her precursor without willfully misreading the maternal story.

Kim Chernin's memoir *In My Mother's House*[28] also writes especially large this pattern of faithful restorying through sustained, conflicted engagement rather than rupture. Allowing her mother's, her grandmother's, and her own stories their separate spaces within the single memoir, Chernin conserves the integrity of each narrative as she surfaces their effects on one another. From the grandmother's story, Chernin's mother draws the courage and inspiration that drives her to become a political activist. And in her mother's story, Chernin discovers the power to both deviate from and honor her mother's choices. Entering into her mother's narrative, Chernin realizes after long resistance the gift that it has to give her. Suddenly enlightened, Chernin understands that "the value of her [mother's] life's work did not depend upon" the work itself, but upon her mother's faithfulness to her own vision. "When I am eighty years old," Chernin writes, "I shall be happy if I have managed to remain true to myself, against all the passionate contradiction that cries out in my nature."[29] In part, the difference these stories describe between rupture and continuing engagement may be psychologically oriented. Nancy Chodorow and others have helped us to understand that women and men relate differently to mothers and fathers in their earliest years in the family. But I suspect this difference in the ways male and female American-Jewish writers deal with parental stories also exists, ironically, because of the silence that Jewish tradition imposed on its women. Traditional Judaism, as we all know, silenced and excluded its women's stories in many ways. But like everything else that human beings try to repress or exclude, they became powerful in exile. And when they found their way into more homely modes of discourse, maternal stories became particularly powerful for American-Jewish women writers, many of whom identify their own narrative gifts as part of their mothers' legacies. Like Gornick, Kate Simon, for example, recalls that her Jewish mother at the kitchen window interpreted the neighborhood, making narrative sense of tenement babble, stilling desire for the world beyond the kitchen.[30]

Theoretically, of course, the mother's link to language has come very clear in recent feminist writings. Bella Brodzki writes that "As the child's first significant Other, the mother engenders subjectivity thru language; she is the primary source of speech and love. And part of the maternal legacy is the conflation of the two."[31] The novelist Tova Reich understands the mother's role in this process in this fundamental way: "My mother had been my muse," Reich writes. "She had fed me the words."[32] Here there is neither usurpation nor perverse, willful revision. Instead, as Brodzki suggests, Reich acknowledges language itself as her mother's gift, as the very source of her own power with words.

Connected in this way with language in a child's earliest memory, mothers' voices can empower daughters by showing them how to conceive and articulate themselves as subjects. Thus, Kate Simon learns from her mother's stories the power of a narrating persona to give or withhold sympathy from her characters.[33] Indeed, when she remembers that "the voices that filled our world were those of women, the Mothers," she invokes a subjective maternal presence powerful enough to shape a child's sense of the world and to "fill" it as well, but not to drown her.[34] The verb's associations with completeness and satiation recall Tova Reich's metaphor of feeding that speaks so directly to these women's sense of verbal empowerment by their mothers.

For some women writers, however, maternal stories can also connect a daughter to the accommodations mothers have made to cultural restrictions that subdue and devalue women. Violet Weingarten's eponymous Mrs. Beneker, for example, is in part a relic of the 1950s in that she has been devalued by cultural pressure to efface herself in her roles as wife and mother.[35] She mothers largely by self-suppression and self-effacement. But she transmits, nevertheless, messages that handicap and infuriate her daughter and would-be daughter-in-law. Isadora Wing's mother in Erica Jong's *Fear of Flying* is similarly complicit in the culture's frustration of active professional women.[36] If, as Marianne Hirsch reports, feminists accuse mothers in our culture of denying "the truth about their own experience of bondage and frustration,"[37] Mrs. Beneker reveals the shape such denials often take and also the effects on daughters' disempowerment by stories that mothers either will not or cannot speak.

Filial stories by women, then, are complicated by the mixed effects on daughters of the frustrations, deprivations, and restrictions of their mothers' lives. But where some male protagonists fictionalize their father's lives to make a ground for their own stories of self, women writers like Broner, Gornick, Chernin, Simon, and many others carry forth the precursor's story even as their own narratives revise it. For example, in the stories of their precursors, the activist Jewish women of nineteenth-century Europe, contemporary Jewish feminists like Grace Paley hear not only a call to move into the wide, public world from the cramping pieties of traditional female domesticity but also a fierce cry of rebellion against the ethnic and gendered bonds that connect women with their families and communities. For Paley's protagonist Faith Darwin, however, activist commitments rise from, coexist with, and even deepen the powerful bonds that earlier activists needed to sever.[38] Mothering accompanies the activist agenda of Faith's own mother, and sets the activist agenda for Faith herself when the "heartfelt brains" of her son turn her outward from the family to work in a world whose neediness and vulnerability make it seem, sometimes, like yet another—profoundly recalcitrant—child.

Phyllis Chesler moves even further into a radical, activist revaluation of traditional family imperatives for Jewish women by bringing forward into the light of story the physical experience of childbirth and nursing.[39] By speaking through the body, as Adrienne Rich instructed, Chesler restories motherhood in its most intimate context, surfacing the power that lay silent in it for so many generations and thus drawing it into the political arena. The political activism of the European precursors, here, is restoried to accompany the family priorities of American immigrant mothers from whom Paley and Chesler descend.

Rich herself, thinking back through the European activist women with whom she identifies, metaphorically affirms the value of maternal devotion even as she critiques the specific political causes that failed them. Rich shares with these European radical women the determination "that the life she gives her life to/shall not be cheap/that the life she gives her life to/shall not turn on her/that the life she gives her life to shall want an end to suffering."[40] Like Maxine Kumin, who writes of carrying forth our mothers in our bellies, Rich exploits the trope of childbearing here to suggest that generations of women carry forward their precursors like women pregnant with the next generation of children.

Perhaps metaphors of pregnancy and childbirth are inescapable in a study of the ways women restory their mothers. Even Harold Bloom reaches into the experience of being mothered when he wants to imagine a kind of relationship between precursors and their descendants that falls outside the limits of the exclusively agonistic, androcentric system he has created. He speaks, briefly, of a "matrix of generous influence" that is profoundly different from the kind of influence that engenders male anxiety.[41] For him, that "matrix" is illusory. Within it, however, recent stories of American-Jewish women seem to find their source.

NOTES

1. Victoria Aarons, *A Measure of Memory: Storytelling and Identity in American Jewish Fiction* (Athens: University of Georgia Press, 1996), 1.

2. Harold Bloom, *The Anxiety of Influence: A Theory of Poetry* (New York: Oxford University Press, 1997), 13.

3. Bloom, *The Anxiety of Influence*, 6.

4. Bloom, *The Anxiety of Influence*, 30.

5. Bloom, *The Anxiety of Influence*, 56.

6. Bloom, *The Anxiety of Influence*, 57.

7. Bloom, *The Anxiety of Influence*, 154.

8. Bloom, *The Anxiety of Influence*, 85.

9. Herbert Gold, "The Heart of the Artichoke," in *Jewish American Stories*, ed. Irving Howe (New York: New American Library, 1977), 299.

10. Bloom, *The Anxiety of Influence*, 51.

11. Gold, "The Heart of the Artichoke," 299.

12. Aarons, *A Measure of Memory*, 172, 173.

13. Norman Finkelstein, *The Ritual of New Creation: Jewish Tradition and Contemporary Literature* (Albany: State University of New York Press, 1992), 22.

14. Finkelstein, *The Ritual of New Creation*, 3.

15. Vivian Gornick, *Fierce Attachments* (New York: Farrar Straus Giroux, 1987).

16. Gornick, *Fierce Attachments*, 137.

17. Gornick, *Fierce Attachments*, 15.

18. Gornick, *Fierce Attachments*, 152.

19. Gornick, *Fierce Attachments*, 110.

20. Gornick, *Fierce Attachments*, 204.

21. E. M. Broner, *Ghost Stories* (New York: Global City Press, 1995).

22. Broner, *Ghost Stories*, 64.

23. Broner, *Ghost Stories*, 124–27.

24. Broner, *Ghost Stories*, 132–33.

25. Broner, *Ghost Stories*, 36.

26. Broner, *Ghost Stories*, 149.

27. Broner, *Ghost Stories*, 180.

28. Kim Chernin, *In My Mother's House: A Daughter's Story* (New York: Harper & Row, 1984).

29. Chernin, *In My Mother's House*, 263–64.

30. Kate Simon, *Bronx Primitive: Portraits in a Childhood* (New York: Harper & Row, 1983).

31. Bella Brodzki, "Mothers, Displacement, and Language in the Autobiographies of Nathalie Sarraute and Christa Wolf," in *Life Lines: Theorizing Women's Autobiography*, ed. Bella Brodzki and Celeste Schenck (Ithaca, N.Y.: Cornell University Press, 1988), 245.

32. Tova Reich, "Hers: My Mother, My Muse" in *New York Times Magazine* (November 6, 1988), 30, 32.

33. Simon, *Bronx Primitive*, 4–5.

34. Simon, *Bronx Primitive*, 36.

35. Violet Weingarten, *Mrs. Beneker* (New York: Simon & Schuster, 1967).

36. Erica Jong, *Fear of Flying* (New York: Signet, 1996).

37. Marianne Hirsch, *The Mother/Daughter Plot: Narrative, Psychoanalysis, Feminism* (Bloomington: Indiana University Press, 1989), 165.

38. Grace Paley, "Faith in a Tree," in *Enormous Changes at the Last Minute* (New York: Farrar Straus Giroux, 1960), 75–100.

39. Phyllis Chesler, *With Child: A Diary of Motherhood* (New York: Crowell, 1979). See also Janet Burstein, *Writing Mothers, Writing Daughters: Tracing the Maternal in Stories by American Jewish Women* (Urbana: University of Illinois Press, 1996), which analyzes this book, among others.

40. Adrienne Rich, *Sources* (Woodside: Heyeck, 1983).

41. Bloom, *The Anxiety of Influence*, 122.

3

Never One without the Other: Empowering Readings of the Mother-Daughter Relationship in Contemporary Spain

María-José Gámez-Fuentes

The representation of mothering as an oppressive experience for the child is a familiar topic that feminist scholarship has widely researched and attempted to subvert by reading against the grain.[1] In the context of contemporary Spain, such a representation has not been dealt with widely until the reemergence of democracy when the complexities and contradictions of the idealizing and monolithic Francoist discourse on motherhood promoted by national-socialist ideals and the Catholic Church during the dictatorship (1939–1975) could be exposed.[2] The dictatorial regime constructed the notion of the maternal as a superior position within the private sphere of the home. This constituted a role for women that, although unrewarding, would place them in an apparently powerful and influencing situation with respect to the rearing of their offspring.

It can be argued that such a conceptualization of the mother figure falls within the parameters of the constitution of the mother as phallic. This term refers to those representations that situate her in a position of power with regard to her children. On the one hand, this conceptualization perpetuates the patriarchal construction of the mother as the one in control of the processes of absorption and separation that permeate the mother-child relationship, and, on the other hand, it obscures the ideological mechanisms at stake within such a positioning.

The representation of the mother as phallic obviously overlooks the complexities of the mother's subjectivity in having to conform within such a role.[3] With the return of the democracy there have been film and

47

literary texts that tackle, on the one hand, the contradictions between the official discourse and women's everyday experience of mothering and, on the other, the different ways in which children experienced it. It is precisely because of the special emphasis that Francoism put on the reconstruction of the mother figure as the embodiment of Spain that different narratives uncover the difficulties of children growing up with a mother figure who in one way or another, by trying either to perpetuate or to oppose the dictatorship's discourse, ended up exiled from/within herself.[4]

This chapter attempts to explore alternative models of thinking about motherhood as portrayed in the volume of short stories *Madres e Hijas* [Mothers and Daughters].[5] They move away from the reductionist and/or suffocating perspectives promoted in the Francoist period, in particular, and patriarchal societies, in general. The representation of the maternal carried out in the volume not only perpetuates the critique of patriarchal constructions of motherhood emerging in the democracy but it also explores new models of thinking about the mother-child dyad in relation to the mother-daughter experience. Following Kristeva's idea of "permanent alternation"[6] I will examine how, despite cultural constraints on women's bodies, the short stories chosen are able to deconstruct the image of the phallic mother by giving voice to the maternal and also to offer a space in which mothers and daughters are able to identify with each other without losing their own identity. Kristeva uses the term "permanent alternation" to refer to a critical strategy against patriarchal positioning based on the idea of both mother and daughter assuming and criticizing each other's role within society. This chapter focuses only on the analysis of three of the short stories: "Al colegio" [On the way to school] by Carmen Laforet, "De su ventana a la mía" [From her window to mine] by Carmen Martín Gaite, and "Primer amor" [First love] by Cristina Peri Rossi.[7] The choice of those three narratives is based on the especially empowering and positive portrayals of the mother-daughter relationship.

During the dictatorship the exaltation of the mother figure attempted to obliterate the voices of women's experiences as mothers. The regime's emphasis on the maternal resulted from a notable decline in the male population after the Spanish Civil War. The solution, which the regime looked to, was its regeneration, and thus the efforts centered around the woman as procreator, as mother, a role that was going to be the object of a vigorous propaganda by the government. Furthermore, faced with a population divided by the war, the regime set up the mother figure as the cohesive element of the two Spains: "The National-Syndicalism affirms the Brotherhood among Spaniards and there is no one better than the woman to consolidate this union among them."[8] Thus, the figure of an all-embracing mother emerged as a personification of the Francoist state.[9] No wonder, when the opportunity came in the democracy to criticize the

Francoist period, was the mother used as a metaphor of the oppressive regime.

Among the set of texts that try to account for different ways of thinking about the mother figure in Spain, the book *Mothers and Daughters* epitomizes in the field of literature the current interest in Spain both in theorizing women's experiences and in offering alternative literary models of representation. The book is a collection of fourteen short stories written by female writers which constitute innovative readings of the mother-daughter relationship. In the introduction, Freixas contextualizes the relation of such a compilation within the area of women's studies in English and French scholarship, emphasizing the need for literature in Spanish by female writers that would voice the similarities and differences of women's experiences. Through the different stories, various views of the experience of mothering are portrayed, passing through analyses and criticisms of prevailing social values. These go from the representation of such an experience as either fatal or uplifting, but frightening, to a declaration of love between a mother and a daughter. Although one also finds familiar themes of mothering as a repressive experience, alternative spaces are created in which to comprehend and/or project the complexities and ambiguities of the mother-daughter dyad. The texts are viewed from a historically informed perspective of the mother role in Francoist Spain as well as from a radically critical reading of patriarchally established stereotypes. The three stories under consideration represent a dialogue between two female characters who, despite culturally imposed constraints on their bodies, manage to build a bridge that allows them to negotiate, in a creative and constructive way, their own different identities without rejecting or repressing each other.

This process of reciprocal identification is paradigmatic of what Gallop[10] proposes, following Kristeva's idea of "permanent alternation," when criticizing Irigaray's argument of the engulfment of the daughter by the phallic mother.[11] According to Gallop, despite Irigaray's lyrical affirmation of a new kind of love between women and her attempt not to repeat or reproduce the patriarchal history, she falls into the trap of the patriarchal construction of the phallic mother by positioning the latter as the obstacle the daughter has to overcome in order to avoid paralysis. In her paper "And the One Doesn't Stir without the Other,"[12] Irigaray addresses the mother in her own plea for separateness. The mother is therefore placed in the position of the receiver of the daughter's demand, which, as Gallop points out, "presumes that the mother has the power to understand and fulfil the demand."[13] Kristeva, on the other hand, exposes the mechanism of defense at work when trying to assign separate identities, since the breakdown of these differences would be threatening both to the patriarchal order and to the daughter positioned within it.[14] Ac-

cording to Kristeva, the patriarchal order needs to objectify the figure of
the phallic Mother as the silent interlocutor, who is supposed to be in
command of the processes of life and death, meaning and identity.
Women need, in turn, language and the paternal symbolic in order to
identify with the mother. Kristeva, unlike Irigaray, speaks from the mother's place in her article "Stabat Mater,"[15] and in doing so she exposes the
fraudulence of conceiving the subject speaking from that place as the one
in command of the processes taking place between mother and child. The
critic assumes and exposes the complexity and paradox of such positioning. In Gallop's words:

> Irigaray's refusal to speak from that place, her resentment of the power of
> that place, leaves the mother phallic, that is, leaves the mother her supposed
> omniscience and omnipotence. Kristeva's presumption to speak from the
> place which no one has the right to speak from, combined with her constant,
> lucid analysis of that place and the necessity of such a presumption, works
> to dephallicize the Mother.[16]

What for Irigaray implies paralysis, for Kristeva is the condition of
movement. Representation is needed to avoid infantile passivity, powerlessness, and anxiety. The distance provided by the female subjects' inscription in the symbolic order of culture and society enables them to negotiate a place from which to exercise power and criticize it, for criticism
is required to overcome the paralysis of a rigid identity. As Kristeva suggests, what is needed is a process of a "permanent alternation: never the
one without the other"[17] through which "each must exercise and criticize
the power; each must be both mother and daughter."[18]

"On the Way to School," "From Her Window to Mine," and "First
Love" stage precisely the attempt to conceptualize the mother-daughter
process as a permanent alternation in which the I and you of the discourse are subverted, enabling mothers and daughters to identify with
the other's position without losing their own identity. The voicing of experience is also diverse since the narrative voice of the different stories
moves from the daughter's to the mother's and vice versa. "On the Way
to School" is told from the mother's perspective. Her voice opens the narration and the reader encounters her thoughts on the first day that she
has to take her daughter to school. Through her words the text communicates, apart from the mother's love for her daughter, the contrast between
the idealization of the maternal role and the actual vulnerability of the
woman in that position. The avoidance of catching a taxi in her daughter's
first trip to school, for example, triggers a reflection on the expectations
and stimulating plans she usually conceives before she goes for a walk
with her daughter, and the real and exhausting experience of having to

dress her up, clean her, and prepare her for the outing so that when they eventually go out:

> I, her mother, am almost as tired as the day I brought her into the world. . . .
> I am exhausted, walking with my coat hanging around me like a cloak; without any lipstick on (because I forgot about that at the last minute), almost dragged along by her, by her unbelievable energy, by the never-ending "whys" of her conversation.
> —Look, a taxi. —That is my desperate cry of salvation and collapse when I am with my daughter. . . . A taxi.[19]

Although this day represents for the mother a painful separation from her daughter, the reflection that we encounter brings the realization that she will also find some space for herself in this detachment. This mixture of feelings is also met when thinking about the choice of school for her daughter. Despite the mother's fondness for the chosen school, she reiterates the fact that it is very far and that they have to take several means of transport to get there. This widening space that opens between the home and the school is paradigmatic of the separation that the school as a cultural institution signifies for the two characters.[20] The different means that communicate both spaces can thus be read as emblematic of the representational bridges that mother and daughter are going to try to build to reach the gap separating them. The school acts as one of the cultural institutions that contribute to the symbolic separation between mother and daughter. It is one further step in the incardination of the daughter within the axis of representation. Not only does it open a physical breach within the maternofilial space of the home where the mother, in her own words, had the daughter at her disposal all the time,[21] but it also contributes further to the sociopsychic distance needed between them.

The fissure opened is not perceived as insurmountable though. The mother acknowledges the differences and similarities that exist in their respective experiences. For the first time she realizes on the way to school that her own hand and her daughter's are the same, and despite the fact that her narrative voice refers to the daughter as *she* and herself as *I*, she says that they both look with the same eyes. It could be argued that this game re-stages affirmatively and positively the freezing position that Irigaray exposes when talking about mother and daughter:

> You look at yourself in the mirror. And already you see your own mother there. And soon your daughter, a mother. Between the two, what are you? . . . There's just a pause: the time for the one to become the other. . . . Until there is only this liquid that flows from the one into the other, and that is nameless.[22]

According to Irigaray, this liquid prevents movement and action. How-ever, as in Kristevian fashion the text under study utilizes "this liquid that flows from the one into the other" to uncover the complexities of such a relationship, as well as its vulnerability and power. From there it con-structs an enabling experience of motherhood. The game between iden-tity and separation is obvious in Laforet's text, and the mother's voice plays precisely with the interchangeability of their position. Their dis-tance will bring them near, in a way, as expressed in the following para-graph:

> . . . [W]hat she [my daughter] will learn every day in this white house, what will gradually separate her from me—work, friends, new dreams—will bring her so near to my soul, that eventually I will not know where my spirit ends nor where hers starts.[23]

This alternation of identities is symbolized at the end of the tale, when the mother envisages herself in the classroom assuming her daughter's position at the start of the child's educational process.

"From Her Window to Mine" is told from the daughter's position. The title already announces the pendular movement that the story is going to represent. The event that triggers the narration is the happiness felt by the female narrator from a dream in which she intended to write a letter to her dead mother telling her things about New York. The form of writ-ing used in her oniric experience is a very peculiar one. It is not based on words but on the reflections of the light on a small mirror that her mother would collect from the other side of the river. Through the mirror, the daughter sends the message to her mother using a code the latter taught her. Such a way of communicating is a game secretly shown to her by her mother, which nobody except the two could share. The encoded message with playful overtones serves as an excuse to emphasize the possibility of an alternative means of language between mother and daughter.[24]

The window acts as a metaphor of the distance needed at the onset of the communicative process. The window is for the daughter a device that has been used by women to escape from the enclosed spaces of the house: "Nobody can put the eyes of a woman as she approaches a window be-hind bars, neither can they prohibit her ploughing through the world towards unknown boundaries."[25] Her mother was also very fond of such an opening, and during the hours of dusk the daughter recalls how her mother used to enjoy seeing the blurring of frontiers between day and night: "And in that silence falling with the dusk over her needlework and my notebooks, by envying and looking at her so much, I am not sure how but I too learnt to escape."[26]

It is in the fissure between lights that the daughter learnt how to flee the confines of enclosed spaces and could guess all the inner ones that her mother kept inside herself. They enabled her mother to fly to the un-known and far away places she once dreamt in her youth but she could never reach in her life as a married Spanish woman during the dictator-ship:

> And I am sure that before I knew her [my mother] she traveled through the window even more. In that time back in her youth and childhood—so novel, like for me—from those inner spaces that I never knew, I am sure that one day she must have got as far as New York itself. . . . To get lost in New York! The city of money and skyscrapers! The city of the emerging cinema and of dreams! How could my mother not have got to New York during one of those flights of a young window-dreaming woman who had fed on exotic novels?[27]

The daughter's reading of the mother's experience subverts the mono-lithic view of motherhood promoted by the Francoist dictatorship by con-sidering alternative ways in which her mother could escape the reduced private sphere of the home. Although she carried out her duties as mother and wife demanded by the official discourse, she is perceived as a woman capable of negotiating an empowering space, not trapped subjectively into the alienating diatribe of the regime. She managed to inscribe her own desire for freedom through filmic and literary narratives and flights of inner nature, as the public domain was in men's hands.

The daughter ends up realizing that the happiness she feels in her dream has originated not only from the fact that she eventually learned how to send a message to her mother using the light code the latter taught her, but also from the acknowledgment that her capacity for fleeing was nourished by her mother. It was her mother who enabled her to establish an alternative means of communication by cultivating in her daughter the will and desire to break frontiers, limits, confinements. This other means of communication stems from the mother, but it constitutes a form of pos-itive agency only in being acknowledged by the daughter in her histori-cally empowering reading of the maternal figure. So what started as a message from the daughter to the mother, ends up also being the result of the experiences the mother passed down to her daughter. From the one to the other, from the other to the one in a pendular movement of en-abling identification:

> Of course she had to have been there [in New York] some time; and that day, whenever it was, the wandering birds of her eyes built a glass nest which was so secret, rare and perennial that until last night nobody had discovered it. There was such a long path, such a rough track, such a labyrinth to reach what took place last night, that coded emission of signals between my mother and myself, from her window to mine![28]

"First Love" is also narrated from the point of view of the daughter who, from an early age, desires to marry her mother. The psychoanalytical connotations are evident, and even more so when the girl acknowledges that her desire goes against the laws of society.[29] However, thanks to the continuous linguistic game between the mother and the daughter, a basic element of their relationship, the protagonist grows neither estranged from the mother nor in jealous rivalry against her (as Freudian psychoanalysis would try to present the development of the female subject[30]), but, quite the contrary, she is able to subvert the law in her later years.

As a little girl she sees that her mother's married life offers the latter no happiness. The narrator compares her own relationship with her mother, with the one between the two spouses. The figure of the father appears interestingly associated to power:

> The little time my father was at home (appearing and disappearing without warning was for him a form of power), they used to fight, to reproach each other and a dark threat would glide through the air—like a black, stormy cloud.[31]

He is also made responsible, in the daughter's eyes, for the lack of adventurous spirit in her mother.[32] The negative portrayal of her mother's marriage is underlined in several occasions, especially when the daughter sees herself as her mother's female troubadour, for the former thinks the latter needs protection, a conclusion that is obviously deducted from the unhappiness she senses and the fights she has witnessed.[33] Moreover, the narrator concludes at the end of the story that the sexual lives of our mothers have to be dealt with sympathetically, as in many occasions, like in her mother's case, they were irrelevant or, even worse, disgusting.

In contrast, the protagonist perceives herself and her mother as a perfect couple because they have equal tastes, although they themselves "weren't exactly the same."[34] Again we encounter the paradigm of identity versus difference that we dealt with in the previous short stories: the reflection of one female body in the other and vice versa; the possibility of a reproduction of the mother's story from a critical standpoint that is actually enabled by the mother. Contrary to the power structure reproduced in her marriage, the mother establishes a relation of negotiation with her daughter through language: "my mother and I knew how to negotiate whenever there was a conflict."[35]

The mother appears from the beginning as the socializing agent through which the daughter acquires her command and love for language, and the knowledge about the laws of society. Thus although the mother is represented as the original object of love, she is also the one that has to pass onto her daughter the prohibitions that come with culture. This is portrayed in an exemplary way when the mother has to instruct the daughter about the reasons why they cannot get married. This prohibition acts metonimically to symbolize the law of culture and society that comes to mediate the mother-daughter relationship through language.

Language permeates the whole relationship between mother and daughter. The association of the mother with language and with the voice is emphasized in several occasions as the daughter recalls their conversations and the explanations she was given. She also had a beautiful soprano voice, as her daughter tells us. All that contributed to the daughter's love for language. The shaping of reality by words is manifested in the different talks they shared. Her mother always listened to her very attentively before she would give her any answer according to her age. For example, when asked by her daughter to marry her, the mother answers that their marriage could not be celebrated because she was still too young. Some time later when the protagonist is told she is old enough to go to school she takes the chance to remind her mother about their marriage. This time the mother tells her that as she has to go to school against her wish because the law requires it, the same law prohibited a mother to marry her daughter. It is, of course, noticeable that in none of the explanations does the mother use the argument of the different sexualities needed for marriage. The mother justifies the impossibility of their official union putting the social law between them. As the girl very precociously realizes:

> The law, then, prevented our marriage. I accepted it bravely, but secretly I was determined to do anything in my power to change it, since the law stopped people from accomplishing their desires.
>   I remember that [on] that afternoon (the one in which the law was revealed to be the obstacle of desire) . . . I reflected and concentrated on that new knowledge about life which my mother had provided me with: desires can go against the law—even those that seem to be the most just and noble—and the law is very difficult to change.[36]

Thus, the phallus emerges between the mother and daughter to mediate the daughter's desire towards her mother. This can be read as paradigmatic of the incardination of the female subject within the axis of desire and the subsequent emergence of the lack. However, this distancing from the mother through the Law of the Father does not leave either of them without voice; it does not repress the relation to the mother's body or what it means, either. Quite the contrary, it is precisely this distancing from one another that makes their respective actions of pendular approach possible. The impediment does not stop them from attempting al-

ternative ways to relate to each other. Rather than accept it, they try to
subvert it by reading their relationship culturally and herstorically.
Through language the mother offers a subversive view of the relation between the sexes to her daughter, and she in turn learns to use it to reconstruct a two-way link to access the subjectivity of her mother, the source
of her own identity. In doing so, the daughter tries to undermine the separation that culture establishes between their bodies. As an adult, the
daughter ends the narrative by saying, "Not only have I grown up
enough to reach her [my mother], but, sometimes, I am the mother and
she is the daughter. This has been our own particular way of changing
men's law."[37]

Indeed, one can also say that the stories analyzed subvert "men's law"
from a variety of perspectives by giving voice to the mothers and daughters portrayed here. Through the pendular communications enacted
within and between the different stories the reader explores some of the
richness, tensions, and complexities of a multivocal relation that has either been strongly suppressed by dictatorial regimes, such as the Francoist one, in favor of a reductionist inscription of the mother as phallic, or
distorted by the all-encompassing unifying discourse of patriarchy.

NOTES

1. See C. N. Davidson et al., eds., *The Lost Tradition: Mothers and Daughters in
Literature* (New York: Ungar, 1980); Lucy Fischer, *Cinematernity: Film, Motherhood,
Genre* (Princeton, N.J.: Princeton University Press, 1996); S. N. Garner et al., eds.,
The (M)other Tongue: Essays in Feminist Psychoanalytic Interpretations (Ithaca, N.Y.:
Cornell University Press, 1985); S. M. Gilbert and S. Gubar, *The Madwoman in the
Attic: The Woman Writer and the Nineteenth-Century Literary Imagination* (New
Haven, Conn.: Yale University Press, 1979); Christine Gledhill, ed., *Home Is Where
the Heart Is: Studies in Melodrama and the Woman's Film* (London: British Film Insti-
tute, 1987); Marianne Hirsch, *The Mother/Daughter Plot: Narrative, Psychoanalysis,
Feminism* (Indianapolis: Indiana University Press, 1989); Ann E. Kaplan, *Mother-
hood and Representation: The Mother in Popular Culture and Melodrama* (London:
Routledge, 1992); Silvia Tubert, ed., *Figuras de la madre* (Madrid: Catedra, 1996).

2. During the Francoist dictatorship, we can find several works, though, that
preclude the critical representations of the mother emerging from 1975 onward.
In the field of literature: Merce Rodoreda, *La plaça del diamant* [The Time of the
Doves] (Barcelona: Club Editor, 1962), and Miguel Delibes, *Cinco horas con Mario*
[Five hours with Mario] (Barcelona: Destino, 1966), constitute a perfect example
of the mother figure who is not aware of the brutal repression her subjectivity has
undergone in order to carry out the role that is expected from her. In the cinemat-
ographic arena, two exceptional films attempt in a subtle way to criticize the official discourse: *La tía Tula* [Aunt Tula], dir. Miguel Picazo (1964), based on the hom-
onymous novel by Miguel de Unamuno, and *Calle Mayor* [Main Street], dir. Javier

Bardem (1956). Both of them touch on the narrow choices women had and show the frustrated destiny of those who did not manage to attain the ideal state of wife and mother, thus becoming spinsters.

3. See Jane Gallop, *Feminism and Psychoanalysis: The Daughter's Seduction* (London: Macmillan, 1982), 115–31, for a detailed analysis of the fraudulent subject position offered to the woman in that place. For an investigation of the phallic mother represented as a castrating figure in film, see Barbara Creed, *The Monstrous-Feminine: Film, Feminism, Psychoanalysis* (London: Routledge, 1993).

4. Among the works that portray the tensions of a mother figure who tries to be on the side of the official discourse are films such as *Cría cuervos* [Raise Ravens], dir. Carlos Saura (1975); *Furtivos* [Poachers], dir. Jose Luis Borau (1975); and *Camada Negra* [Black Brood], dir. Manuel Gutiérrez Aragón (1977). The different female characters attempting to personify the Francoist ideal on motherhood expose critically the damage resulting from such a task: the alienation and/or annihilation of the female protagonist. In *Raise Ravens* the alienation of the female subject is represented metonimically through the representation of the mother as a dead figure, and in *Poachers* and *Black Brood* the critique of the mother as embodiment of Spain is achieved through a brutal portrayal of phallic mothers. These two films, by representing two female figures who ferociously assume and try to retain the phallic position, deconstruct the way the economy of the phallus works and expose the destructive effects both on the women's subjectivity and on those under their care. This narrative strategy is emblematic of that proposed by critics such as Gallop who à propos of Lacan argues that "if 'the phallus can play its role only when veiled,' then to refuse and deny the phallic position may mean to veil it and be all the more phallic, whereas blatantly, audaciously, vulgarly to assume it may mean to dephallicize" (Gallop, *Feminism and Psychoanalysis,* 120). On the other hand, there is another set of texts that exemplify instances of female resistance against the dictatorship. In this sense, Josefina Aldecoa's novel *Mujeres de negro* [Women in Black] (Barcelona: Anagrama, 1995) is a perfect example of the difficult and, in certain circumstances, almost impossible task of juggling one's own integrity as a woman against a tyrannical patriarchal state and an optimum state of body and mind to establish an affective and effective link with the subsequent female generations. This is the case of the protagonist of this novel who, despite being a brave and stimulating example to her daughter, is enclosed into an inner exile, originated in the need to protect her inner self from the years of material despair and dryness of feeling of the postwar years. Thus, she becomes in her daughter's eyes one of the many women dressed in black, symbol of traditional Spain, and whom her daughter wants to break away from.

5. Laura Freixas, ed., *Madres e hijas* (Barcelona: Anagrama, 1996).

6. Julia Kristeva, *About Chinese Women*, trans. Anita Barrows (London: Marion Boyars, 1986).

7. It is relevant to mention at this point the fact that Peri Rossi is not a Spanish-born writer but a Uruguayan one who arrived in Spain as an exile in 1972 and has been living in Spain as a Spanish national since 1974. The biographical geographical difference of the author does not invalidate, though, either the project of the volume or the purpose of my analysis; rather, it adds a further layer of diversity

in the exploration of the complexities of the mother-daughter relation in Spain, in particular, and patriarchal societies, in general.

8. Maria Pastor I Homs, "La educacíon femenina en la postguerra (1939–45)," in *El caso de mallorca* (Madrid: Ministerio de Cultura, Instituto de la Mujer, 1984), 26.

9. For an analysis of the historical influence of the Church and the Falange on the construction of the ideal of "the new woman" during the Spanish dictatorship, see M. T. Gallego Mendez, *Mujer, falange y franquismo* (Madrid: Taurus, 1983); Pastor I Homs, *La educacíon femenina en la postguerra;* Carmen Martín Gaite, *Usos amorosos de la postguerra espanola* (Barcelona: Anagrama, 1992); and H. Graham and J. Labanyi, eds., *Spanish Cultural Studies: An Introduction: The Struggle for Modernity* (Oxford: Oxford University Press, 1995), 182–95.

10. Gallop, *Feminism and Psychoanalysis.*

11. Luce Irigaray, "And the One Doesn't Stir without the Other," trans. Lelene Vivienne, *Signs* 7, no. 1 (Autumn 1981): 60–67.

12. Irigaray, "And the One Doesn't Stir."

13. Gallop, *Feminism and Psychoanalysis,* 115.

14. Kristeva, *About Chinese Women.*

15. Toril Moi, ed., "Stabat Mater," in *The Kristeva Reader* (New York: Columbia University Press, 1986).

16. Gallop, *Feminism and Psychoanalysis,* 117.

17. Kristeva, *About Chinese Women,* 38.

18. Gallop, *Feminism and Psychoanalysis,* 121.

19. Freixas, ed., *Madres e hijas,* 36. All the quotations from *Madres e hijas* are my own translations.

20. Let us remember precisely that the title of the short story is "On the Way to School," underlining the separating process of the experience.

21. Freixas, ed., *Madres e hijas,* 37.

22. Irigaray, "And the One Doesn't Stir without the Other," 63.

23. Freixas, ed., *Madres e hijas,* 37.

24. This project obviously echoes Cixous' work in her advocation for an alternative women's language that would disrupt the patriarchal structures in which female experience has been conceptualized by Western philosophical and the literary canon. See Hélène Cixous, "The Laugh of the Medusa," trans. Keith Cohen and Paula Cohen, *Signs* 1, No. 4 (Summer 1976): 875–93; Hélène Cixous, "Castration or Decapitation," trans. Annette Kuhn, *Signs* 7, no. 1 (Autumn 1981): 41–55.

25. Freixas, ed., *Madras e hijas,* 42.

26. Freixas, ed., *Madras e hijas,* 43.

27. Freixas, ed., *Madras e hijas,* 43–44.

28. Freixas, ed., *Madras e hijas,* 44.

29. Freixas, ed., *Madras e hijas,* 104.

30. See Sigmund Freud, *On Sexuality: Three Essays on the Theory of Sexuality and Other Works* in the Penguin Freud Library, vol. 7 (Harmondsworth: Penguin, 1991), 338–39.

31. Freixas, ed., *Madras e hijas,* 97.

32. Freixas, ed., *Madras e hijas,* 97.

33. Freixas, ed., *Madras e hijas,* 102.
34. Freixas, ed., *Madras e hijas,* 97.
35. Freixas, ed., *Madras e hijas,* 98.
36. Freixas, ed., *Madras e hijas,* 104.
37. Freixas, ed., *Madras e hijas,* 106.

4

Journeying Back to Mother: Pilgrimages of Maternal Redemption in the Fiction of Michèle Roberts

Cath Stowers

How successful is contemporary women's writing in developing maternal narratives and letting the mother speak? This chapter explores the fictions of Michèle Roberts in the light of this question, drawing from psychoanalysis, *l'écriture féminine,* postcolonial theory, and feminist theorizing on motherhood. Roberts's work is veined through with myriad journeys and travels, and I will be questioning the extent that journeys in women's writing can decolonize and activate difference, the ways a white woman writer can journey. Travel here becomes a repeated means of allowing maternal difference. To Roberts's mind, her books are "about women who learn to love journeying," and journeys here are not of conquest but of pilgrimage back to the mother, maternal redemption and reparation.[1]

But although journeys here are often of the daughter journeying to rejoin the mother, Roberts's work still successfully explores the mother as other, allows mothers to tell their own stories, and offers alternative narrative structures to those of Oedipality. For Roberts, her novels are "maternal narratives," and, opening up spaces for multiplicity and for spiraling stories, she has "allowed mothers to have voices in my fiction" as an "homage to the subjectivity of the mother."[2]

Given the grounding of Roberts's fiction in feminist thinking and theory, it is perhaps not surprising to find that her work mirrors the present, and continuous, fracturing of the feminist movement by discourses of difference. Roberts's work offers a fictional illustration, a tracing, of central developments within both feminist thinking and women's literary input. In particular, this fiction parallels certain shifts that have occurred within feminist theorizing of the maternal, motherhood and mothers. Roberts's work is a perfect illustration of those shifts that Marianne Hirsch has observed in women's writing from the voice of the daughter berating or mourning the lost mother, to texts in which mothers and daughters speak to each other, to maternal narratives that let the mother speak.[3]

This fiction deliberately draws from psychoanalytic theorizing whereby the very structure of Oedipality involves a journey and a return, a necessary integration in the same place of an identity secured by a difficult journey. More specifically, Roberts explicitly follows Melanie Klein's rewriting of the Oedipal drama, making the mother and her body, and their departure, the central figures in infantile development. Roberts's characters typically have absent mothers, and she has talked of the "fruitful, inspiring absence" of the mother.[4] For Klein, the infant oscillates between "seeking, finding, obtaining, possessing with satisfaction" and "losing, lacking, missing, with fear and distress."[5] These are the sorts of oscillations figured by fluxing, fluctuating journeys away from and back to the mother in Roberts's work.

Roberts's texts further illustrate feminist (re)interpretations of psychoanalytic theories, pushing gender asymmetry back to the mother-child pre-Oedipal, focusing on the primacy of the mother-daughter bond, on the dual process of separation-individuation, and on the growth into masculine and feminine persons. And, of course, many features of French feminist thinking can also be found in Roberts's fiction. Like *l'écriture féminine*, her work is rich with both quests and maternal metaphors and often speaks from what Jan Silverman Van Buren has called "babybody discourse."[6]

It has been suggested, however, that the focus on the space of the maternal by Hélène Cixous and others still enacts an erasure of the mother's voice and stories. Psychoanalysis itself has also been, as Gallop argues, "a theory of childhood," being both about childhood, and a childhood theory theorized from the child's point of view.[7] Roberts's claim that the mother's absence enables her to "imagine, invent, what life she's having, what her dreams are" may suggest that she too is writing of no more than a maternal object.[8] The problem becoming clearer, then, is how to symbolize the mother without objectifying her again? I want to suggest that Roberts's fiction does let the mother speak and goes beyond the figure of the mother in search of the mother's subjectivity.

Now, if we follow Jane Gallop's line that the "glorification of the figure of the mother is parallel to the erasure of differences among women," then it becomes clear that Roberts's explorations of the real (m)other behind the mother-as-object enact a strategy of opening up of difference.[9] And this is a strategy shared, I think, with another contemporary woman writer: Toni Morrison. Indeed, the reuniting of mother and daughter in

Roberts's fiction is often figured in passages of pre-Oedipal symbiosis, of mother-baby body discourse, where the return to the mother and her body is quite literally a return back to the womb. Such passages are also a central feature of Morrison's writing. To my mind Roberts's restitutory quest to the mother is paralleled by a pilgrimage, a homage, to Morrison. Like Morrison, Roberts accommodates maternal subjectivities, and I will be suggesting certain interactions between these two writers.

In her book *The Mother/Daughter Plot*, Marianne Hirsch specifically highlights Morrison's *Beloved* as the epitome of the truly maternal text. Hirsch further argues that the mythologies of, among others, Persephone and Demeter "suggest alternative economies which may shape different plot patterns" to Freud's focusing on Oedipus.[10] Journeys in Roberts's fiction in fact enact that cyclical mother-daughter reparation suggested by this very myth. And yet Hirsch argues that texts that have mothers as the object of a quest still silence and other the mother. I want to question some of Hirsch's assumptions and suggest that Roberts's fiction does rotate around the "maternal focus" that Hirsch identifies in black women's writing. For Roberts certainly explores the meanings of the (female and maternal) body, acknowledges the specificity of maternal experience, and portrays mother-daughter anger—all features Hirsch assigns to truly maternal writing.[11]

Tracing Roberts's intellectual debts to Morrison, I will be suggesting that, like Morrison's, Roberts's work effects strategies of decolonization. And I will be reading Roberts's fiction as an illustration of Hirsch's argument that a focus on mothers as others can achieve an actual redefinition of the notion of difference:

> Difference here is not merely gender difference. It encompasses the (maternal) difference within the feminine and the multiple differences within the maternal, the differences among women, the individual woman's difference from Woman . . . and the difference of maternal plots and stories.[12]

The fluctuating, to-ing and fro-ing journeys of Roberts's texts give difference free rein, in the mother, the self, and gender, and bring difference to bear on psychoanalytic and French feminist theorizing.

Roberts's first two novels, *A Piece of the Night* and *The Visitation*, establish mother-daughter conflict and the daughter's feelings of rejection by the mother as major themes. Both these novels appear to be concerned with what Naomi Schor has called "the myth of a sort of prelapsarian pre-Oedipus." Journeys are initiated by the loss of the mother and the maternal body, and become a kind of pilgrimage back to the mother. *The Wild Girl* and *The Book of Mrs. Noah*, Roberts's next two novels, mark a shift away from the confessional realism of the first two fictions to a growing

concern with the maternal principle and with mothers. Journeying leads
to the conciliatory site of the mother and to maternal desire and tale telling, that "tale telling" that, according to Minh-ha, is "what it takes to expose motherhood in all its ambivalence."

Roberts's fifth novel, *In the Red Kitchen,* makes space for the daughter
and mother to speak to each other, exploring the realities of mothering
across different classes and centuries and for the first time portraying a
specifically maternal house. In Roberts's fiction this house becomes a
place where the mother and her stories can be secreted away. Peculiarly
accommodating, chattering and bodily, such a house is most prominent
in *Daughters of the House* where the oscillating journeys back to and away
from the mother also become condensed into the image of the sea crossing. This is a text in which daughters mother the mother, and as such
Daughters of the House is one of Roberts's novels in which the similarities
with Morrison are particularly rich. As in *Beloved,* a daughter travels back
to a house full of maternal anger and grief, journeys back to the pre-
Oedipal, and mothers the mother. What *Daughters of the House* makes
clearer is that Roberts, like Morrison, is interested in the passage of the
self into the acquisition of full subjectivity. Journeys seem to be a particularly suitable means of narrativizing this theme, a means that can, simultaneously, suggest paradigms for a decolonizing, mobile identity. As the
scene of Léonie's channel crossing from England to France makes clear,
the state of in-betweenness, of to-ing and fro-ing, of duality, is made into
a position in itself, where identity is productively unstable and open to
difference.

This migratory, maternal aesthetic is also a major feature of the work
of many black women writers. Jamaica Kincaid, Elean Thomas, Michele
Cliff, and Joan Riley all deal with the opposing pulls of the "motherland"
and the "Mother Country," and the journeys between the two.[13] Roberts's
treatment of journeying can clearly not be aligned with such migratory
writings without qualification. Her earlier works could, after all, be
charged with veering toward Orientalism. Bangkok and Thailand repeat-
edly feature as sites for (Western) travels, and Roberts's explicit alignment
of the mother's body with "the Orient that travelers wish to plunder,
rape, explore" in her early fiction is clearly problematic.[14] The object-
relations work, psychoanalysis, and French feminism that are central theoretical bases in Roberts's work have also all been the focus of a sustained
backlash, becoming embroiled in debates on relevance and ethnicity.

But in *A Piece of the Night* Julie determines that although "others travel
to the East, to map it and explore and bring back booty, explanations. I
choose a different voyage."[15] And in spite of the aesthetic of mobility and
crossings in Roberts's work, she is nonetheless continually aware of location, whether of herself, of the theory she draws from, or of whiteness in
general. So, I now want to move on to discuss the ways that Roberts's

fiction can be read not just as a pilgrimage to the mother but also as to difference, suggested by similarities shared with Morrison's work. My intention here is not simply to point to motifs shared by Roberts and Morrison. My attempted alignment of a white and a black woman writer is clearly a matter for tricky negotiation. Morrison's writing is founded on a strongly non-white experience: as *Beloved* makes clear, psychic journeys are aligned with the suffering and horror of the Middle Passage, and the maternal here is a question not just of Cixous' white ink, of milk, but of blood. Journeys are not free floating and self-determined but enforced migrations and loss is not just of individual mother-daughter separation but of a people severed from their roots. *Beloved* makes clear that the reunion of mother and daughter cannot be any permanent peace; with Sethe finally being eaten away by Beloved in a desperate, destructive, cannibalistic confusion of boundaries, the dangers of being stuck in the pre-Oedipal are made explicit, in particular the potentiality for the engulfment of the mother. The pre-Oedipal in Morrison, then, is much more a regressive rather than a privileged site, and the pre-Oedipal daughter is not the penitential traveler returned as in Roberts but a clutching terror to be exorcised.

In spite of these disconnections between Roberts's and Morrison's journeying fiction, what I am attempting is a questioning of Hirsch's observations of maternal fiction in black women's writing only. It could be argued that the desire to privilege black women writers comes from a middle-class, liberal, and white guilt over an ongoing and active racism. I am not, of course, challenging the need for terms such as "black women's writing." What I am suggesting is that fencing black women's writing off into a field that cannot be trespassed into or traversed by a white foot is an easy option, easier than confronting our own whiteness, location, and racism. Like Carole Boyce Davies's concept of "migratory subjects," I am offering the trope of the fluctuating, to-ing and fro-ing journey as a figure for a new critical practice, a particular form of located journeying that can be an intervention into and escape from binary schemes that condition the ways we read black, postcolonial, and white women's writing.[16]

Both Roberts's and Morrison's journeys explore the same kind of territory. Both are concerned with the passage of the self within family dynamics, journeys maneuvering from the pre-Oedipal to the Oedipal and back again, enacting a quest for self-discovery. Such fictions expose the fictions of motherhood, counteract the myths of maternity, and write in the realities of mothering. It is in this light that I think Roberts can be added to Hirsch's list of women writers who offer major voices attempting to explore maternal subjectivity.[17] For these are texts that celebrate mothers—Mrs. Noah, for example, ending her litany praising mothers with the call "I want to join in. I want to worship, to praise. My own mother. All mothers."[18] Roberts's novels show mothers speaking, telling their own stories, creating and writing. And just as in *The Song of Solomon*, where Milkman realizes, "Never had he thought of his mother as a person, a separate individual, with a life apart from allowing or interfering with his own," so in Roberts's "Une Glossaire/A Glossary," the mother is seen "as a woman not just (a) mother," who, "long before [her children] came into existence . . . had a life of her own."[19]

So, Roberts's novels are not just written articulating the daughter's constructions. Roberts is well aware of the dangers of letting only the daughter speak; in *The Book of Mrs. Noah* the Correct Sibyl asks, "The voice of the angry daughter . . . is the only one heard in our land. What of the mother?" and Roberts's texts are indeed composed of mothers' stories.[20] Pilgrimages here, then, enable a return not only to the mother but also of the mother. Indeed, the figure of the writing, creating mother is a central one in Roberts's fiction, explicitly aligned with that of the mother/wanderer. The implication is that for mothers to be able to create, and write, they too need to journey.

Far from elevating motherhood to some spiritual or psychoanalytic abstraction, Roberts draws attention to its historical, economic, social, political, and cultural contexts. She also tackles areas of mothering usually glossed over by conventional myths, portraying mothers who cannot cope, mothers who do not want to mother, mothers who've lost their children. The combat at the heart of familial and sexual structures and a recognition of murderousness and maternal anger are central in the work of both Morrison and Roberts. In both, it is often the angry mother who is uncovered in all her difference by journeys in these fictions. In both, maternal rage and abuse/infanticide are symptoms of the highlighting of maternal difference and the historicizing of the maternal. And in both, this theme has been growing in prominence throughout earlier works until meeting its epitome in Morrison's *Beloved* and Roberts's story "Anger."

Like Morrison's other works, *Beloved* is a text of journeys: the daughter journeys back to the mother, the story is initiated by the return of a journeying male, and the mother journeys into self-discovery. As in Roberts's fiction, the journeys in *Beloved* seem to be initiated by severance from the mother, and both start and lead to a maternal house. As in Roberts, mothers are absent here in a myriad of ways. As in Roberts, such mother starvation can lead to vision and haunting.

Beloved's errantry back to the mother is from beyond the grave, and Morrison makes the suggestions of the pre-Oedipal (water, an alternative language, maternal milk—and blood) clear. In the "babybody" section of *Beloved* the separation from the mother leads to a severance and desire for reunion articulated in terms of eating and orality:

I reach for her chewing and swallowing she touches me she knows I want to join she chews and swallows me. I am gone. . . . I see me swim away a hot thing. . . . I am alone I want to be the two of us I want the join.[21]

This redemptive site, the place of babybody discourse and pre-Oedipal language, achieves the symbiosis of mother and daughter before the time when "Daddy is coming for us": "I am not separate from her there is no place where I stop her face is my own."[22]

Now Roberts's story "Anger" and her 1994 novel *Flesh and Blood* both contain a core section of maternal-baby-body discourse that is remarkably similar to that of *Beloved*. Like Roberts's fiction, *Beloved* centers around the Demeter and Persephone myth of cyclical mother-daughter reunion. As in Roberts, the loss of the mother is "the source of the outrage," the concern not only with the child's longing for the lost maternal object but also with the immense loss experienced by the mother who is unable to keep her children alive and rear them.[23] Both Roberts's and Morrison's fiction deals with the "rage" of the daughter but also lets the mother speak, journey, recover—and ultimately discover a self for herself.

In her discussion of *Beloved*, Hirsch speaks of the "transmission of unspeakable stories" as a distinctly "maternal act."[24] Throughout Morrison's work, those stories that are "unspeakable" are often of mothers far removed from maternal myths, of mothers who would be classified as "bad," of mothers who rebel against the costs and demands made on them with maternal anger. Roberts's fiction is also often concerned with "unspeakable stories," frequently shared by females. As in Morrison, these are recurring stories of infanticide, of baby blood. The story "Anger" from *During Mother's Absence*, is a case in point. It does, after all, close with Roberts's direct acknowledgment of the inspiration provided by Morrison's work, and a number of shared features can certainly be identified. These include the figure of the unwilling or "bad" mother; the mother's engulfment by the daughter; the intervention by the father/husband, and the effect this has on mother-daughter relations; the scarring and separation concomitant on the loss of the mother; temporary reunions with the mother; breast-feeding as a central symbol of mother-daughter dynamics; and fire as a symbol of maternal anger and violence.

Whereas in the traditional Melusine story, the lost paradise is the father's kingdom, here, as in Roberts's other fiction, it is the old mother-daughter unity. In *Beloved*, the separation from the mother is portrayed as a quite literal severance marked by the scar etched around the daughter's throat. "Anger" also explores the mother-daughter separation in terms of scarring, with Melusine "a damaged person" dropped in the fire by her mother. And in "Anger," as in *Beloved*, the mother is engulfed and eaten up and away by the daughter: "They watched her feed what was left of her soul into her daughter's rosy mouth which ardently sucked it in."[25]

In the babybody section of "Anger," a section written in the style of
Beloved's mother-daughter reunion passage, the fire is identified as the
place of separation from the mother: "Dead people go to Purgatory, to
have all the badness burnt out of them by a great fire. But the fire happens
when you are born, not after you are dead."[26] Simultaneously, however—
and more so than in Morrison—the fire is the site of reunion with the
mother. Even after the daughter has been banished from the mother into
marriage, she can "come into the kitchen to warm myself at the fire . . .
and the mother will never turn me away."[27] The fire is the element of the
mother in all her diversity, not just her anger but her love, her creation
and birthing as well: "out of the love between us comes the fire, and the
warm kitchen and the mother in the kitchen. . . . Out of the fire between
us comes the baby."[28] Here an eternal mother-daughter link is almost religious in its force; the fire can be returned to, and the daughter healed by
the mother: "my mother dropped me in the fire, but she will heal me. She
will heal me with her tears."[29] So, here we have a decidedly pre-Oedipal
narrative section that has obvious debts to Morrison's novel. As in *Beloved*,
this passage figures a restitutive reunion between mother and daughter,
an interior journey that rediscovers the mother and celebrates the female
body:

> Look in the mirror, the mother says, and see how beautiful you are. . . . See
> the red fire glowing there, in the secret place between your legs. . . . You are
> like me. You are my daughter. . . . You can leave me and you can always come
> back. . . .
>   I threw my mother in the fire. I shall heal her. I shall heal her, with my
> tears.[30]

Flesh and Blood, like "Anger," contains a central maternal/babybody
section, but in this novel its position as the core of the narrative is made
more blatant. This is a spiraling, circling text, its myriad stories and sections rippling out from its heart, the excerpt of mother-child symbiosis.
Roberts's works certainly swerve and spiral away from any linearity of
plot or structure. The figure of the labyrinth recurs throughout her novels.
The maternal body at the heart of Roberts's labyrinths—and I mean here
both the labyrinths in the texts and of the texts—is only reached by circling journeys of return and departure that become, most clearly in *Flesh
and Blood*, symbolized by the figure of the spiral.

Flesh and Blood is, out of all of Roberts's fiction, the text that most explicitly uses the spiraling journey back to the maternal body as an active
form-giving principle. This is a novel of sensations of mother-memory, of
multiplicity and tale telling. Roberts weaves and reassembles narrative,
an example of Hirsch's maternal texts that effect a differing narration of

development, one where linear progression is superseded by fits and starts and tentativeness. Roberts has explained how the journeys of Fred/ Frederica in *Flesh and Blood* represent a "going backwards when in trouble," a "jumping back to go forwards"; here the to-ing and fro-ing pilgrimages that I have been trailing through her work meet their epitome in a constant movement between inner and outer, maternal separation and reunion, Oedipality and pre-Oedipality, England and France.[31]

Journeys in *Flesh and Blood* again effect a return to the mother and her body as redemptive site, as Paradise, and, to quote Roberts, "explore what would happen if a character went (back to the mother's body)— would they want to stay or leave?"[32] The outer journeys, she continues, "metaphorize the personal, inner journey," and this inner journey is one that never ceases, for "rebirth happens," the subject is "squeezed out again, grieving."[33] It seems, then, that the pilgrimage is not just to the mother, but to a newly acquired self as well. This is not travel by any conquesting, monarchic self but rather one that changes the journeying self, which opens not only the mother but also the self itself to difference. This is a further way that I think Roberts's pilgrimages can be read as decolonizing, as decided strategies of difference. As the editors of the *Travellers' Tales* collection have suggested in their consideration of concepts of travel:

> The voyage out of the (known) self and back into the (unknown) self. . . . Travelling can . . . turn out to be a process whereby the self loses its fixed boundaries—a disturbing yet potentially empowering practice of difference.[34]

Journeys in *Flesh and Blood* spiral in two directions: those that separate daughter from mother, and those that reconnect. So, for example, we have the story of Frederica Stonehouse, the daughter journeying from mother-child unity to her first primary school. In another story, Eugénie is a daughter similarly severed from the mother via a coach journey to her new marital home. It is the story of "Rosa," however, which most powerfully portrays these journeys that signify the loss of the mother. Here the mother literally runs away from her five daughters, disappearing like Frankenstein's monster into frozen wastes and leaving Rosa as another of Roberts's daughters hungering for mother love: "I felt my stomach was very large, emptied by her going, then blown out with fear. I wanted to eat, to fill myself with her."[35]

But Rosa makes reparation, journeying back to the maternal body. The Angel Cherubina who appears to Rosa acts as guide—"your mother is in Paradise, and I have come to tell you how to get there"—leading both daughter and reader back to Paradise and the pre-Oedipal: "My country is called Paradise. . . . Most people . . . are certain it is now lost forever.

. . . Yet some adventurers spend their lives trying to discover it. Archaeologists. . . . Explorers."[36]

So access to the lost maternal realm is dissociated from traditional paradigms of travel and exploration:

> Put together the desire and the maps, . . . but you have not found it. . . .
> Though the travellers come back and tell their tales and the scholars distill
> their theories and the explorers boast about the distant exotic places they
> have seen. . . . My country is somewhere else.[37]

Just as in *A Piece of the Night* Julie chose "a different voyage" from that to "the Orient," here the maternal can only be reached by a journeying that avoids repeating patterns of conquest and Otherizing—by, that is, decolonizing journeys.

So, *Flesh and Blood* is a text in which journeys again reunite mothers and daughters. And it is a text, like *Beloved*, like "Anger," in which journeys reach the babybody not as their end point but as their turning point. The first five stories tracing the loss of and departure from the mother lead to the central five stories, and the last five stories then depict the returned, refound mother.

The "love messages" that are at the heart of *Flesh and Blood* are pre-Oedipal messages between mother and daughter. Re-creating the pre-Oedipal Paradise, here mother and daughter are inseparable, indistinguishable, "I" and "you" merging to "us," "we" and "you/me"; with "us so close skinskin," the daughter is "allowed love home flesh my mamabébé."[38] Journeys have led us, then, to that stage *Beloved* yearns for when "I" is "the two of us." This is the site of reparation, redemption and unity, a place where, as in *Beloved*, "I am not separate from her there is no place where I stop": "we is one whole undivided you/me broken now mended you/me restored mamabébé."[39]

But the journey does not cease at this site of revisited symbiosis. Instead, the baby is "born out of you/ bébé born crying wanting you mamabébé."[40] Rebirth in this novel is partly a propulsion towards the mother's story. Roberts has identified this novel as being "about storytelling," and after the symbiotic turning point of *Flesh and Blood*, stories are told by the mother.[41] The journeying return to the maternal does not, then, colonize and silence the mother but rather decolonizes and gives her her own voice, calls for us to "listen hush now bébé hush listen what mama say."[42]

Returning to the story of Rosa, we are told of her rescue and resurrection of the mother. Rosa finds her mother dead in a sled, but the mother is quite literally brought back to life, reparation made for her earlier murder with which the text opened, a reparation reminiscent not only of the pre-Oedipal sea but also of that desperate greedy orality of *Beloved*'s

babybody section: "I put my lips to the ice that held and surrounded her
like love. I kissed her. . . . I kissed her again and again, I sucked and bit
her glass flesh, . . . I held her in my arms and nibbled and licked her, my
waterfall."[43] The daughter in Roberts's novel journeys not just to find the
mother but to bring her back; the daughter mothers the mother.

Flesh and Blood certainly ends with the maternal body, making the "fe-
cund and abundant" maternal body temporarily and "newly available to
us."[44] In Georgina's own love-making, where she is the active one, un-
peeling and cracking Clem open, her revelation that she learnt her fellatio
techniques "at my mother's breast of course" "magically" transforms
male lover into milk-giving mother, "turned into Gladys, her big white
body, and he was a plump white cocky breast at which she sucked her
fill, as long as she wanted."[45]

Journeys throughout this text have, then, signaled both separation from
and reunion with the mother. The final two stories of *Flesh and Blood* bring
together these two pulls. "Louise" is a mother's story about losing a
daughter, a daughter called Frederica or Freddy. This daughter leaves the
mother, runs away from home, in a storm of sexuality, to "make films
about art."[46] This final section in a sense provides the solutions to the puz-
zles of *Flesh and Blood*, revealing that Georgina/George is in fact Frederica, the daughter, who is also Freddy from the start of the book. This final
story is "an elegy for the mother I remember, whose breast my tiny hands
patted as I searched for her with my mouth . . . She talked to me in a
secret language of mamabébé."[47] Like *Beloved*'s lament of separation, this
is a mourning "for the mother I lost, when the skin that bound us ripped
away, our separate skins tore off and we were miserable being two beings
so different she couldn't like me being unlike herself."[48] Simultaneously,
however, "this is also an elegy for the mother I found again," a mother
permitted all her power, corporeality, and sex:

> My mother was my first great love, she was my paradise garden, and she
> was the Queen of Heaven, she was not that soppy lady Mary but someone
> far more beautiful and fierce, she was lion-soft and flushed and sexy, she
> smelled of herself, of her own body, she shouted out, she was powerful.[49]

Journeys into and away from pre-Oedipality are identified as necessary
for the subject formation of both mother and daughter: "she thought I
had abandoned her and given her up for ever but I had not. I needed to
go away so that I could come back just as she did."[50] This daughter comes
back as an expectant mother, *Flesh and Blood* "closing," like Roberts's
other texts, with a potential mother, presented as a link with the "lost
Paradise" of the mother. The unborn child "swims inside me . . . my flesh

and blood, made of love in the land of milk and honey, the land of spices and stories."[51]

Frederica, we learn, fled home disguised as a man to escape the denigration of her sexuality, the abusive (sexual) insults of her mother and father: "I put on a disguise so that someone else could feel the bite and sting of those words but not me. . . . I had to cover myself with a man's clothes then run."[52]

This, then, is the fleeing Fred "on the run" that *Flesh and Blood* opened with. This novel certainly backs up Hirsch's claim that maternal texts demand that we "revise our very notion of resolution," closing in a circularity which returns to the novel's start, with the daughter and her partner walking "back through Soho and into the next story."[53] Spiraling back to Fred's original journey through Soho that opened the text, we realize that Fred is the daughter, searching for the mother killed by the daughter's rage and running away. By the end of the journey, the spiraling stories of wandering and fleeing mothers and daughters, we know the daughter has been reunited with the mother, for we ourselves have traveled through the narrative's circles to the core of the book—the pre-Oedipal maternal body. *Flesh and Blood* ends with hope, with the potential of dual parenting, and with the image of the expectant mother and father walking forwards yet backwards, spiraling into a series of mediating concentric circles and spiraling out again, the traveler reborn. Ultimately *Flesh and Blood* exemplifies Karen Elias-Burton's arguments that women writers are reclaiming the mother:

> as a metaphor for the sources of our own creative powers. Women are creating new self-configurations in which the mother is no longer the necessary comfort but the seed of a new being, and in which we are no longer the protected child but the carriers of the new woman whose birth is our own.[54]

NOTES

1. Michèle Roberts, interview with Cath Stowers, London, March 1997.

2. Roberts, interview, March 1997.

3. Marianne Hirsch, *The Mother/Daughter Plot: Narrative, Psychoanalysis, Feminism* (Bloomington and Indianapolis: Indiana University Press, 1989), 8.

4. Michèle Roberts, reading and talk, the University of York, United Kingdom, autumn 1995.

5. Jacqueline Rose, *Why War? Psychoanalysis, Politics and the Return to Melanie Klein* (Oxford: Blackwell, 1993), 151.

6. Jan Silverman Van Buren, *The Modernist Madonna: Semiotics of the Maternal Metaphor* (Bloomington: Indiana University Press, 1989), 14.

7. Jane Gallop, ''Reading the Mother Tongue: Psychoanalytic Feminist Criticism,'' *Critical Inquiry* 13 (Winter 1987), 314–29.

8. Roberts, reading and talk, autumn 1995.

9. Kahane in Gallop, ''Reading the Mother Tongue,'' 328.

10. Hirsch, *The Mother/Daughter Plot*, 5.

11. Hirsch, *The Mother/Daughter Plot*, 161, 166.

12. Hirsch, *The Mother/Daughter Plot*, 12–13.

13. Elaine Showalter in Hirsch, *The Mother/Daughter Plot*, 125.

14. Michèle Roberts, *A Piece of the Night* (London: Women's Press, 1978), 55, 26.

15. Roberts, *A Piece of the Night*, 35.

16. Carole Boyce Davies, *Black Women, Writing and Identity: Migrations of the Subject* (London: Routledge, 1994).

17. Marianne Hirsch in Donna Basin, Margaret Honey, and Mahrer Kaplan, eds., *Representations of Motherhood* (New Haven, Conn.: Yale University Press, 1994).

18. Michèle Roberts, *The Book of Mrs. Noah* (London: Minerva, 1987), 43.

19. Toni Morrison, *The Song of Solomon* (New York: Signet, 1977), 75; Michèle Roberts, ''Une Glossaire/A Glossary,'' in *During Mother's Absence* (London: Virago, 1993), 142, 173.

20. Roberts, *The Book of Mrs. Noah*, 139.

21. Toni Morrison, *Beloved* (London: Picador, 1988), 213.

22. Morrison, *Beloved*, 210.

23. Morrison, *Beloved*, 4.

24. Hirsch in Basin et al., eds., *Representations of Motherhood*, 109.

25. Michèle Roberts, ''Anger,'' in *During Mother's Absence*, 11.

26. Roberts, ''Anger,'' 25.

27. Roberts, ''Anger,'' 25.

28. Roberts, ''Anger,'' 25.

29. Roberts, ''Anger,'' 26.

30. Roberts, ''Anger,'' 25–26.

31. Roberts, reading and talk, autumn 1995.

32. Roberts, reading and talk, autumn 1995.

33. Roberts, reading and talk, autumn 1995.

34. George Robertson, Melinda Mash, Lisa Tickner, Jon Bird, Barry Curtis, and Tim Putnam, eds., *Travellers' Tales: Narratives of Home and Displacement* (London: Routledge, 1994), 23.

35. Michèle Roberts, *Flesh and Blood* (London: Virago, 1994), 96.

36. Roberts, *Flesh and Blood*, 104.

37. Roberts, *Flesh and Blood*, 104–5.

38. Roberts, *Flesh and Blood*, 109.

39. Morrison, *Beloved*, 213; Roberts, *Flesh and Blood*, 109.

40. Roberts, *Flesh and Blood*, 110.

41. Roberts, Reading and Talk, Autumn 1995.

42. Roberts, *Flesh and Blood*, 110.

43. Roberts, *Flesh and Blood*, 116.

44. Roberts, *Flesh and Blood*, 165.

45. Roberts, *Flesh and Blood,* 167.

46. Roberts, *Flesh and Blood,* 171.

47. Roberts, *Flesh and Blood,* 173.

48. Roberts, *Flesh and Blood,* 173.

49. Roberts, *Flesh and Blood,* 173.

50. Roberts, *Flesh and Blood,* 173–74.

51. Roberts, *Flesh and Blood,* 174.

52. Roberts, *Flesh and Blood,* 174.

53. Hirsch, *The Mother/Daughter Plot,* 35; Roberts, *Flesh and Blood,* 175.

54. Karen Elias-Burton, "The Muse as Medusa," in *The Lost Tradition: Mothers and Daughters in Literature,* ed. Cathy N. Davidson and E. M. Broner (New York: Unger, 1980), 205.

Part II

Dismantling Patriarchal Motherhood

5

Bitches with Broomsticks: The Bad Mother in American Maternity Poetry

Susan MacCallum-Whitcomb

Adrienne Rich has said that poetry emerges from society's "points of stress" as if "the stress in itself creates a search for a language in which to probe and unravel what is going on."[1] If this is indeed the case, then we should not be surprised that so much fine work was produced by those American poets who, like Rich herself, became "mother[s] in the family-centered, consumer-oriented, Freudian-American world of the 1950s."[2] After all, being a mother, in an era when motherhood was considered a woman's raison d'être, was a very stressful thing.

As Betty Friedan explains:

> There was, just before the feminine mystique took hold in America, a war, which followed a depression and ended with the explosion of an atom bomb. After the loneliness of war and the unspeakableness of the bomb, against the frightening uncertainty, the cold immensity of the changing world, women as well as men sought the comforting reality of home and children.[3]

Yet the homes members of this postwar generation would create bore little resemblance to the ones they themselves grew up in. The new suburban ideal changed irrevocably both the physical design of the house and its relationship to the community, while new household technology raised the standards for domestic comfort and cleanliness. The vision of parenthood for this postwar generation was similarly "new and improved."[4]

Logistically, there was the issue of family size, as baby boom mothers were expected to bear and raise more children than their predecessors.[5] Moreover, they were also expected to rear them in a different way. As Martha Wolfenstein observes, in the opening decades of this century, chil-

dren were seen as "sinful" creatures "endowed with strong and dangerous impulses." However, in the years immediately following World War
II, they were suddenly transformed into "harmless" little beings whose
impulses were both "pleasant and good."[6] Children became the hope for
the future, peace and innocence personified, and if America was truly to
be a kinder, gentler nation, they had to be nurtured at any price. Of
course, the physical and psychological cost to their mothers was great,
especially after innumerable child care "experts" stepped in with their
trickle-down translations of Freud, making it clear that mothers were no
longer just responsible for their children's bodies and souls but for their
ids, egos, and superegos as well.

It could be (and indeed was) argued that the added responsibility and
renewed sense of purpose that now came with mom's job description
were empowering; however, the reality was quite different. In many respects, maternal power was merely an illusion, a consolation prize
granted by a patriarchal society that had found it expedient on multiple
levels to turn Rosie the Riveter into June Cleaver. (The fact that male "experts" felt justified in guiding mothers through virtually every step of the
child-rearing process validates this claim.) Moreover, mothers often perceived their power to be illusory. With a host of "experts" looking disap-
provingly over their shoulders (to say nothing of the hoards of children
glaring accusingly from cribs and corners and potty chairs), mothers
began to feel anxious, inadequate. In a word, they began to feel powerless.[7]

The spectre of failure loomed large for mothers because, in the Institution of Motherhood, passing grades were hard to get. In fact, it took a
great deal of labor just to fail. According to John Bowlby, the influential
psychiatrist and psychoanalyst of the 1940s and 1950s who popularized
attachment theory:

> even a bad parent [read "mother"] who neglects her child is none-the-less
> providing for him. Except in the worst cases, she is giving him food and shel-
> ter, comforting him in distress, teaching him simple skills, and above all is
> providing him with that continuity of human care on which his sense of se-
> curity rests.

To excel, Bowlby argued:

> a mother needs to feel that she belongs to her child, and it is only when she
> has the satisfaction of this feeling that it is easy for her to devote herself to
> him. The provision of constant attention, night and day, seven days a week,
> 365 days in the year, is only possible for a woman who derives profound
> satisfaction from seeing her child grow from babyhood, through the many

phases of childhood, to become an independent man or woman, and knows that it was her care which made this possible.

It is for these reasons that the mother-love which a young child needs is so easily provided within the family, and is so very very difficult to provide outside it.[8]

Simply put, the "good" postwar mother was expected to not only put herself "unreservedly" and "continuously at the disposal of others,"[9] but she also had to find her work wholly fulfilling. She still had to wash out diaper pails, to wipe up baby barf and baby bums, but she no longer had a right to complain—let alone ask for assistance—because such tasks were suddenly of supreme importance and could be completed satisfactorily by her alone. She had to whistle while she worked: the future of her family—no, the future of the free world—seemed to depend on it. And she couldn't fake this kind of pleasure. Small children, it seemed, could easily distinguish between the "good" mother and every other variety. Like some other small mammals, they could apparently smell insecurity, insincerity, and fear.

Using only slightly more scientific methods, the "experts" too could readily separate the "good" mother from the "bad"; and when they set their minds to it, they began to find the latter everywhere. As Friedan explains:

It was suddenly discovered that the mother could be blamed for almost everything. In every case history of a troubled child; alcoholic, suicidal, schizophrenic, psychopathic, neurotic adult; impotent, homosexual male; frigid, promiscuous female; ulcerous, asthmatic, and otherwise disturbed American could be found a mother. A frustrated, repressed, disturbed, martyred, never satisfied, unhappy woman. A demanding, nagging, shrewish wife. A rejecting, over-protecting, dominating mother.[10]

It does not require a huge stretch of the imagination to see in this era of mass finger-pointing and blame-laying, during which women could be convicted of large crimes on little evidence, a parallel to another unfortunate era in American history: the latter part of the seventeenth century, age of the witch-hunt. One need only substitute "It's Mom's fault that I had a nightmare" or "My milk was sour" for "It is the witch's fault that evil spirits visited me in the night" or "My cow produced foul-tasting milk" to see the similarities. Certainly this was recognized by a number of America's literary mothers, women who were already using the magic power of words to translate experience into art.[11]

Like the witches, these mothers lived dangerous lives. Although they were often vulnerable beings, hobbled by economic dependency and isolated in suburbia, they were seen to have the power to do great harm.

Furthermore, they too were aware that they risked persecution if their behavior fell outside the established norms. These women, particularly those who openly acknowledged their own dark side, came, therefore, to define their "alienation as witchery"[12] and to identify themselves with the figure of the witch. As a result, she became a common feature in the maternity poems they wrote.

For them, the witch served a variety of purposes. On one level, the witch offered an alternative paradigm for female behavior: something that neither the child care manuals nor the popular television programs of this era could provide. If a woman couldn't meet the exacting membership requirements of the sorority club that worshiped Harriet Nelson and Donna Reed, she could, at least, find companionship among the weird sisters.

On a different level, employing the figure of the witch added a certain credibility to the maternity poets' art. Since the confessional genre that many of these women worked within was still being criticized as narrow and overly personal, their identification with the witch allowed them to demonstrate both the accessibility and broader significance of their poetry, because through it the writers of maternity poems could tap into history, mythology, anthropology. But the figure of the witch also had the added advantage of being firmly rooted in their subject matter. In poems about the relationship between mother and child, what image could be more appropriate than one that is an integral component of children's literature? We all know the witch's stories. They have been read to us or told to us; we've seen them acted out in drama or dance or animated films. Thus, the witch is at once a piece of our popular culture and part of that private vocabulary that exists between parent and child.

Among the earliest, and arguably the most notable, of the maternity poets to make use of the witch figure was Anne Sexton. It seems to have come naturally to her. According to Maxine Kumin, the friend and fellow poet with whom she coauthored four children's books, Sexton had always been "attracted to the fairy tales of Andersen and Grimm": they were for her "what Bible stories and Greek myths had been for other writers."[13] Proof of this fascination came in 1971 when Sexton published *Transformations*, a collection of poems based on stories by the Brothers Grimm, which was inspired by and dedicated to her daughter Linda.

In this work, Kumin notes, the poet places "the family constellations in a fairy tale setting," focusing "on women cast in a variety of fictive roles: the dutiful princess daughter, the wicked witch, the stepmother."[14] But two clarifications must be made here. First, the roles are often conflated so that the witch and the mother (step- or otherwise) become one. Second, the roles are not entirely "fictive": in introducing the poems, Sexton announces that "the speaker in this case / is a middle-aged witch, me,"[15] and she confides in a letter that "it would . . . be a lie to say that they [the poems in *Transformations*] weren't about me, because they are just as much about me as my other poetry."[16]

Thus, it is significant that the witch of *Transformations* is not a frightening figure. Instead, she is "profoundly maternal, offering to her children revisions of patriarchal myths to reveal the truths that women know."[17] It is significant as well that in Sexton's re-visions those maternal characters who were hitherto seen as evil, from Mother Gothel in "Rapunzel" to the witch-queen in "Snow White and the Seven Dwarves," are sympathetically portrayed.[18]

As suggested, variations on these fairy tale figures can also be found throughout her confessional poetry. Sexton the mad woman called herself "a possessed witch/haunting the black air"; Sexton the poet admitted that she practiced the "Black Art."[19] But she was understandably more reticent in assuming the mantle of the witch-mother.

Anne Sexton produced her first child in 1953, the same year that John Bowlby published *Child Care* and the *Growth of Love*; however, her mothering style differed greatly from that which Bowlby prescribed. She admitted to being a mentally unstable, suicidal adulteress who was estranged from her children when they were young and who made them suffer a variety of abuses as they grew. Living in a different part of suburban Boston 250 years earlier, she wouldn't have had a prayer. And she knew it.[20]

So it is perhaps logical that in "The Double Image," Sexton's initial foray into maternity poetry, she would choose to describe herself as one who communes with witches rather than as a witch herself. Here, in attempting to explain the events surrounding her three-year separation from her youngest child, Joy,[21] Sexton writes that she was motivated by the "witches" at her "side."[22] When dealing with the same situation six years later in "A Little Uncomplicated Hymn," Sexton still does not use the word "witch" outright, but she certainly presents herself as a reasonable, hand-drawn facsimile of one. In this poem, as in "The Double Image," Sexton is clearly aware of the grave consequences of her actions. Nevertheless, she does everything save cackle as she dumps the infant in the "ditch" and then flies off "in madness/over the buildings" while the candles on her small daughter's birthday cake glitter in the background.[23]

By the time "The Witch's Life"[24] was written a decade later, the question of Sexton's identity has been resolved. Here she recalls a woman from her past whom the neighbourhood children called "The Witch":

> All day she peered from her second story window
> from behind the wrinkled curtains
> and sometimes she would open the window

and yell: Get out of my life!
She had hair like a kelp
and a voice like a boulder.
Now, Sexton confesses, she has become just like her:
My shoes turn up like a jester's.
Clumps of my hair, as I write this,
curl up individually like toes.
I am shovelling the children out,
scoop after scoop.

"Yes," Sexton confirms at the poem's end, hers is "the witch's life." Yet we should not be too quick to dismiss her as the quintessential "bad" mother on that basis alone, because "the witch's life" is not always anti-maternal. For example, in Sexton's signature piece, "Her Kind,"[25] the poet-as-witch takes pride in filling her "warm caves" with "innumerable goods" (the image itself suggests the womb) and in fixing "suppers for the worms and the elves" that reside with her. Thus, while she may disdain the "plain houses" of ordinary mothers, she revels in the domesticity of her own unconventional home. Sexton the witch, in other words, is not a "bad" mother, only a "misunderstood" one. Indeed, if we review "The Double Image" and "A Little Uncomplicated Hymn," it could be argued that she is actually a "good" mother because she believes that she is acting in her daughter's best interest. After all, the poet does not so much abandon her child as sacrifice herself so that Joy might live. Addressing the child in "The Double Image," the poet writes:

I, who chose two times
to kill myself, had said your nickname
the mewling months when you first came;
until a fever rattled
in your throat and I moved like a pantomime
above your head. Ugly angels spoke to me. The blame,
I heard them say, was mine. They tattled
like green witches in my head, letting doom
leak like a broken faucet;
as if doom had flooded my belly and filled your bassinet,
an old debt I must assume.

Death was simpler than I thought.
The day life made you whole
I let the witches take my guilty soul away.[26]

In relinquishing her Joy (in both the uppercase form and the lower), the poet is not being self-serving. Rather, like the young, gold-spinning mother in "Rumpelstilskin," Sexton has made a bargain and she can only live up to it by dying.

Seen in this light, the title "The Double Image" takes on new significance. Although it initially refers to the portraits Sexton and her own dying mother had painted during this time, it is also clearly extended to include the relationship between the poet (herself a variation on the dying mother) and her child. But ultimately the central symbol of the poem becomes like the crazy-house mirror at a carnival, reflecting the poet simultaneously as daughter and mother, and also reflecting her dual aspects within each of those roles. Just as Sexton is at once the dutiful and devouring daughter, she is both the "bad" mother and the "good."

The same duality can be found in the maternity poems of Maxine Kumin, one of the writers with whom Sexton was most closely associated. Both Kumin's life and her relationship with her children appear, at least from the outsiders' perspective, to be much more stable than Sexton's: indeed, though Kumin may be extraordinarily gifted in some ways, she appears to be a rather ordinary American mom. Nonetheless, Kumin also makes use of the witch figure when discussing her interaction with her offspring.

A case in point is "The Fairest One of All."[27] In this poem, Kumin watches admiringly as her adolescent daughter Jane stands ironing in an "acre of whiteness." Moved by the scene, the poet envisions the beautiful, deserving young woman as a princess, giving herself the role of the "middle-aged queen." Yet we know from the title, with its allusion to "Snow White and the Seven Dwarves," that Kumin really is, like the speaker in Sexton's *Transformations*, "a middle-aged witch."[28] Therefore, the abruptly altered tone of the poem's final stanza should not be wholly surprising.

> So far so good, my darling, my fair
> first born, your hair black as ebony
> your lips red as blood. But let there be
> no mistaking how the dark scheme runs.
> Too soon all this will befall:
> Too soon the huntsman will come.
> He will bring me the heart of a wild boar
> and I in error will have it salted and cooked
> and I in malice will eat it bit by bit
> thinking it yours.
> And as we both know, at the appropriate moment
> I will be consumed by an inexorable fire
> as you look on.

Here Kumin plots to kill her daughter, to feed off the child she once nurtured and nursed. Such is the stuff nightmares are made of; still, there is much to be said in the speaker's defense.

For instance, she suggests that the scenario described here, shocking as it may seem, is not unnatural. The poet is simply playing her part in the age-old parental drama, and on account of this she earns some sympathy. Kumin earns more by giving us a variation on Sexton's "double image," presenting herself both as the child's true, biological mother and as a stepmother who just happens to be the wickedest of witches. The importance of such "splitting up," at least from the child's perspective, has already been recognized by Bruno Bettelheim. In his book *The Uses of Enchantment: The Meaning and Importance of Fairy Tales*, Bettelheim explains that:

> although Mother [in fairy tales] is most often the all-giving protector, she can change into cruel stepmother if she is so evil as to deny the youngster something he wants. Far from being a device used only in fairy tales, such a splitting up of one person into two to keep the good image uncontaminated occurs to many children as a solution to a relationship too difficult to manage or comprehend. With this device all contradictions are suddenly resolved.[29]

For the child, Bettelheim adds, "the fantasy of the wicked stepmother not only preserves the good mother intact, it also prevents having to feel guilty about one's angry thoughts and wishes about her."[30]

On the personal level, this doubling process may work in much the same way for the mother. By employing the surrogate to do the dirty work for her, Kumin transfers responsibility for those actions to a [m]other. Thus she articulates the resentment and rage that all mothers, at some point or another, invariably feel, while at the same time alleviating (or at least lessening) the guilt her behavior causes by means of a distancing device. Through it she can become, in Adrienne Rich's words, "like the terrible mothers we long and dread to be,"[31] and she can do this without jeopardizing the integrity of her socially sanctioned "good" self.

However, on a public level (and it must be remembered that these poems—no matter how personal the subject matter—are public utterances), this "splitting up," ironically, allows for a form of maternal reintegration. The audience, after all, is not composed of children. We do not truly believe that some black magic has been used to transform the "all-giving protector" into a hook-nosed hag. Instead, use of the device forcefully reminds us that one woman can play both roles. In fact, Kumin would say she must, for in her view the dual aspects of motherhood are interdependent rather than mutually exclusive. Kumin would further argue that regardless of the role the woman chooses, whether she acts as a "good" mother or a "bad" one, she remains, at heart, a witch because it is only through employing the witch's power that she has the ability to act at all.

To clarify this point, let us briefly consider two of Kumin's works, both of which were originally published in *The Retrieval System* (1978): "Changing the Children" and "Seeing the Bones." From the outset the former poem is startling.[32] The title, for instance, conjures up images of routine maternal chores like changing the children's diapers or clothes. But it is immediately apparent that Kumin fantasizes about using the power of the witch to place a "cruel spell" on them, literally changing her "little loved ones" into lower life forms. "Anger," she says, "does this."

> Soon enough, no matter how
> we want them to be happy
> our little loved ones, no
> matter how we prod them
> into our sun that it may
> shine on them, they whine
> to stand in the dry-goods store.
> Fury slams in.
> The wilful fury befalls.

It is important to note that Kumin here is not motivated by a desire to make her own life easier: she does not transform her young into model children but rather into waddling porcupines, maggot-infested crows, web-spinning spiders, and wart-spewing toads. Nor is she endeavoring to teach her children a lesson (as the witch in many fairy tales was attempting to do): she doesn't seem to care that the son remains a "berater" while the daughter is filled only with "false repentance." The speaker transforms them because she feels like it—and because she can. In "Changing the Children," Kumin refuses to make apologies for using her power as a witch. In part, the reason is that she sees no need to: her actions, arising out of the "legitimate rage of parents," are perfectly justified. But it is also because she recognizes that her ability to do good derives from the same source. This becomes evident in "Seeing the Bones."[33]

The poem calls to mind one of Kumin's earlier works, "Making Jam without You," in which she uses her magic to alter the dreams of her daughter Judy. "I am putting a dream in your head," Kumin announces, "and it is a good one."[34] However, in "Seeing the Bones" the mother emerges even more clearly as a witch, for in this instance the jam maker's kettle is transformed into a witch's cauldron, and the woman who formerly preserved fruit now has the power to preserve one of her children. Addressing herself to her "daughter of the file drawer," her "citizen of no return," Kumin writes:

> Working backward I reconstruct
> you. Send me your baby teeth, some new

> nail parings and a hank of hair
> and let me do the rest. I'll
> set the pot to boil.

Here she employs her power not to destroy the girl, but to demonstrate her love for her through an act of regeneration. Here the cauldron, which she had anticipated using in "The Fairest One of All" to turn her daughter's heart into a tasty snack, becomes an agent for rebirth. In short, Kumin revises the image of the witch and, in doing so, reclaims her cauldron by restoring it to its original position as a symbol of life.[35]

In the end, then, Kumin the witch-mother is a complex woman. Like many other maternal witches she has the potential to be both death dealing and life affirming as well. She may shake off a hungry child like a "leech," or she may offer her body as a sacrifice. She may invent "fabulous lies," or she may use her "crone's voice" to impart life's hard truths.[36] She may be ruthless, resentful, or she may be extravagant with her affection. In any event, she resists simple definitions.

Such a woman not only rejects what I call the Margaret Anderson model of motherhood (Mother is a paragon of virtue, and Father always knows best). Ultimately, she rejects the Samantha Stephens model[37] as well: the model that begrudgingly admits that even a witch can be a "good" mother, as long as she tries hard to conduct herself like a "normal (?) American housewife."[38] Such a woman contends that she is a good mother precisely because she is a witch, and on closer inspection we can see that Anne Sexton, too, is one of "her kind."

If we return to "A Little Uncomplicated Hymn" and "The Double Image," for instance, we can see that from the beginning the witches in Sexton's confessional poems have had the capacity to be wondrous as well as wicked. In the first of these, the witchlike mother flies: something that a regular mom, as Darrin Stephens constantly reminded us, just shouldn't do. But the fact that her favoured mode of transportation is an "umbrella"[39] rather than a broom suggests that she may be related to Mary Poppins: the magical, umbrella-laden, surrogate mother made popular by Walt Disney in 1964, one year before Sexton's piece was written. Similarly, in "The Double Image" the unearthly beings who commune with Sexton are called both witches and "angels" (albeit "Ugly" ones).[40] For the reader well acquainted with Sexton's body of work, this brings to mind "Consorting with Angels," a poem that not only features another odd-looking assortment of angels, but one that focuses on history's most saintly witch, Joan of Arc.

In both cases, the witches in question may be eccentric, but they aren't evil: indeed, they have the power to do considerable good. The same can be said for Sexton when she becomes a witch herself. Consider the poem

"LIVE,"[41] which details her gradual acceptance of the witch's role. Although Sexton initially thinks of herself as "a killer" who repeats "The Black Mass" and anoints herself daily with "little poisons," she comes to realize that she can be a satisfactory wife and mother, despite her deviant behaviour. "Even crazy, I'm as nice/as a chocolate bar," the poet asserts: "Even with the witches' gymnastics/They trust my incalculable city,/my corruptible bed."

But as the poem draws to a close Sexton goes further still, herself acknowledging that it is only by virtue of being a witch that she has the power to be a good mother. Without it, she wouldn't be a better parent: she'd just be a dead one. "O dearest three," Sexton says to her husband and children:

> The witch comes on
> and you paint her pink.
> I come with kisses in my hood
> and the sun, the smart one,
> rolling in my arms.
> So I say *Live*
> and turn my shadow three times round. (italics hers)

In this poem, Sexton, as both witch and mother, transcends the stereotypes. She is at once the woman of nightmare and "dream," the woman of "shadow" and light. She has intimate knowledge of what Adrienne Rich has called the "Heart of Maternal Darkness,"[42] yet she can still carry the sun like a babe in arms. And in the end, she is, like Maxine Kumin, a woman who not only accepts but celebrates her contradictions.

It is not, perhaps, surprising that Sexton and Kumin would both arrive at this point: they were, after all, "intimate friends and professional allies."[43] However, they do not stand alone. Sandra Gilbert, Susan Griffin, Marilyn Hacker, Alicia Ostriker, Adrienne Rich, Robin Morgan, Anne Stevenson, Marilyn Nelson Waniek: these are only some of the other American maternity poets who do not shrink from using the witch's power, who have the courage to cast off the simplistic maternal role that society has defined for them.

As Alicia Ostriker points out in *Stealing the Language*, "Good motherhood, in our culture, is selfless, cheerful, and deodorized. It does not include resentment, anger, violence, alienation, disappointment, grief, fear, exhaustion—or erotic pleasure."[44] But these maternity poets embrace every aspect of the maternal experience. Indeed, the honesty and urgency with which they write ultimately force us to reevaluate those social assumptions that have traditionally allowed us to separate the "bad" mother from the "good."

NOTES

1. Bill Moyers, *The Language of Life: A Festival of Poets,* ed. James Haba (New York: Doubleday, 1995), 338.

2. Adrienne Rich, *Of Woman Born: Motherhood as Experience and Institution* (New York: Norton, 1976), 25.

3. Betty Friedan, *The Feminine Mystique* (New York: Laurel, 1983), 182.

4. It should be noted at the outset that this vision of parenthood was inherently elitist.

5. As Betty Friedan explains:
The baby boom of the immediate postwar years took place in every country. But it was not permeated, in most other countries, with the mystique of feminine fulfilment. It did not in other countries lead to the even greater baby boom of the fifties, with the rise in teenage marriages and pregnancies, and the increase in family size. The number of American women with three or more children doubled in twenty years.
See Friedan, *The Feminine Mystique,* 183.

6. Martha Wolfenstein, "Fun Morality: An Analysis of Recent American Child-training Literature," in *Childhood in Contemporary Cultures,* ed. Margaret Mead and Martha Wolfenstein (Chicago: University of Chicago Press, 1955), 169–72. Wolfenstein's observations are based on her study of the U.S. government's Infant Care bulletins between 1914 and 1951.

7. For a moving account of a postwar mother's life and the sense of powerlessness that envelopes her, see Anne Stevenson's "The Suburb" in *Selected Poems 1956–1986* (Oxford: Oxford University Press, 1987).

8. John Bowlby, *Child Care and the Growth of Love* (Harmondsworth, England: Penguin, 1965), 77–78.

9. Bowlby, *Child Care,* 78.

10. Friedan, *Feminine Mystique,* 189. Friedan here is not overstating her case: Rene Spitz, for instance, makes such connections throughout *The First Year of Life: A Psychoanalytic Study of Normal and Deviant Object Relations* (New York: International Universities Press, 1965).

11. In *The Crucible* (1953), playwright Arthur Miller drew parallels between the Salem witch trials of 1692 and the hearings of the House Un-American Activities Committee, led by Senator Joseph McCarthy during the early 1950s. Since finding a "bad" mother in America at this time was just as easy as finding a Communist, it is not surprising that America's literary mothers would connect the witch trials to events in their own lives.

12. Jane McCabe, "'A Woman Who Writes': A Feminist Approach to the Early Poetry of Anne Sexton," in *Anne Sexton: The Artist and Her Critics,* ed. J. D. McClatchy (Bloomington: Indiana University Press, 1978), 218.

13. Maxine Kumin, "Foreword," in *The Complete Poems of Anne Sexton,* ed. Linda Gray Sexton (Boston: Houghton Mifflin, 1981), xxviii.

14. Kumin, "Foreword," xxviii.

15. Sexton, "The Gold Key," in *Poems,* 223.

16. Anne Sexton, *Anne Sexton: A Self-Portrait in Letters,* ed. Linda Gray Sexton and Lois Ames (Boston: Houghton Mifflin, 1977), 362.

17. Elaine Showalter, Lea Baechler, and A. Walton Litz, eds., *Modern American Women Writers* (New York: Scribner, 1991), 464.

18. Sexton expects us to sympathize with these characters, just as she herself did. For example, in "A Reminiscence," the illustrator of *Transformations,* Barbara Swan, recalls saying to Sexton, "I don't know about you but I identify with the poor old queen" in "Snow White." Sexton agreed, so Swan "made a drawing that portrays the universal problem of the aging beauty, needing every beauty prop available, and the young girl, smug and indifferent, temporarily secure in her glorious youth." See *Anne Sexton: The Artist and Her Critics,* 86.

19. Sexton, "Her Kind," in *Poems,* 15; and "The Black Art," in *Poems,* 88.

20. See Sexton's interview "With Gregory Fitz Gerald," reprinted in *No Evil Star: Selected Essays, Interviews, and Prose,* ed. Steven E. Colburn (Ann Arbor: University of Michigan Press, 1986), 195.

21. Sexton suffered a serious mental crisis when Joy was seven months old and was forced to leave the child in the care of her paternal grandparents. During the separation, the poet attempted suicide. For details, see Linda Gray Sexton's *Searching for Mercy Street: My Journey Back to My Mother, Anne Sexton* (Boston: Little, Brown, 1994).

22. Sexton, "The Double Image," in *Poems,* 39.

23. Sexton, "A Little Uncomplicated Hymn," in *Poems,* 150.

24. Sexton, "The Witch's Life," in *Poems,* 423–24.

25. Sexton "Her Kind," in *Poems,* 15–16.

26. Sexton, "The Double Image," in *Poems,* 36.

27. Maxine Kumin, "The Fairest One of All," in *Our Ground Time Here Will Be Brief* (New York: Penguin, 1982), 175–76. For a poem which is similar both in theme and its use of the fairy tale motif, see Marilyn Nelson Waniek's "Mama's Promise," in *Mama's Promises* (Baton Rouge: Louisiana State University Press, 1985), 11–12.

28. Sexton, "The Gold Key," in *Poems,* 223.

29. Bruno Bettelheim, *The Uses of Enchantment: The Meaning and Importance of Fairy Tales* (New York: Knopf, 1976), 67.

30. Bettelheim, *Enchantment,* 69.

31. Adrienne Rich, "Hunger," in *The Dream of a Common Language: Poems 1974–77* (New York: Norton, 1978), 13.

32. Kumin, "Changing the Children," in *Ground Time,* 59–60.

33. Kumin, "Seeing the Bones," in *Ground Time,* 62–63.

34. Kumin, "Making Jam Without You," in *Ground Time,* 170.

35. In *The Woman's Encyclopedia of Myths and Secrets,* Barbara G. Walker confirms that, in pagan tradition, the cauldron symbolized "the Great Mother's cosmic womb" (New York: HarperCollins, 1983), 150.

36. Quotes in this paragraph are taken, in order, from the following: Alicia Ostriker, "Mother/Child," in *The Mother/Child Papers* (Santa Monica, Calif.: Momentum, 1980), 22; Anne Stevenson, "Generations," in *Selected Poems,* 24; and Margaret Atwood, "Solstice Poem," in *Two-Headed Poems* (Toronto: Oxford, 1978), 84. This final poem by Atwood bears a striking resemblance to Sexton's "A Little Uncomplicated Hymn."

37. Margaret Anderson was the perfect mother on the TV program *Father Knows Best* (1954–1963). Samantha Stephens was the loveable witch-wife on *Bewitched* (1964–1972) who tried to suppress her power to please her mortal husband, Darrin. See Tim Brooks and Earle Marsh, *The Complete Directory of Prime Time TV Shows, 1946–Present* (New York: Ballantine, 1988).

38. Sexton, *Letters,* 270.

39. Sexton, "A Little Uncomplicated Hymn," in *Poems,* 150.

40. Sexton, "The Double Image," in *Poems,* 36.

41. Sexton, "LIVE," in *Poems,* 167–70.

42. Rich, *Of Woman Born,* 256.

43. Maxine Kumin, "A Friendship Remembered," in *Anne Sexton: The Artist and Her Critics,* 103.

44. Alicia Ostriker, *Stealing the Language: The Emergence of Women's Poetry in America* (Boston: Beacon, 1986), 179.

6

Rewriting "Cinderella": Envisioning the Empowering Mother-Daughter Romance

Jeanne Wiley

As recorded in many popular fairy tales, the story of mothers and daughters is typically fraught with ambivalence and conflict—that is, when it is not marginalized through silence or absence. If and when the maternal agent appears, she is often indicted and repudiated as the instrument of her daughter's repression.

Psychoanalytic readings of popular fairy tales (as well as recent Disney versions), legitimize the practice of silencing or demonizing the maternal agent in relation to the daughter's subject formation.[1] The purpose of this essay is to revisit the site of this highly charged mother-daughter relation as it appears in the canonical and conservative "Cinderella" and to explore the transgressive and emancipatory potential of a revisionary handling of the tale published more recently by Angela Carter.[2] First, I aim to deconstruct the alleged conflict between mothers and daughters and the mother blaming that it solicits (in particular, as it applies to the figure of the active maternal agent who appears in the guise of the stepmother); second, I will recount the return of the repressed feminine (as it applies to the figure of the dead or absent mother, who appears, in the case of "Cinderella," in the guise of the fairy godmother); and third, I will propose and assess a revision of the mother-daughter relation, namely, one that is foregrounded and empowering rather than silenced and/or repressive—that is, causing the silencing, mutilation, or subjugation of female agency. My overall goal is to explore a progressive model of intersubjective relations beyond the mother-daughter relation, a model not structured by zero-sum oppositionality (i.e., self versus m/other) and one not committed to the destructive trap of adversarial and asymmetrical hierarchical arrangements (i.e., self over and against m/other).³ I hope to demonstrate that the model of the enabling and reciprocal mother-daughter relation poses the possibility of an exit route from those impoverished and destructive models of intersubjective relations and is, in that sense, potentially transformative in the quest for greater justice in the fabric of human relations.

THE CANONICAL CINDERELLA

"Cinderella" is the "best known folktale in the world."⁴ Indeed, most of us can recite the story on command. This alone should alert us to the possibility that something other than entertainment is going on. The bare bones version of the tale with which most of us are familiar is that of an innocent girl victimized by the cruelty of her stepmother and stepsisters and subsequently rescued by a prince after she is magically endowed with the accoutrements of wealth by a helpful fairy godmother. Apart from and complicit with the many other highly significant cultural forms alluded to and affirmed in this story (e.g., the drama hinges on the disclosure of hidden royalty—a Christian fabula—and, moreover, Cinderella's happy redemption requires a magical leap into the upper class—a capitalist fiction), the story "Cinderella" records of the relation between mothers and daughters is not a happy tale. If it were not so numbingly familiar as to be passed over without notice, we would be startled, I think, to realize that "Cinderella" is not simply a heterosexual romance but, in a central way, a story about the conflict between women and between generations of women as they compete for the questionable privilege of allying themselves with powerful husbands.

Two maternal agents appear in the popular version of "Cinderella." On the one hand, there is the memorable and exciting although wicked stepmother. She is active and ambitious; hence, by conservative fairy tale logic, she is an evil woman who is cruel and repressive in relation to her daughters but most memorably to Cinderella. The wicked stepmother is, of course, a cautionary tale about mothers to daughters, affirmative of patriarchal arrangements. For, given this background context, every daughter needs to learn that ambitious mothers, like ambitious women, are perversions. They are strident, aggressive, and selfish. They steal power from men and from other women, especially from their daughters with whom they compete for male attention and patronage.

The other maternal agent who appears in "Cinderella" is the less memorable and much less plausible fairy godmother. She represents the fantastic projection of Cinderella's desire to be rescued from her alienated condition. In a sense, she represents the displaced agency of Cinderella. Since the fairy godmother acts on Cinderella's behalf, she permits Cinderella to realize her ambitions without acting on her own behalf—without, that is, despoiling her image as innocent victim with the stain of active ambition. In Carter's rendition, the fairy godmother is the ghost of Cinderella's dead mother; this is not obvious in the canonical version and it is not necessary that it be obvious. What is obvious and necessary is that as the figure who represents the model of the good mother in the canonical version, the fairy godmother must be mystified and instrumentalized as well as fantastically implausible and ghostly. This too accords with the agenda of conservative fairytale logic. The good mother, like the good woman, is a background figure—ideally passive. If and when she is active, her sole function is to serve the needs of others; in Cinderella's case, the function of the good mother or the fairy godmother is to assist her daughter in being conscripted into a patriarchal economy by providing Cinderella with, for example, the right clothes.

Continuing to read and to analyze "Cinderella" from a critical and feminist perspective, it is worth noticing at this point that the model of ideal femininity underwritten by the tale is unabashedly regressive. Ambitious women, namely, the stepmother and her daughters, are unambivalently demonized whereas the poor, humble, and victimized Cinderella is sanctified. The fairy godmother is, in turn, depersonalized and marginalized to the realm of ghostly apparitions. Her only exercise of agency—her only function and dimension in the tale—is in service to Cinderella. Notice that the fairy godmother is, indeed, a spectre of subjectivity. She is insubstantial and asexual. She is not a subject or a person in her own right—that is, one who is the bearer of desires and not merely the mediator of others' desires.

Finally, if the critical eye steps back from the internal dynamics of the conflict between women in "Cinderella" and from the regressive model of femininity it promulgates to notice what all the women have in common, one thing is certainly clear. All the women aim at marriage and only at marriage. That is, the furthest reach of their ambitions—the outer limits of their imagined desires—is to become wives (or to assist their daughters in becoming wives). This is a self-defeating ambition that reflects and prescribes the asymmetrical arrangements between the sexes in patriarchy. For if (as is the case in so many tales that describe the desires of female protagonists) female ambitions are confined to erotic fulfillment or romance—that is, to the desire to become wives or to the desire to be the objects of another's desire—then they are seeking, ironically, to forfeit the capacity for executive agency—that is, to be self-determining subjects in their own right and not the objects of another's agency. In other words, if it is the case that the sole ambition of all the women who appear in "Cin-

derella" is marriage and the dubious state of "happily ever after" alleged
to follow, then these women are questing to confine themselves to passivity and dependence in relation to masculine agency and desire. As such,
the singular quest to achieve agency and maturity through romantic fulfillment is necessarily self-defeating.[5] How can you be self-directed if you
are riding in harness?

Assessed from this feminist perspective, it becomes undeniably clear
that the popular version of "Cinderella" is a conservative and regressive
fantasy. It is complicit with patriarchal and Freudian versions of the family romance as well as heterosexist and capitalist cultural mores. In service to these arrangements, "Cinderella" proposes a zero-sum conflict between the female agents (only one of the daughters can become the
prince's beloved) and prescribes heterosexual marriage into wealth as the
ultimate goal of female ambitions (by way of the artifices of beauty, hu-
mility, and daintiness). In concert with the Freudian version of the family
romance and femininity, this conservative fantasy not only represses and
instrumentalizes the passive mother—the fairy godmother—but, more
importantly and more dramatically, it demonizes the active maternal
agent in relation to the daughter's subject formation. The stepmother
graphically represents the threat such mothers pose to their daughters in
patriarchy. When active, ambitious, and overinvolved, they are stifling
and dangerous—the material agents of castration. They disempower their
daughters by hampering their daughter's subject formation as they compete with their daughters for male attention and patronage. According to
this Oedipalized "mother-blaming" logic, such mothers make it seem
that the only reasonable course of action open to daughters who wish to
escape the jealous aggression of these willful maternal agents is to transfer their allegiance to the patriarchy by subordinating themselves to masculine prerogatives. Marriage is, as the story would have us believe, what
rescues daughters from their castrating mothers.

THEORETICAL TRANSITION

As framed in the prior analysis, the story "Cinderella" tells about the con-
flictual relations between women and between generations of women is
certainly frightening and destructive in its capacity to model an impoverished view of female agency and misogynist and patriarchal norms. But,
of course, this is not the whole story. Given an alternative perspective, one
could easily read the tale in a more generous light, noting that it foregrounds female desire and has a utopian ending—however much those
narrative elements are constrained by patriarchal limitations. The very
longevity of the tale, the proliferation of regressive and progressive ver-

sions of it, together with the wealth of critical material that has grown up around it, attest to its power to fascinate and delight. My objection to "Cinderella" is not with this power or this pleasure. My critique centers, rather, on the tale's insistent deformation of the relations between mothers and daughters and the effect this has on our ability to imagine not only active female agency in a positive light but also intersubjective reciprocity. As I will argue here, the deformation of the relation between mothers and daughters—the distortion of the mother-daughter romance—advanced in the canonical "Cinderella" is instrumental in underwriting a model of intersubjective relations that not only gives rise to mother blaming, romantic mystifications, and female passivity; it is also a model that underwrites sexist hierarchies and the self-other oppositionality they assume.

CARTER'S "ASHPUTTLE"

To make this argument, consider the features of the canonical tale as they undergo subversion and transformation in "Ashputtle or the Mother's Ghost: Three Versions of One Story," Angela Carter's feminist revision of "Cinderella." Carter's story is broken up into three abbreviated vignettes, each of which progressively narrows its focus to concentrate finally, in a singular way, on the mother-daughter relation.

The first vignette, titled "The Mutilated Girls," is an explicit exercise in metafiction in that it is a story about the story of Cinderella more so than it is the story itself. In this way, "The Mutilated Girls" signals that its aim is to install the distance requisite to a subversive interrogation of the context of the story (i.e., the patriarchal sociocultural and familial conditions that form the background to the tale), rather than to a retelling of the tale per se.

The narrator of the outer frame argues that the story of Cinderella is ostensibly but not really a story of a battle between women. Not only is the reason for the stepmother's cruelty toward Cinderella made explicit (they are rivals for the patronage of Cinderella's father), but Carter reintroduces what Disney has excised from the popular version, namely, the shocking dismemberment of the stepsisters' feet by the stepmother. Recall that the motive for the stepmother's cruelty is her desire to see her daughter's foot fit the shoe that will mark the wearer as the prince's beloved. Carter's reintroduction of the element of dismemberment explicitly dramatizes, in a pronounced way, the patriarchal and Freudian view of femininity as a castrated form of subjectivity. That is, given the asymmetrical arrangements between the sexes in patriarchy, only the appropriately disempowered or passive woman will fit the feminine role. From the perspective of the outer frame narrative, moreover, what is also thrown into sharp relief is that although the stepmother acts as the material instrument of her daughters' castration, it is the absent father, and later the prince, who are central in instigating and sustaining the conflict among the women. In Carter's version, it is the men who are indicted as the formal agents of castration. The women are merely puppet antagonists in a battle that is predetermined and manipulated by powerful men.

Hence, as seen through the eyes of Carter's metafictive narrator, the story of Cinderella becomes not so much a story about the conflict between women or a heterosexual romance; rather, it is a story about the contest between two groups of women over which daughter (Cinderella or one of her stepsisters) will assume the legitimate position in the father's house and which daughter will, in turn, win the position as the prince's bride. According to the conservative logic of the canonical tale, the daughter who wins this oppressive zero-sum contest is the one who will, presumably, escape the maternal sphere of the home and thereby achieve the semblance of agency, however limited or derived. In either case, what Carter's metafictive subversion makes clear is that the men control the distribution of wealth and power and hence, represent the women's only avenue to agency in this context. In short, Carter's first reworking of the canonical tale argues that although the story of Cinderella seems to be a story about the conflict between women and between mothers and daughters, in reality, it is a story about the constraints on women in a patriarchal context in which the avenues to agency and status are predetermined by and for men.

The second vignette, titled "The Burned Child," turns away from a metafictive reflection on the story of Cinderella to focus on the dynamics of the relation between Cinderella and her mother. The death of Cinderella's mother as well as her father's neglect and remarriage to Cinderella's stepmother has consigned Cinderella to the position of servant in her stepmother's house. In this competitive context, the stepmother rightly perceives that Cinderella can no longer be the "legitimate" daughter of the newly configured household as she represents a threat to the stepmother's claim to her father's patronage. However, in Carter's rendering, Cinderella's status as household servant takes on psychological as well as economic and political meaning. Cinderella is at home in the ashes—the "cinders"—because she is mourning her mother. She clings to the hearth—symbolic of the home's center—as she would to her absent mother. In this way, the narrative suggests that the relation Cinderella has with her absent mother is identificatory, but also infantile or characteristic of a pre-Oedipal level of development; that is, she is quasi-symbiotically fused with her mother. Cinderella's mother is, conversely, so overinvested in her daughter's marriagability and return to legitimacy that she awakens from death itself in response to Cinderella's pitiful state.

With her mother's assistance, Cinderella develops to maturity and wins the prince. However, in aiding in her daughter's subject formation, which, in this case, involves Cinderella's transformation from a pitiful child to a marriageable woman, the mother expends herself to the point of exhaustion. To her daughter, she exclaims, "You've milked me dry."[6] The price of Cinderella's rehabilitation, maturation, and entrance into the patriarchal economy, it seems, is the life energy of her mother.

The third and final vignette, titled "Travelling Clothes," is even more abbreviated than the first two versions, although it manages to spotlight the mother-daughter relation and rescue the story of the mother's agency from the repressed margins, from what Elaine Showalter calls the "wild zone" of the literary unconscious.[7] Here, the kiss of the mother's ghost together with the gifts she bestows on her daughter release Cinderella from her psychological immaturity and lowly servant status, transforming her from a child and victim of her stepmother's household into an independent adventurer. To signify the way in which Cinderella's mother enables her psychological transformation and her economic and political emancipation, the text uses dense symbols. For example, the mother's kiss erases rather than inflicts the scars suffered by Cinderella at the hands of her crippling stepmother. Further, the mother bestows on Cinderella three gifts: jewels, symbolic of economic independence; a coach, symbolic of autonomy and the ability to act in the public domain; and third, perhaps most significantly, a red dress—arguably, a symbol of active and passional desires. As the mother gives Cinderella the dress, she claims, "I had it when I was your age."[8] Finally, as the story ends, the enabling mother prompts her daughter to leave the nest rather than seek the prince, exclaiming, "Go and seek your fortune, darling."[9]

What is crucially different about the portrayal of the mother-daughter relation in the third vignette from that depicted in the second vignette is that, first, the mother is not instrumentalized and expended or sacrificed in order to enable her daughter to mature and become marriageable; second, this mother is unrepressed and exciting. She is self-determining and autonomous—that is, clearly self-possessed and the executive authority with respect to her own active desires. And, finally, the maternal agent who appears in the third vignette empowers her daughter to become an active and executive subject outside the patriarchal economy by mirroring this possibility to her daughter. In other words, as an active "adventurer" herself, the mother makes that choice a viable possibility for Cinderella.

INTERPRETATION

What is the significance of this revisionary handling of the tale of Cinderella by Carter? In the argument that follows, I demonstrate that the subversive revision of the canonical tale gives rise to a model of the enabling and empowering mother-daughter relation, one not structured by asymmetry or conflict and one not shaped by patriarchal constraints. Moreover, in line with my overall goal, I show that this revision leads not only to an affirmation of female agency and desire outside patriarchy—outside the "father's law"—but to an alteration in the oppositional and asymmetrical character of the self-other relation that informs conventional notions of sexual difference.

Notice first that each of the three vignettes in Carter's tale proposes a different way of constructing and assessing the mother-daughter relation and that the different versions form a sequence which progressively alters the character of the mother from that of a repressive or marginalized agent to an enabling and foregrounded one in which, first, she is objectified and exhausted by means of her daughter's subject formation (in the second vignette) and, finally (in the third vignette), she is affirmed as an active subject in her own right (i.e., an executive subject capable of being the subject of desires rather than just the object or instrument of them).

In the first vignette, a classic version of the patriarchal and Freudian family romance is critically interrogated and shown to have a destructive effect on the relations between women and the possibility of active female agency. This critique suggests that when relegated to a secondary position with respect to male privilege, the effect on women is divisive and disabling. Women compete with each other for male patronage in a zero-sum game and mothers become the material (although not the formal) agents of their daughters' repression. For, in the familial, psychological, and economic arrangements predetermined by patriarchy, only the castrated woman will fit; that is, only the passive woman who is willing to forfeit her agency to become the object or the instrument of another's agency will fit in.

The second vignette in Carter's rendering bears the marks of the female family romance as defined by Marianne Hirsch.[10] That is, although the maternal agent is enabling with respect to her daughter's maturation and subject formation, there is a distinct lack of reciprocity in their relation. Cinderella achieves separation and agency by instrumentalizing and exploiting her mother; that is, Cinderella achieves agency at the expense of her mother. Ultimately what Cinderella achieves by means of this tactic is a problematic and impoverished form of agency; she sacrifices her mother only to become a somewhat handicapped "player" in the patriarchal matrix as the object of the prince's desire.

According to Hirsch, a female family romance is a text that seeks to protest patriarchy by foregrounding the daughter's struggle to achieve active agency. Yet, ironically, the price of the daughter's entrance into the patriarchal economy is the rejection or silencing of the maternal agent—

the textual situation so predictable in the canonical fairy tale. This occurs, according to Hirsch, because in the effort to articulate an active female agency, female family romances seek to disidentify with conventional notions of femininity and these conventional notions include attributes of passivity and maternity.[11] Hence, paradoxically, in their efforts to promote an active female agency, female family romances repeat the silencing and repudiation of maternal agency so common in conventional plot structures. Carter's second version of the tale of Cinderella reveals the catch-22 or self-contradictory nature of the emancipatory textual strategy utilized by female family romances. By exploiting her mother to achieve agency, a daughter may indeed win a place in patriarchy, but she does not model the possibility of an active female agency outside the limitations of the patriarchal configuration. The only way this is conceivable, as Carter's third vignette demonstrates, is if the price of the daughter's agency is not the agency of her mother.

Carter's third vignette, "Travelling Clothes," completes the progressive and emancipatory transformation of the mother-daughter relation. Here, in a transgressive narrative gesture that radically distinguishes Oedipalized familial relations from the Freudian and patriarchal paradigms, a maternal subjectivity is accessed and articulated. Significantly, this maternal subjectivity is formed neither in relation to the patriarchal matrix and nor to the needs of—as the instrumentalized object of—the daughter's maturation and subject formation. In this way, the third vignette illustrates the features of Hirsch's feminist family romance; that is, the mother is a subject in her own right, and the mother-daughter relation is foregrounded.[12]

Notice that for Carter, the key to the radical difference between the disabling and disabled mothers that appear in the first two vignettes and the enabling mother that appears in the third is that the active subjectivity of the maternal agent in the third vignette is envisioned apart from its relation to the patriarchal matrix. In fact, to sharpen the textual focus to the maximum extent on the mother-daughter relation in this version, the father-daughter relation and/or the prince-daughter relation is completely absent. Instead, the mother who appears in the third vignette is, unmistakably, an outlaw from the "father's law." She is described as a traveler, a symbolic attribute that suggests that she is an adventurer in her own right (i.e., self-directed—the subject and not merely the object of desires). Moreover, she possesses a red dress, suggestive of a passionate rather than passive sexuality. But, most importantly, what marks her as a transgressive agent is that her status is not derived from her relation to her husband or to her daughter. As a traveler, she is not beholden or reducible to or circumscribed within her familial relations. The result of this mother's clearly articulated and unmoored executive agency is a profound alteration in the mother-daughter relation as conceived in more conservative models. As a subject in her own right, this traveling mother is the possibility condition by means of which her daughter, Cinderella, achieves an executive subjectivity that is not premised on her castration (her passivity) so much as it is premised on its overcoming. This adventurous mother enables this particular daughter to become the subject and the author of her own desires, that is, this mother makes it possible for this daughter to become another adventurer outside the patriarchal matrix rather than another victim, object, or object of exchange relative to masculinist desires.

Ultimately, I think that the mother-daughter relation envisaged in "Travelling Clothes" models the mutuality and reciprocity of an identification or mirroring of two executive subjects neither of whose affirmation is contingent on the exploitation, domination, or exclusion of the other. This mother-daughter reciprocity thus broaches the radical possibility of an intersubjective relation—a self-other relation—that is not structured by asymmetrical oppositionality and one that is, moreover, made possible only by the recuperation and articulation of an active maternal agency— perhaps even an active maternal sexuality—outside the constraints of a patriarchal matrix.

CONCLUSION

In conclusion, the critical claims I have made with respect to the canonical "Cinderella," and other stories that repeat its mother-blaming and/or mother-silencing logic, are very simple and very crucial. To recapitulate briefly: the portrayal of the mother-daughter relation in the story of Cinderella tells an all too familiar tale that prescribes the rejection of the maternal agent, and this, in turn, gives rise to the inevitable subordination and passivity of female agency in relation to male privilege as a whole. The familial romance textually dramatized in the canonical "Cinderella" is a repetition of the logic that reinscribes and underwrites patriarchy. It is premised on the deceptive and contradictory equation of female maturation with female subordination and it virtually guarantees the installation and transmission of hierarchical and oppositional intersubjective relations, not only those between generations of women but also those between the sexes.

And while the costs of this logic have been exposed and critiqued elsewhere in theoretical and empirical studies, notably by Carol Gilligan,[13] the insights gained from the disruption of the canonical "Cinderella" through a close reading of Carter's feminist revision are worth careful meditation. For Carter's revision draws attention to the crippling costs of such fantasy. That is, by demonizing or marginalizing the maternal agent in relation to the daughter's subject formation, we lose the emancipatory and transgressive potential of the model of intersubjective reciprocity revealed in the enabling mother-daughter relation. This revolutionary model promotes an active female agency; it recognizes the political power of female relations, intergenerational and otherwise; and it plants the possibility of nonoppositional and nonhierarchical relations, heterosexual and otherwise, within the realm of the imagination.

Let me close with a cautionary note. Of course, it would be an arrogance to suppose that theoretical works such as this one that address the realm of fantasy and the imagination are any substitute for the hands-on practical work needed to enable the empowering mother-daughter relation. As always, the relation between theory and practice is problematic. Nevertheless, I think that a convincing argument can be made and has been made—although this is not the place to rehearse its steps—concerning the power of fairy tales as repeatedly exercised in the socialization of children.[14] Suffice it to say here that fairy tales undeniably and powerfully shape the expectations and imaginations of children, generation after generation. In light of this, we who operate in the realms of both theory and practice need to be reminded to become increasingly and critically aware of the costs of their delights. Furthermore, although these recommendations seem impotent when faced with the fabulous might of the Disney corporation, we need to tell our children other stories. At the very least, we need to empower our children to approach stories such as "Cinderella" with a skeptical eye. Because the real fantasy is not that mothers disable daughters or that men rescue daughters from demonic mothers in order that they may live happily ever after. The real story is otherwise, and the story of "Cinderella" not only disrespects that but blinds us to the emancipatory potential of other possible intersubjective configurations.

NOTES

1. See Bruno Bettelheim, *The Uses of Enchantment: The Meaning and Importance of Fairy Tales* (New York: Vintage, 1989). For criticism of this practice, see, especially, Andrea Dworkin, *Woman Hating* (New York: Dutton, 1974). By subject formation, I mean the process of maturation and individuation through which a person becomes an executive subject (i.e., relatively autonomous and self-determining within the fabric of human relations). It is the process dramatized in psychoanalysis by means of the Oedipal and castration complexes.

2. Angela Carter, "Ashputtle or the Mother's Ghost: Three Versions of One Story," in *Angela Carter: Burning Your Boats: The Collected Short Stories* (New York: Penguin, 1995), 390–96.

102   *Chapter 6*

3. The unusual construction of the term *m/other* is borrowed. See Jane Flax, *Thinking Fragments: Psychoanalysis, Feminism, and Postmodernism in the Contemporary West* (Berkeley: University of California Press, 1991), 18.

4. See "Cinderella," *Funk and Wagnalls Standard Dictionary of Folklore, Mythology, and Legend* (New York: Funk & Wagnalls, 1972).

5. Both Freud and Carolyn G. Heilbrun explain the compromised and self-contradictory nature of female desire when it is aimed solely at the wish for erotic and/or romantic fulfillment (as lived and as expressed in fantasy and life stories). See Sigmund Freud, "The Relation of the Poet to Day-Dreaming," in *On Creativity and the Unconscious: Papers on the Psychology of Art, Literature, Love, Religion* (New York: Harper, 1958), 44–54; and Carolyn G. Heilbrun, *Writing a Woman's Life* (New York: Ballantine, 1989).

6. Carter, "Ashputtle or the Mother's Ghost," 395.

7. Elaine Showalter, "Feminist Criticism in the Wilderness," in *The New Feminist Criticism: Essays on Women, Literature, and Theory*, ed. Elaine Showalter (New York: Pantheon, 1985), 243–70.

8. Carter, "Ashputtle or the Mother's Ghost," 396.

9. Carter, "Ashputtle or the Mother's Ghost," 396.

10. See Marianne Hirsch, "Female Family Romances: A More Archaic Murder," *The Mother/Daughter Plot: Narrative, Psychoanalysis, Feminism* (Bloomington: Indiana University Press, 1989), 43–67.

11. Hirsch, "Female Family Romances," 10–11.

12. See Hirsch, "Feminist Family Romances: Life before Oedipus," in *The Mother/Daughter Plot*, 125–61.

13. See especially Carol Gilligan, "Joining the Resistance: Psychology, Politics, Girls and Women," *Michigan Quarterly Review* 29, no. 4 (1990): 501–36. Gilligan argues that adult women can best help girls minimize the costs of navigating through adolescence in patriarchy if they, the adult women, model selves that have not been silenced for the sake of relationships.

14. See Maria Tatar, *Off with Their Heads: Fairy Tales and the Culture of Childhood* (Princeton, N.J.: Princeton University Press, 1992); and Jack Zipes, *Fairy Tales and the Art of Subversion: The Classical Genre for Children and the Process of Civilization* (New York: Routledge, 1983).

7

Heterosexual and Lesbian Mothers Challenging "Feminine" and "Masculine" Concepts of Mothering

Andrea Doucet and Gillian Dunne

This chapter explores how heterosexual and lesbian mothers create new forms of mothering that attempt to challenge and ultimately dismantle patriarchal motherhood. Drawing on our interviews with ninety-seven mothers (and twenty-three fathers) carried out in Britain during the early to mid-1990s, we employ a wide conception of mothering, one that includes a revitalized conception of caring combined with economic independence. Our chapter aims to reconceptualize mothering practices and provide new insights on gender relations. We also hope to contribute toward developing alternative feminist conceptions of mothering, as distinct from both a "feminine" conception of mothering and a "masculine" model of mothering.[1] Our chapter builds from the narratives of the women we interviewed, and we interweave these narratives with selected writings from feminist theoretical debates on care, gender equality, and gender differences.

The chapter arises out of an active dialogue between us, the authors, over the past seven years on the relationship among gender, sexuality, and the organization of work and family life. More specifically, it is informed by our involvement in two different research projects, with some aspects of our research methodology in common.[2] Doucet's work considers the arrangements of heterosexual couples who define and describe themselves as "sharing" parenting, housework, and employment,[3] while Dunne explores similar issues in relation to cohabiting lesbian partnerships with dependent children.[4] One of the key themes, which brought these two studies together, was our shared interest in how gender permeates the lives of couples trying to be "equal." These investigations of divisions of labor in lesbian partnerships and in heterosexual couples who described themselves as sharing parenting took us deeper into an empirical and theoretical understanding of the significance of the social production of gender differences for shaping outcomes. We share a common interest in illuminating the limitations and possibilities for change offered within a wide range of partnerships. Furthermore, Dunne was particularly interested in exploring the extent to which egalitarianism could be sustained in lesbian partnerships when children were present. Given that the women in Dunne's study have the advantage of negotiating their relationships within a context of gender similarity, she sought to illuminate what can be achieved when gender difference as a structuring principle is minimized.

The chapter is organized into three sections. First, we introduce the qualitative research studies that inform this chapter. Second, we draw out two shared findings from our research studies that demonstrate some of the ways in which these mothers challenged patriarchal motherhood and male conceptions of mothering. Finally, in concluding, we point to some ways of theorizing mothers' efforts to create alternative and critical conceptions of motherhood within patriarchal cultures.

TWO QUALITATIVE RESEARCH STUDIES

Research Sample: Doucet's Study

Doucet's research was conducted with a "critical case study" of twenty-three heterosexual British couples with dependent children who identified themselves as "consciously attempting to share the work and responsibility for housework and childcare." These were not couples who claimed to be involved in "50/50 parenting"[5] or "coparenting"[6] as she was interested in household variation in the meaning and structure of sharing with regard to household work. Furthermore, the emphasis was on socially situated "choice" rather than necessity, such as in cases of male unemployment, since research suggests that the latter most often revert back to traditional divisions of labor once the man is employed full-time once again.[7] Her initial interest in speaking to these couples was to investigate where gender differences were most resistant to change in households who were attempting to minimize strict gender divisions of labor.[8] The "sharing" couples that Doucet interviewed exhibited enormous variation in the meanings attached to, and the structured patterns of, "sharing" housework and childcare. It is important to point out that seven of the mothers accepted gender differentiation in parenting, housework, and employment; thus, for them, "sharing" meant working within these "natural" gender differences. As Karen, a part-time lab technician, puts it, "Men are men and women are women. And they're different and they do different things." The other mothers challenged gender differences and attempted to create patterns in which gender differences were eliminated or minimized. This proved to be much more difficult than originally anticipated, partly because of the gendered social institutions and social structures within which they lived their lives. In spite of the constraints, sixteen of the twenty-three women struggled to create new patterns of mothering.

Research Sample: Dunne's Study

Dunne's research is based on the experiences of thirty-seven lesbian couples living in six major English cities.[9] A wide range of strategies was employed to recruit participants, with snowballing through different sources being the most successful. The only selection criteria used were that respondents be currently cohabiting and that dependent children were present. Interestingly, most respondents had become parents via donor insemination and were raising their children as a joint project. As both parents usually thought of themselves as mothers and/or were biological mothers (in 40 percent of households) the term *birthmother* is used to describe the biological mother of the child/children or youngest child and *coparent* to describe the partner. Furthermore, the majority had at least one child under five years old, thus providing the opportunity to explore arrangements at a point in the life cycle when polarization is often at its most extreme for heterosexual parents.[10] While there was some variation in the two samples in terms of ethnicity and class, participants in both studies were predominantly white, well educated, and middle class, although many came from working-class origins and had experienced social mobility. In relation to Dunne's study, educational and occupational advantage among her sample was theoretically predictable given the material dimension to the construction of sexual identity. A similar observation can be made about issues of gender equity and the challenging of traditional gender ideologies for Doucet's study. Moreover, the social class composition of her sample should not, however, be surprising given that patterns for sharing housework and childcare were relatively rare in Britain in the late 1980s and early 1990s.[11]

Methodology

Both studies employed a diversity of methods, mainly qualitative, to gain a sense of how employment, parenting, and housework were allocated between partners. A semistructured joint interview (approximately two to three hours)—which revolved around the use of a visual participatory method of data collection called the Household Portrait technique[12]—was conducted for each partnership in the two studies. These were followed by individual interviews. In addition, each of Dunne's participants completed time-task allocation diaries for seven days. Doucet analyzed her interviews by using an adapted version of the voice-centered relational method of data analysis,[13] while Dunne's method of analysis was informed by a grounded theory approach.[14]

Findings

As our conversations about our two research projects progressed, it soon became clear that sexuality did mediate gender with respect to the organization of work in the home and in the labor market, so that both kinds of labor were more symmetrically balanced or "equal" in lesbian households. Moreover, we observed that the majority of women in both studies shared a common commitment to taking responsibility for young children. This was particularly revealing in Doucet's study, in which couples presented themselves as "consciously attempting to share housework and childcare." Nevertheless in spite of good intentions, the gendered discourses, the social institutions, and social structures within which these couples lived out their lives proved more pressing than had been anticipated. Meanwhile, Dunne, whose previous work had examined issues of gender, sexuality, and employment[15] in relation to childless/childfree lesbians, was initially taken aback by her respondents' commitment toward caring for their children. She had anticipated that most would resolve the contradiction between the demands of income generation and child care by making use of public or private child care provision. As the different kinds of work that we are examining—earning a living, managing and maintaining a household, and caring for children—are all essential foundations for living, we then begin to think about why it is that women, rather than men, retain this commitment, while also reflecting on how to make sense of the persistent link between women and caregiving. Our thinking led us through the maze of literature on the theoretical relationship between gender equality and gender differences[16] and to two theoretical points that we elaborate on, in conjunction with our findings, in the next section of this chapter. We came to these theoretical points through our interpretations of women's narratives, and thus we will weave the empirical findings and the theoretical points together.

A FEMINIST CONCEPTION OF CARING AND MOTHERING

Marianne Hirsch points out in the introduction to *The Mother/Daughter Plot* that many of the "daughterly" white feminists being raised in the 1960s and 1970s had grown into mothers who struggled to reconcile their continued ambivalence toward their mothers' situations with their own mothering practices and experiences.[17] While some of the women in our studies expressed these sentiments of ambivalence toward their own mothers' caring, what was even greater was their critical questioning of culturally and socially defined "mothering scripts"[18] and the gender scripts that define particular conceptions of caring practices and identities for mothers. These scripts, as Hilary Graham has pointed out, hold that "caring defines both the identity and activity of women in Western society."[19] The majority of the women in both studies struggled with the dilemma of wanting to question dominant feminine conceptions of caring, which precluded women's autonomy and independence, while also recognizing the value of care work and mother's work. In the end they were attempting to resolve a classic dilemma that has been grappled with by feminist theorists, that of focusing on the positive side of care rather than its frequently portrayed "downside."[20] In this sense, we would argue that the majority of women in our studies were rejecting a feminine conception of care and embracing and developing a feminist conception of care. This distinction between a feminine and a feminist approach to caring is well articulated by Joan Tronto:

> [T]he feminine approach to caring carries the burden of accepting traditional gender divisions in a society that devalues what women do. . . . *A feminist approach* to caring, in contrast, needs to begin by broadening our understanding of what caring for others means, both in terms of the moral questions it raises and in terms of *the need to restructure broader social and political institutions if caring for others is to be made a more central part of the everyday lives of everyone in society.*[21]

Tronto also highlights that "feminist theory will also need to describe what constitutes good caring."[22] The majority of women in both studies (sixteen of twenty-three in Doucet's and all of Dunne's) were providing everyday examples of feminist examples of "good caring." They reconceptualized caring so that its positive qualities were maintained, and also transcended, so as to balance caring with autonomy, dependence, and independence.

Doucet's Study

Although the women in Doucet's study were grappling with the tensions between feminine and feminist conceptions of caring, they were also confronted with the dilemma of living with male partners who were largely not involved in these reflections. Or if they were, these were reflections that stopped short of questioning the primacy of employment versus home life. Of course, nobody said this in direct ways, but her interpretations of the individual interviews with men brought her to these views.

In the same way, even where women were emphasizing that a career was very important to them, they also had not relinquished traditionally female domains such as caring and domestic responsibility. Mandy, a university administrator, points to how she combines her need for economic independence with caring. She begins by saying:

> But one important imperative for me, and I wouldn't like to quantify it or put it in a blanket, is to feel okay about money. To me, money is security. And my money is security. I think I would feel immensely uncomfortable living off somebody else's salary.

At the same time, she also says, "My ideal world would be that I worked probably three-quarters time with the hours arranged so that I could meet Jessica from school."

After speaking about her wish to combine some degree of autonomy with caring, Mandy notes that she is also bothered by the fact that it is mainly her, and not her husband, who is thinking along these lines:

> I think the other thing is that I would like to achieve a better mutual understanding with Christian about the relative importance of our two jobs so that we don't have the misunderstandings that we do. We still have tussles about whether or not one persons' work is prioritized over the other's. He feels that I prioritize mine. And I know that he prioritizes his.

While it was the case that the men in Doucet's research contributed a great deal to the children and to the domestic sphere, women retained the overall responsibility for domestic life, and this posed tensions and difficulties as they attempted to balance full-time paid employment with home life. In the end, five of the sixteen women accepted this state of affairs and arranged their hours into part-time work while the children were young. For the other eleven women, it was a continual source of discussion and negotiation as women coaxed and battled with men to get more involved. In the case of Laura and Stephen, the couple with the longest marriage in the study (twenty-seven years), Laura describes in meticulous detail how every five years "she went on strike" with certain aspects of household life and how she just pressed on with her demands as the years went on and as she moved up the career ladder from nurse to health visitor, to college lecturer in health studies. With some weariness, she says that she and Stephen finally arrived at a position where she felt more comfortable with their respective roles in caring for the children. She says:

> In fact, for the first time I feel that if anything ever happened to me, I know that they would be OK. I'm sure they would have been OK before—I'm sure Stephen would have been reasonably fine coping at an earlier stage. But now I know that I could disappear from the face of the Earth and they'd be all right.

Dunne's Study

In the case of Dunne's households where parenting was described as a joint project, both birthmothers and their partners shared this responsibility for the overall care of the children, or at least they expressed that they were trying to share it. Cay, birthmother of two young boys, describes how she sees their approach to parenting differing from their understanding of heterosexual arrangements:

> It's just so much more equal; the responsibilities are shared. Like with her friends with children the same age . . . like Simon, and he's a new man and he's very involved and very supportive, but he doesn't say to his partner, "I'd like to go out on Wednesday night—is that OK with you?" He just says, "I'm going out Wednesday night." It appears that it's up to the woman to sort out child care. Whereas if one of us is going to go out we discuss it first because it is not a given right.

Like the rest of the sample, they describe a flexible approach to the organization of work in the home with both partners entering the rhythm of domestic life—which was supported in the diary analysis.[23] This is understandable given their similarities as women and the absence of gender scripts to inform practice. Cay's partner Vivien, who had been married and has a grown-up son, describes some advantages of their arrangements:

> I think what we do is try and expand the idea of roles. . . . What we tend to do is swap them around all the time and we share a lot of things. So one minute I'll be doing this sort of thing and then Cay will do the same thing at other times. And now [that I am in full-time employment] I don't come back . . . like I was married for quite a long time, and when my husband came home from work, as far as he was concerned the day was finished in terms of work, whereas when I come home from work . . . I take off my coat and assess what's going on and act—get on with it. If they're in the bath, I go and get their pajamas or whatever. And you don't have that kind of demarcation line. . . . I can enjoy the mothering in a new and exciting way, because

even though I was in a relationship I didn't have the sort of freedom and sharing that I have in this relationship, so I had the weight of responsibility for the child squarely on my shoulders. . . . So I felt I couldn't allow myself so much time to actually enjoy just being a mother.

Vivien's words illuminate a feminist concept of caring that highlights the pleasures associated with caring in a social context where assumptions about who does what are less fixed and where each partner also has a certain degree of autonomy. The approach of these mothers to sharing domestic work and their valuing of the pleasure and work of care help explain why both partners in this study were able and willing to devote a far greater amount of time to child care than is usual in heterosexual partnerships.[24]

CHALLENGING A "MALE MODEL" OF PARENTING, HOUSEWORK, AND EMPLOYMENT

While sixteen of the mothers in Doucet's study and all of the mothers in Dunne's sample were challenging patriarchal motherhood, they were, almost without fail, also questioning a "male work norm" and a "male model of employment."[25] In this sense, they were giving life to some of the theoretical insights developed by feminist authors who have been critical of some of the tenants of liberal feminism and "equality feminism." That is, although the equal rights tradition has been important as a theoretical tool and a political strategy for women's struggles to gain equal entry into and access to the rewards of the public world of work and politics, it also has its limitations. As argued by Elizabeth Meehan and Selma Sevenhuijsen, "The employment of equality as a concept and as a goal supposes a standard or a norm which, in practice, tends to be defined as what is characteristic of the most powerful groups in society."[26]

In a similar vein, Deborah Rhode has eloquently argued for the creation of a "society truly committed to caretaking values"; this would be achieved "not only through fundamental changes in employment structures and welfare policies" but also through a recognition that the important questions at stake are *"not only of gender equality but also of cultural priorities."*[27]

Doucet's Study

For even the most successful of the career women in Doucet's sample, whose salaries outweighed those of their male partners, there was still a sense—particularly while the children were in their preschool years—that employment should be balanced with home life and moreover that the workplace should recognize the value of parenting. Marie is one of the highest earners of the sample, earning 28,000 pounds (approximately $46,000 U.S. dollars/year) as a tax consultant. Her views have changed gradually, particularly after she had her second child:

> When I first had Oliver, you know, it was very important to me that I didn't, that having the children didn't interfere with my work because it mattered to me that people at work could see that I was able to carry out my job now. Well, I'm actually coming to the view, well, you know, work shouldn't be like that. . . . Work environments should actually respect the fact that you're a parent. . . . I know that would be viewed detrimentally. I feel I should say that the children are important and that Jake [partner] should be able to say it at his work too. People's awareness of the fact that families should be accommodated with work should increase by doing that. I feel that's a more important battle, really. I know I can carry on my job perfectly well having children. But I mean, I shouldn't feel awkward about wanting to go home early one day because I want to do things with Oliver or having a day off. I shouldn't feel that I've got to sort of not tell people that I'm doing something with my children. They feel it's sort of sapping my enthusiasm for my job. That's ridiculous. . . . More fundamentally, men think that if you've got children, you change as a person. And I have changed as a person. But I don't think it makes me less capable of doing my job well. I think, in fact, the demands of having family and holding down a job are strengthening things. They mean you've got to compartmentalize your time even more. I think it means I work better when I'm at work because I have to switch off and I have to get it done and get home. And I want to work efficiently so I get my job done in the day.

In a similar way, Mandy points to the dangers for women in assuming that men have an ideal situation with regard to work: "What happens in the workplace doesn't let men do what would achieve equality for them in the family sphere. And it's now also preventing women from doing that."

While women across the sample voice similar reservations, these sentiments about balancing home life and paid employment were clearly gender differentiated. That is, although the overwhelming majority of full-time employed women sought to achieve a better balance between paid work and child rearing, these expressions were conspicuously absent from all of the men interviewed. Many of the men did comment that they wished they could take sick leave days to be with their children as well as on how they would like to have the opportunity to take paternity leave within a supportive working environment. However, not one of the twenty-three men interviewed mentioned the lack of fit between the working day and the children's school hours. Joe and Lilly, for example, discuss how they combine two full-time careers with caring for their daughter. Lilly says that "I do feel guilty sometimes and if Hannah [their daughter] is having a problem, then I think, 'Well, would she be having it if I was looking after her?'" On the other hand, her partner Joe says that he doesn't feel guilty about working full-time because "I suppose it's expected that the man goes out to work."

Only two men slowed down their careers around the children, but this was due to their partner's insistence that one parent should do so, and since both of these men were self-employed (with variable earnings), it made sense that they did rather than their partners, who were in full-time high-paying jobs. Both of these men came to appreciate the gains they had achieved by being the primary caregiver of young children as well as the importance of politically and socially recognizing caring as "work." In the words of Adam: "I enjoy the fact that being at home with the baby is just so unquestionably necessary as work." Nevertheless, Adam and all the other men in the sample still felt the hold of "hegemonic masculinity."[28] That is, they constantly assessed how they were holding up under the gaze of other men and "what other men think." This left men in a position whereby as much as they may have desired to do so, they never fully crossed the dividing lines between traditional fathering and new conceptions of fathering where they might have found something in common with feminist conceptions of mothering. In the case of Doucet's couples, there was, thus, a strong overarching sense across the entire sample that mothers suffered from guilt if they were not spending enough time with their children while fathers experienced guilt if they were not putting enough energy into their jobs. Ultimately this proved to be difficult for women. Because men were not taking on a comparable share of the care and responsibility for the children, women were left to compensate, which only deepened their feelings that both their mothering and their commitments to employment were being compromised. In questioning malestream notions of the distinct separation of home and work while parenting with partners who did not share this critical stance, women were left to deal with the frustrations of deciding to "opt out" of the male model or remain within it. Five of the sixteen women opted out while the remaining continued to work full-time hours within a predominantly "male model" of work that made it difficult for women, and men, to parent.

Dunne's Study

For Dunnes' couples, a high level of flexibility and even-handedness characterized the allocation of employment responsibilities between partners, regardless of the age of the children. Being a birthmother or the birthmother of the youngest child was a poor predictor for employment differences (hours, status, pay, etc.) between partners. Their thinking about employment was shaped by a view that both partners had a right to, and would benefit from, an identity beyond the home and that level of pay was a poor indicator of the value of work performed. It was unusual to find one partner's "career" taking priority over the other's. A strong sense that caring for a child was important, demanding, and pleasurable work balanced this, however. For example, Dunne asked both birth mothers and coparents whether the arrival of children had influenced their view on the centrality of paid employment. Helen and Maggie are both part-time social workers, who divide the care of their three-year-old son between them. Maggie explains her changing attitudes to paid work:

> It has changed, yes. Yes, and work is not as important to me now. I think the original reason for working part-time was to share Paul [their son]. But actually I'm not sure now even if I'd want to go back to full time—probably not back to being a totally work person, which would be stressful and horrible. . . . The motivation behind it was to do with Paul, and to make sure that he was equally cared for—because neither Helen nor I wanted to be either the one that was at work or the one that was at home all the time.

What is interesting to note is that Maggie is not Paul's biological mother. Importantly, this shift in attitude towards paid work was common for both birthmothers and coparents alike. With persistent regularity respondents spoke of seeking balance in their lives. Thus, it was not unusual to find both partners in half-time employment, particularly when they had preschool-age children, and this was the "ideal" for many other couples in the study. For example, one working-class couple with children from a previous marriage, where neither had formal qualifications, bought a catering van, and each worked half-time selling hot dogs so that one was always at home for the children.

Another common approach was to take turns in developing paid work opportunities and taking "career breaks." Within reason, they were prepared to experience a reduced standard of living, and indeed many did, to enable what they perceived to be a fairer outcome. For the mothers in Dunne's study, respondents' decisions about how to balance child care with paid employment seem to confound "rational" economic models, which see traditional divisions of labor as the logical outcome of men's superior earning potential. This kind of model illuminates the taken-for-granted nature of privileging employment considerations over caring. Further, in Dunne's households it was not unusual for the partner with the higher-paying job to reduce her hours of employment. This was often seen to make sense because that person held more power in relation to her paid working life. This again exposes the masculine thinking underpinning rational economic models.[29]

Furthermore, the experiential insights gained through lack of specialization facilitated the development of empathy. Thus, the performance of paid work, the domestic routine, and child care afforded no mystery. This view is well summarized by Louise. She and her partner Thelma each have half-time employment and share the care of their two preschool-age children between them:

> I think that because you have been through the situation yourself you have a real understanding. If you are at home all day with a baby you cannot think of anything that is more demanding than that, or more tiring. But if you have been out at work all day, you cannot think of anything more tiring than that. But because we have done both, we can really understand. There wouldn't be an argument about who has had the hardest day because we both had a very clear understanding of the experience of being at home all day and the experience of being at work all day. They are both very demanding in different ways.

Finally, Thelma sums up the advantages of both partners working with a more even balance:

> I think we go about things in our own way; we don't have the role definition. We get the best of both worlds, really. We get to continue along the road with our careers and also to spend time as a family and to enjoy the time with the children. Disadvantages? We could earn more money, I suppose, if we worked full-time, but then it takes away the point of having children I would say.

CONCLUSIONS

Karin Davies in her Swedish study of women, work, and time argues that when women have the option to work part-time, particularly where part-time work is not equated with poorly paid, insecure, or temporary work, they may reap many personal and political benefits.[30] She writes:

> In one sense, women choosing and taking part-time work, and thereby being instrumental in bringing about one of the major changes that has occurred in the last twenty years, can be seen as a rejection, on their part, of wage labor as the over-riding structure and an unconditional adherence to male time. It is a strategy . . . for women to retain the totality of their daily lives. . . . [B]y limiting the time spent in wage labor, a soil is provided *whereby visions of what is important to fight and strive for can find a space.*[31]

Ultimately, however, it was Dunne's couples who were best able to find ways whereby they could follow these "visions" and "find a space" for "what is important to fight and strive for." The women in Doucet's study did this largely in conjunction with other mothers, but they constantly found themselves in a double bind whereby they wanted to reconceptualize caring and yet to do so would mean giving up their simultaneous goals for achieving "equality" with their male partners. While Dunne's couples certainly suffered inequalities with their male colleagues and friends, they nevertheless had a "feminine space" in which to mother. This was a space that existed somewhere between traditional conceptions of the feminine and masculine, somewhere between equality and difference, and indeed beyond equality.[32]

The class implications of our arguments cannot be underestimated. The sixteen women in Doucet's study who were most successfully challenging gender differentiation and the majority of women in Dunne's sample were educationally advantaged. Thus, these creative options and sets of negotiations may not be open to working-class or economically disadvantaged households in the same way. Nevertheless, the argument remains that the absence of gender differences and gender scripts was an asset for Dunne's couples, both working-class and middle-class. That is, female partners did not have to make their decisions around mothering and employment in relation to the major gender differences in pay and status as well as within the hegemonic masculinities that face most heterosexual couples.

In this chapter we have argued that rather than move from a patriarchal notion of motherhood to a "male" way of mothering, the women we interviewed sought to balance work and home life in ways that recognized the value of economic independence as well as emotional interdependence. Our findings suggest that mothers who are attempting to translate a "feminine" conception of mothering and caring into "feminist" ones are creating critical and strategic practices of mothering. In doing so these mothers, particularly the lesbian mothers in Dunne's sample, are also recreating gender. Judith Butler has written, "In an important sense, gender is not traceable to a definable origin because it is itself an originating activity incessantly taking place."[33] The mothers in both studies, but particularly those in Dunne's research, are "incessantly" re-creating mothering and re-creating gender. One of the reasons for the imbalance in parenting and caring in heterosexual relationships lay with fathers' resistance or inability to mirror the mothers' versatility with regard to balancing paid employment with the work and pleasures of home life. Our work underlines the necessity to problematize the centrality of paid employment in the lives of men, and associated discourses of hegemonic masculinities, rather than simply the desire for women to care.

NOTES

We both owe a debt of gratitude to the individuals who agreed to be part of our studies and who so patiently shared their wisdom and precious time with us. The research reported in this chapter was funded by the Commonwealth Association of Canada and the Social Sciences and Humanities Research Council in Andrea Doucet's case and by the British Economic and Social Research Council (reference number R00023 4649) in Gillian Dunne's project. For encouragement and guidance in their projects, both authors thank Bob Blackburn as well as, in Doucet's research, Carol Gilligan, and in Dunne's, Henrietta Moore. Particular thanks to Dunne's overworked and underpaid, yet always enthusiastic, colleagues Kim Perren, Esther Dermott, and Jackie Beer who assisted her project over the three years.

1. Barbara Katz Rothman, "Women as Fathers: Motherhood and Child Care Under a Modified Patriarchy," *Gender and Society* 3, no. 1 (March 1989): 89–104.

2. See Andrea Doucet, "Encouraging Voices: Towards More Creative Methods for Collecting Data on Gender and Household Labor," in *Gender Relations in the Public and the Private,* ed. Lydia Morris and Stina Lyon (London: Macmillan, 1996); Gillian A. Dunne, "Why Can't a Man Be More Like a Woman? In Search of Balanced Domestic and Employment Lives," LSE Gender Institute Discussion Paper Series, 3 (1997); Gillian A. Dunne, "'Pioneers behind Our Own Front Doors': Towards New Models in the Organization of Work in Partnerships," *Work Employment and Society* 12, no. 2 (1998).

3. Andrea Doucet, *Gender Equality, Gender Differences and Care: Towards Understanding Gendered Labor in British Dual Earner Households,* unpublished doctoral dissertation, University of Cambridge, Cambridge, 1995; Andrea Doucet, "Gender Equality and Gender Differences in Household Work and Parenting," *Women's Studies International Forum* 18, no. 3 (May 1995): 271–84; Doucet, "Encouraging Voices."

4. Dunne, "Why Can't a Man"; Dunne, "Pioneers"; Gillian A. Dunne, "A Passion for 'Sameness'? Sexuality and Gender Accountability," in *The New Family?* ed. Elizabeth Silva and Carol Smart (London: Sage, 1998); Gillian A. Dunne, "Add Sexuality and Stir: Towards a Broader Understanding of the Gender Dynamics of Work and Family Life," in *Living 'Difference'?: Lesbian Perspectives on Work and Family Life,* ed. Gillian A. Dunne (New York: Haworth, 1998).

5. Gayle Kimball, *50/50 Parenting: Sharing Family Rewards and Responsibilities* (Lexington, Mass.: Lexington, 1988).

6. Diane Ehrensaft, *Parenting Together: Men and Women Sharing the Care of Their Children* (London: Collier Macmillan, 1987).

7. Norma Radin, "Primary Care-Giving and Role-Sharing Fathers," in *Non-Traditional Families: Parenting and Child Development,* ed. Michael E. Lamb (Hillsdale, N.J.: Erlbaum, 1982); Norma Radin, "Primary Caregiving Fathers of Long Duration," in *Fatherhood Today: Men's Changing Role in the Family,* ed. Phyllis Bronstein and Carolyn Pabe Cowen (New York: Wiley, 1988); Graeme Russell, *The Changing Role of Fathers?* (St Lucia: University of Queensland Press, 1983); Graeme Russell, "Problems in Role Reversed Families," in *Reassessing Fatherhood: New Observations of Fathers and the Modern Family,* ed. Charlie Lewis and Margaret O'Brien

(London: Sage, 1987); Lydia Morris, *The Workings of the Household* (Cambridge: Polity Press, 1990); Jane Wheelock, *Husbands at Home: The Domestic Economy in a Post-Industrial Society* (London: Routledge, 1990).

8. The couples in Doucet's study were found through snowball sampling through varied community, employment, and parenting organizations in the villages, towns, and small cities of southeastern England. All households had children (between one and four children, and all children over the age of one year) (D. R. Entwistle and S. G. Doering, *The First Birth* [Baltimore: Johns Hopkins University Press, 1980]). Although the majority of respondents came from working-class backgrounds, the sample was largely "middle-class," with 87 percent (*n* = 20) of the sample having educational qualifications, technical or academic, beyond secondary school. Average individual earnings were 16,800 pounds ($27,400 U.S. dollars) per annum. The majority of individuals were employed by the public sector—in teaching, nursing, health services, social work, postal work, and clerical and administrative work within educational institutions. Doucet's sample is predominantly white with two respondents of color (East Indian), one Spanish, and several Welsh respondents. Dunne's sample is varied by ethnic background, but all are white; the sample includes several Irish women, a Greek, an Iranian, and five Jewish women.

9. Overall, parenting was depicted as jointly shared between partners in thirty households (80 percent); generally their children were described as having two mothers. Where parenting was not a "joint project," the reasons given usually related to the relationship being formed when children were older. Respondents tended to be well educated—70 percent hold degrees or professional qualifications and are occupationally advantaged; 78 percent were professionals, administrators, or managers; see Dunne, *Lesbian Lifestyles: Women's Work and the Politics of Sexuality* (Basingstoke: MacMillan, and Toronto: University of Toronto Press, 1997), for discussion of links between lesbian lifestyle and educational and occupational empowerment. They were usually employed in the public sector, as teachers and health and social workers. Some were self-employed in craft occupations or in several cases as cleaners.

10. It is important to add that some partnerships had men involved, such as in cases where donor fathers were also involved in caring, albeit as junior partners.

11. J. Brannen and P. Moss, *Managing Mothers: Dual Earner Households After Maternity Leave* (London: Unwin Hyman, 1991); Morris, *The Workings of the Household;* N. Gregson and M. Lowe, "Renegotiating the Domestic Division of Labor: A Study of Dual Career Households in North East and South East England," *Sociological Review* 41, no. 3: 475–505; N. Gregson and M. Lowe, *Servicing the Middle Classes: Class, Gender and Wages: Domestic Labor in Contemporary Britain* (London: Routledge, 1994).

12. See Doucet, "Encouraging Voices"; Dunne, "Why Can't a Man."

13. See Natasha S. Mauthner and Andrea Doucet, "Reflections on a Voice-Centered Relational Method: Analyzing Maternal and Domestic Voices," in *Feminist Dilemmas in Qualitative Research: Public Knowledge and Private Lives*, ed. Jane Ribbens and Rosalind Edwards (London: Sage, 1998); Andrea Doucet, "Interpreting Mother-Work: Linking Methodology, Ontology, Theory and Personal Biography," *Canadian Women's Studies* 18, nos. 2 & 3 (October 1998): 52–58.

14. Anselm L. Strauss and Juliet Corbin, *Basics of Qualitative Research: Grounded Theory Procedures and Techniques* (London: Sage, 1990). See Gillian A. Dunne, "Balancing Acts: On the Salience of Sexuality and Sexual Identity for Understanding the Gendering of Work and Family Life Opportunities," in *Women and Work: The Age of Post-Feminism?* ed. J. Sperling and M. Owen (Ashgate: Aldershot, 1999).

15. Dunne, *Lesbian Lifestyles*.

16. See also Doucet, "Gender Equality."

17. Marianne Hirsh, *The Mother/Daughter Plot: Narratives, Psychoanalysis, Feminism* (Bloomington: Indiana University Press, 1989).

18. Ann Willard, "Cultural Scripts of Mothering," in *Mapping the Moral Domain: A Contribution of Women's Thinking to Psychological Theory and Education,* ed. Carol Gilligan, Janie Victoria Ward, and Jill McLean Taylor with Betty Bardige (Cambridge, Mass.: Harvard University Press, 1988).

19. Hilary Graham, "Caring: A Labor of Love," in *A Labor of Love: Women, Work and Caring,* ed. Janet Finch and Dulcie Groves (London: Routledge & Kegan Paul, 1983), 30.

20. Deborah L. Rhode, "Theoretical Perspectives on Sexual Difference," in *Theoretical Perspectives on Sexual Difference,* ed. Deborah L. Rhode (London: Yale University Press, 1990), 6.

21. Joan Tronto, "Women and Caring: What Can Feminists Learn about Morality from Caring?" in *Gender/Body/Knowledge: Feminist Reconstructions of Being and Knowing,* ed. Alison M. Jaggar and Susan R. Bordo (New Brunswick, N.J.: Rutgers University Press, 1989), 184–89, emphasis added.

22. Tronto, "Women and Caring," 184. See also Alison M. Jaggar, "Sexual Difference and Sexual Equality," in *Theoretical Perspectives on Sexual Difference,* ed. Deborah L. Rhode (New Haven, Conn.: Yale University Press, 1990).

23. See detailed analysis in Dunne, "Pioneers"; Dunne, "A Passion."

24. See Dunne, "Pioneers."

25. Anne Showstack Sassoon, "Introduction: The Personal and the Intellectual, Fragments and Order, International Trends and National Specifities," in *Women and the State: The Shifting Boundaries of Public and Private,* ed. Anne Showstack Sassoon (London: Unwin Hyman, 1987), 31.

26. Elizabeth Meehan and Selma Sevenhuijsen, eds., *Equality, Politics and Gender* (London: Sage, 1991). See also Carol Lee Bacchi, *Same Difference: Feminism and Sexual Difference* (London: Allen & Unwin, 1990); Iris Marion Young, *Throwing Like a Girl and Other Essays in Feminist Philosophy and Theory* (Bloomington: Indiana University Press, 1990); Deborah L. Rhode, *Justice and Gender: Sex Discrimination and the Law* (London: Harvard University Press, 1989); Rhode, "Theoretical Perspectives."

27. Rhode, "Theoretical Perspectives," 210–11, emphasis added.

28. R. W. Connell, *Masculinities* (Berkeley: University of California Press, 1995).

29. See R. Edwards and S. Duncan, "Rational Economic Man or Lone Mothers in Context? The Uptake of Paid Work," in *Good Enough Mothering? Feminist Perspectives on Lone Mothering,* ed. E. Bortolaia Silva (London: Routledge, 1996).

30. Karin Davies, *Women and Time: Weaving the Strands of Everyday Life* (Lund, Sweden: University of Lund, 1989).

31. Davies, *Women and Time*, 208, emphasis added.

32. See Drucilla Cornell, *Beyond Accommodation: Ethical Feminism, Deconstruction and the Law* (New York: Routledge, 1991); Luce Irigaray, *The Speculum of the Other Woman,* trans. Gillian A. Dunne (Ithaca, N.Y.: Cornell University Press, 1985).

33. Judith Butler, "Variations on Sex and Gender: Beauvoir, Wittig and Foucault," in *Feminism as Critique,* ed. Seyla Benhabib and Drucilla Cornell (Minneapolis: University of Minnesota Press, 1986).

8

The Mammy and the Mummy: Cultural Imaginary and Interracial Coalition

Ivy Schweitzer

> The myth of the strong black woman is the other side of the coin of the myth of the beautiful dumb blonde.
>
> —Eldridge Cleaver, *Soul on Ice* (162)

In a discussion of "certain shared cultural conditions" of black and white women in the United States during the nineteenth century, Hortense Spillers concludes, "In fact, from one point of view, we cannot unravel one female's narrative from the other's, cannot decipher one without tripping over the other." As "twin actants on a common psychic landscape [and] subject to the same fabric of dread and humiliation," black and white women during that period were subject to different, in fact, antithetical, but mutually constituting cultural imagery.[1] My shorthand for this imagery is the "mammy" and the "mummy." Although the contours of these stereotypes have changed since the abolition of slavery, the legacy of such representations has contaminated relations between Anglo- and African-American women, and has been a painful and ongoing source of discord for feminists and feminist movements. This essay revisits two landmark feminist texts of the 1970s and compares their attempts to theorize and address this imagery, to glean directions for future cross-racial coalitions.

In her study of the "myth of Aunt Jemima," Diane Roberts observes, "Representations of whites and blacks fuel a war over the body: the black body, the white body, the female body."[2] And, I would add, as a specific

121

cultural and visual category, the maternal body. Roberts uses a gendered and racialized notion of Bakhtin's opposition of the "classical body"—single, ethereal, sanctioned, and official—and the "grotesque body"—multiple, protuberant, open, and impure—to describe the "mythic" delineations of the embattled, unruly, and perpetually overregulated female body. Her point is that these opposed images are, in fact, interdependent. "Blacks in a slave society were powerless and marginal yet the whites who owned them built their culture around not being black," she observes, a point reinforced by Toni Morrison's explorations of the "Africanist presence" in U.S. literature in her study *Playing in the Dark*.[3] Hazel Carby explores this phenomenon specifically in relation to gender, arguing that nineteenth-century prescriptions for femininity, "the cult of true womanhood," defined the virtuous, submissive and domestic white woman against a promiscuous, unruly, and sexualized dark female.[4] The consequences of this interdependence, however, are often overlooked. In their study of transgression, Stallybrass and White find that the "top" of the social scale often attempts to reject the "bottom," "only to discover, not only that it is in some way frequently dependent upon that low-Other . . . but also that the top includes that low symbolically, as a primary eroticized constituent of its own fantasy life."[5] This explains the psychic tenacity and the libidinal pull of these images for white culture. What, then, of the fantasy life of the so called "low-Other" and its internalization of, or resistance to, the powerful imagery that the "top" assigns it, against which the Other must define itself in order to become a fully human self and political agent?

Historically, motherhood has been a resilient site for a broad range of cultural and ideological work. It has been used for the construction of racial and class-divisive notions of femininity, just as it has been an arena of cross-race and cross-class solidarity. For example, black abolitionists like Harriet Jacobs, in her well-known slave narrative, appealed to northern women as women, on behalf of black women, and more specifically, as her narrative attests, on behalf of black mothers abused by a vicious system.[6] These appeals to the universality of female and specifically maternal experience enabled black and white abolitionists to make the case for the female slave "as a woman and a sister"—that is, as a gendered human being and thus a "natural" political cohort or "sister" of white women, on the analogy of biological kinship.[7] But this strategic identification also allowed suffragists to deploy the trope of slavery in the service of feminine "liberation" that had the unintended effect of disguising real differences among women across race and class, and even made possible, according to Karen Sánchez-Eppler, a further and more insidious differentiation between women. She also points out that identifying with the shackled and silenced black woman enabled white women to assert their own voices to gain access to political discourse and agency denied to the slave.[8]

Given the cultural power and political instability of representations of femininity and maternity, it is not surprising that the most pervasive figurations of black and white women from this period of history in the United States concern mothering. These are the black "mammy" of southern tradition, commercially disseminated on packages of pancake mix as a smiling Aunt Jemima, complete with head scarf and mixing spoon, and her privileged white counterpart whom I call the "mummy," a sensually deadened woman, infantilized and put on a pedestal in the house of sentimental domesticity. Although the twentieth-century versions of these images that I will examine differ in historically significant ways from their nineteenth-century predecessors, they continue to represent powerful and opposing "caricatures," in Adrienne Rich's words, that "still imprint our psyches."[9] Both black and white women have struggled for years, mostly separately from each other, to write ourselves out of these cultural images and their destructive legacy of internalized oppression, guilt, and distrust. However, they are so psychically entangled, that to disentangle ourselves from one image, we must also confront and dismantle or, at least, unsettle the other. This double deconstruction, an important source of cross-racial feminist critique that can also be a source of cross-racial, cross-class solidarity, is illustrated in the enigmatic first chapter of Alice Walker's novel *Meridian*[10] and in Adrienne Rich's accounts of her black nanny in *Of Woman Born: Motherhood as Experience and Institution*.[11] Both were landmark feminist texts published in 1976, as the second wave of the women's movement reached its crest. Although one is fiction and the other is memoir, bringing these texts together creates an interracial dialogue that was only beginning to happen at the time of their publication.

A complex and tenacious mythology has grown up around the white southern practice of bringing slave women into the plantation house to nurse and wet-nurse the master's white children. The "mammy," as this house servant became known, also "served" the reigning ideologies and epitomized the strategies and contradictions of "the peculiar institution." First, the practice brought blacks, regarded by many southern whites including Thomas Jefferson, as subhuman and thus fit only for slavery, into the very heart of white domestic arrangements and made them indispensable. Second, it made black women, characterized by self-interested white masters as uninterested in nurturing their own progeny, surrogate mothers for the precious inheritors of southern white culture. Although literary writers and postwar apologists for the "New South" canonized "Mammy" as an essential and mitigating feature of the region's racially stratified culture, in recent years, historians have found little evidence to corroborate the existence of the mammy of southern tradition—large, maternal, fiercely loyal to her white owners, and stoically strong.[12] M. M. Manring, in the most thorough review of "mammy historiography," calls her "a nest of internal contradictions" that reveals more about the sexual tensions within the white culture that invented her.[13] The question is, Where in reality lay her loyalties? Was she a "white lie," the invention of ruling race/class nostalgia, or a sell-out?

Mammy's meaning in American culture has been hotly contested by commentators, black and white. For example, W. E. B. Du Bois characterized the mammy as "one of the most pitiful of the world's Christs . . . an embodied Sorrow, an anomaly crucified on the cross of her own neglected children," while the prominent black scholar Carter Woodson praised her descendant, the "Negro washerwoman," as the "towering personage in the life of the Negro" and instrumental to racial uplift.[14] Historian Eugene Genovese counters Du Bois's view but modifies Woodson's as well, and he begins to dismantle the myth. The bonded women who filled this role were often courageous and resourceful. "More than any other slave," Genovese argues, Mammy "had absorbed the paternalist ethos and accepted her place in a system of reciprocal obligations defined from above. . . . Her tragedy lay, not in her abandonment of her own people, but in her inability to offer her individual power and beauty to black people on terms they could accept without themselves sliding further into a system of paternalistic dependency."[15]

To factor gender into this revisionist interpretation produces an even more subtle reading. Elizabeth Fox-Genovese argues that slaveholders encouraged the notion of their household as "my family, white and black," an embodiment of their "vision of an organic community." The mammy in particular, as a desexualized, loyal and loving figure, symbolized this elusive, as well as delusive, vision.[16] But this formulation sidesteps the question of the mammy's subjectivity, and the possibility of her strategic dissimulation. Deborah Gray White finds that "the reality of Mammy and female household service does not square with the Mammy legend" and dates the beginnings of the legend to the 1830s when the "Victorian ideal of womanhood" began to take hold. She concludes that mammy was not a historical person, but an ideological construction whose function was to epitomize both "the ideal slave, and the ideal woman" in her all-encompassing, defining maternalism. "As part of the benign slave tradition, and as part of the cult of domesticity, Mammy was the centerpiece in the antebellum Southerner's perception of the perfectly organized society."[17] Alice Walker reminds us that Mammy was named for her mammary glands—the body parts that indicate her primary caretaking role.[18] However, Barbara Christian contends that "Mammy is an important figure in the mythology of Africa," a symbol of the Earth's creativity recapitulated in women, that white slave culture appropriated and debased. In the black oral tradition, she notes, the mammy "is cunning, prone to poisoning her master, and not at all content with her lot."[19]

The traditional construction of Mammy adeptly turns the markers of allegedly threatening and uncontrollable female sexuality—breasts—into benign, asexual means of maternal nurture, available for appropriation by the dominant group. For lurking just behind the mammy image is her counterpart—the Jezebel, a young, seductive mulatta whose supposedly overheated sexuality and insatiable appetite were no match for the rickety morality of white slave masters and their sons and nephews. Whereas the Jezebel provided a handy explanation of slave rape that turned slave owners into victims, the mammy "affirmed the other side of the story, how black women behaved when under proper white control,"[20] and reaffirmed the morality of the slave system that Jezebel jeopardized. Because of her supposedly simple and "loving" nature, the mammy selflessly nursed and nurtured the children of white folks, at the expense of her own children—what we now recognize as a form of "coerced mothering" that nevertheless remains an important source of income for black women and other women of color even at the end of the twentieth century. The economic oppression our inheritance of these social assumptions and arrangements perpetuates is magnified by the residual cultural image of black women, which remains one of subordination and service.[21]

The proximity of the mammy to affluent white southern women helped construct their relationship as antithetical and mutually constitutive. As the mammy image promoted a myth of black women's stoical strength, it abetted the equally corrosive myth of the white woman's frailty and dependence, and her moral purity that required strenuous protection on the part of southern white men, most frequently in the form of segregation, lynch mobs, and eventually the activities of the Ku Klux Klan. Supposedly delicate and helpless as true "ladies" were meant to be, the privileged white woman needed servants to keep her house and maintain her person. Although as a womb she was absolutely essential to the production of legitimate white heirs, the daily care and raising of children compromised her lofty purity. Through the dual images of the slave woman, her mothering duties were relegated to the mammy, and her sexuality was rerouted through Jezebel.

As substitute for the white mother, the trusted and loyal mammy was also depicted as inducting white children into their proper social class and racial privilege. A well-known illustration of this ideological function occurs in Margaret Mitchell's enormously popular epic of southern nostalgia, *Gone with the Wind.*[22] In one of the opening scenes, an ample Mammy disciplines a rebellious Scarlett O'Hara by giving an extra tug to the corset she is tying around the girl's sixteen-inch waist and exhorting her to eat heartily before the Wilkes's barbeque, because a real lady always eats like a bird in public.[23] This moment in the film version of 1939 unmistakably positions Scarlet and Mammy as mirror images, a visual cue that recurs throughout the scene. For example, as they tussle over a shawl that Mammy uses to cover Scarlett's décolletage (Figure 8.1), their bodies, though antithetical in size and dress, are in precisely the same position; their eyes are locked in battle, and though they lean away from each other, they are linked by the garment that symbolizes female modesty, an example of which Mammy wears in a dignified knot around her neck. Frequently represented as the gatekeeper, and thus, ironically, the perpetuator, of southern feminine purity and gentility, the mammy was used by boosters of the region to typify "the mythic Old South of benign slavery, grace and abundance."[24]

Nor were these images confined to the slaveholding South but rather were in full evidence in northern—and abolitionist—culture. A classic example involves the ex-slave and feminist abolitionist activist Sojourner Truth, whose striking appearance and pertinent comments at a women's rights convention in Akron, Ohio, in 1851 have become legendary. Although Truth was not enslaved in the South but in upstate New York and did not bear and lose thirteen children to the slave trade, she has come to epitomize the strong black mammy figure serving the needs of feminists and abolitionists alike. A major contribution to this image is the account of Truth's performance in Akron published over a decade later by Frances Dana Gage, a feminist and abolitionist who presided over the Akron convention. In her report, Gage heightened the drama of Truth's intervention by depicting hostile white clergymen in the audience challenging the women's platform of female and black suffrage by questioning why women deserved the vote when they needed to be helped out of carriages and over ditches. In response, Gage depicts Sojourner Truth rising to the platform and silencing all objections with thunderous repetitions of the ringing question, "Ar'n't I a woman?"[25]

According to Gage, "She had taken us up in her great strong arms and carried us safely over the slough of difficulty, turning the whole tide in our favor."[26] The image of white women being carried over the ditch of misogyny like frightened children by a strong black woman did not, in Gage's mind, prove the clergyman's point. Nell Irvin Painter argues that Gage overdramatized the circumstances and invented Truth's famous speech from words she spoke on other occasions. Nevertheless, according to Painter, the famous question Gage put into Truth's mouth "inserts blackness into feminism and gender into racial identity," thus doing "the very same symbolic work" Truth accomplished through her presence at these meetings.[27] What is significant for this analysis is that Gage rendered Truth as the strong black woman coming to the rescue of confused and divided white women, and that despite the inaccuracies of her report,

Fig. 8.1 Scarlett (Vivien Leigh) and Mammy (Hattie McDaniel) in MGM's *Gone with the Wind* (1939)

Source: Photo courtesy of the Museum of Modern Art Film Stills Archive.

that rendering of Truth as a majestic "mammy" figure remains indelibly inscribed in our collective imagination.

This strong black maternal figure reappears in postwar popular culture, especially in films (just think of Whoopi Goldberg's film career) as the caregiver of color whose "diverted mothering," according to Sau-ling Wong, assuages white guilt by providing the visual illusion of "multiculturalism" and the palliative of individual interracial friendship.[28] The black woman's so-called "natural" physicality enables the white woman's abdication not only of motherhood but of sensuality, eroticism, sexual desire, and cultural agency that masks the social and economic power she often wields over women of color. Gage portrays Truth as capable of refuting patriarchal arguments that day in Akron, but she remained, as Adrienne Rich observed over a century later, "Powerful black mother of us all, the most politically powerless woman in that room."[29]

Rich's essay "Disloyal to Civilization: Feminism, Racism, Gynephobia" is one of the first attempts by a white woman to analyze race relations between women and within the emerging women's liberation movement.[30] She begins by invoking the "history that touches our nerve-ends even though we are largely ignorant of it," charging interracial relationships with pain and anger. That "history" for her is, on the one hand, the "racist and patriarchal home" and culture she was born into and, on the other, "the most unconditional, tender, and I now believe, intelligent love" she received from the black woman who raised her.[31] By examining her own history in the light of women's shared history, Rich is determined to understand and demystify the "mythic" power of that relation: "How black women and white move as myths through each other's fantasies, myths created by the white male psyche including its perverse ideas of beauty . . . how . . . we use each other to keep from touching our own power."[32] To deconstruct these myths of patriarchal racism, she revisits the stereotypes invoked by Gage's version of Sojourner Truth's speech, which continue to "imprint our psyches" with "caricatures of bloodless fragility and broiling sensuality." Rich implies that Truth's rescue and Gage's fantasized need to be rescued are ineluctably linked and that this binary, created and strategically deployed by masculine culture to separate and narrowly define women, is what must be dismantled. Her solution is embodied in a radical revision of Gage's words into a utopian vision of women loving women, laying

claim to ourselves and each other beyond the most extreme patriarchal taboo. We take each other up in our strong arms. We do not infantilize each other; we refuse to be infantilized. We drink at each other's differences. We begin to fuse our powers.[33]

It is a compelling, eroticized vision of interracial sisterhood that owes much to Rich's reading of and conversations with sister poet and black lesbian feminist writer Audre Lorde. In the spirit of Lorde's exhortation that women must come to see our differences "as a fund of necessary polarities between which our creativity can spark like a dialectic,"[34] Rich urges women to refuse the positions of mammy and mummy offered them by patriarchal culture, positions that allow white women to endow black women with cultural agency in the face of social and political disenfranchisement and exclusion. To do so would be to tap a new source of political power, united in goals but diverse in attributes, through our personal/erotic connections. This connection is "that lightning-rod conductor between women" that for Rich animates "lesbian/feminism":

> love experienced as identification . . . a non-exploitative, non-possessive eroticism, which can cross barriers of age and condition, the sensing our way into another's skin, if only for a moment's apprehension, against the censure, the denial, the lies and laws of civilization.[35]

This is a highly subversive and powerful force. However, alongside this idealized vision of healing mutuality, in which women sensually inhabit the other's "skin," Rich leaves in place, at least textually, the role in which silenced black women are expected to protect and support white women, when she opposes the broad and deep culture of white patriarchal racism with the tender loving she received from her black nanny.

Rich makes this explicit in another essay of this period in which she castigates the "two women, one white, one black" who were the first persons to love her but who also "surrendered me to the judgment and disposition of my father and my father's culture: white and male." In her anger at the two "mothers," she states that "they became merged in my inarticulate fury. I did not know that neither of them had had a choice."[36] In trying to recover how women, particularly mothers, betray their daughters—how she was betrayed as a daughter by both her white and black mothers—Rich conflates the white and black women in her early life as if their situations (one as wife, the other as employee), their lack of choices, their collusion with patriarchy, even the anger and contempt the daughter feels for them, could possibly be interchangeable. And she conflates them because she insists on seeing them both as her "mothers," a label by which she intends to express the intimacy and importance, even the equality, of her black nanny, but that, because of its history, obscures through sentimentality the often dehumanizing realities of the domestic worker.

Ann duCille makes a similar critique, arguing that despite Rich's outwardly respectful and loving recovery of the memories of her black nurse

in the course of writing *Of Woman Born,* she fails to see the ways these
memories themselves thrust motherhood, even a metaphorical one, on
this childless black woman, thus depriving her of an identity or even a
voice outside of the role she fulfilled in Rich's life as "my Black mother."
Rich recalls, "She was slim, dignified, and very handsome, and from her
I learned—non-verbally—a great deal about the possibilities of dignity in
a degrading situation."[37] The seeming antithesis of the traditional
"mammy," this woman who remains unnamed throughout Rich's account still fulfills the conventional mammy role as duCille defines it, of
"tak[ing] the ignorant white infant into enlightenment."[38] Rich's "paternal arrogance," as duCille calls it, is magnified by the dramatic feminist
claims that frame this groundbreaking study of motherhood, "not to be
used merely as an instrument, a role, a womb, a pair of hands or a back
or set of fingers; . . . to speak for ourselves, in our own right," claims that
don't seem to pertain to the black woman.[39] Ten years later, in the anniversary edition of *Of Woman Born,* Rich looks back and critiques her earlier
position from a perspective more conscious and self-conscious about race
relations. She remarks how her account of 1976 "overpersonalizes and
does not, it seems to me now, give enough concrete sense of the actual
position of the Black domestic worker caring for white children."[40] Even
here duCille insists that Rich still does not see this woman as a woman
separate from her, "who is not her black mother, but a laborer whose role
as mammy is also constructed."[41]

Despite duCille's critique, it is difficult not to credit Rich's courage and
integrity in letting her patronizing depictions stand, and in revising them
publicly to produce an archaeology of white feminist thinking about race
which has been a touchstone for younger feminists like myself. Unlike
scores of other white feminists at the time, Rich began to recognize the
centrality of race politics to feminist goals of social and personal transformation and the need for white women's "emotional apprehension," as
opposed to merely "intellectual analysis," of their accountability for racism.[42] What she could not yet see clearly was how the multiple burdens
of sexism, classism, and racism (also on the part of white feminists) borne
by women of color prevented the healing sisterhood, the "love experienced as identification," the mutual mothering, she envisions. Ironically,
according to Midge Wilson and Kathy Russell's study *Divided Sisters,* "the
appeals for sisterly solidarity during the first two decades of the modern
feminist movement were issued largely by White women" and betray a
similar incomprehension.[43] Black feminists and writers such as Toni Morrison, for example, produced decidedly distopian representations of interracial relations in which common, daily, and concrete aspects of female
experience, such as gender discrimination or economic deprivation, cre-

ate a bridge across racial difference that provides a more realistic, if temporary, ground for alliance.

It is this expedient and strategic commonality that Alice Walker explores in *Meridian,* her fictional memoir of the civil rights movement that tells the story of Meridian Hill, a young black girl living in the rural South and coming of age in the early 1960s. One of the greatest impediments to Meridian's growth is society's double standard for women, especially her mother's expectation that she, too, blindly and passively accept the inevitability of marriage and motherhood, and the complete self-sacrifice they required of women, black and white, in the postwar period. In this respect, Meridian fights the same war for "personhood" against collusive mothering whose battles Rich elaborates so insightfully in *Of Woman Born.* But Walker also spells out important historical and psychic differences. Getting pregnant in high school because her mother refuses to explain the facts of life to her, Meridian is wracked with guilt for giving away her son in order to attend Saxon, a black women's college, on a scholarship. Her guilt is compounded, however, because she knows that "enslaved women had been made miserable by the sale of their children . . . that the daughters of these enslaved women had thought their greatest blessing from 'Freedom' was that it meant they could keep their own children"[44] and mother them. Meridian thinks of her mother "as Black Motherhood personified, and of that great institution she was in terrible awe, comprehending as she did the horror, the narrowing of perspective, for mother and child, it had invariably meant."[45] This sentence's surprising reversal of meaning echoes Meridian's painful rejection and revision of the awesome but awful "institution" of "Black Motherhood." It also echoes but makes racially specific Rich's radical deconstruction of motherhood from a "natural" or "instinctual" set of personal activities and experiences to a complex social and culture structure shaped by dominant ideologies.

Neither Meridian nor her mother can be construed as a conventional "mammy" figure. Still, black mothering is depicted in this text as imposed and coerced by sexism and intransigent traditions that the black community inherits, in part, from the pervasive ideals of dominant white society embodied in the figure of the "mummy woman." Meridian's confrontation with this figure occurs in the tightly orchestrated and densely symbolic first chapter of the novel that takes place in the small coastal Georgia town of Chicokema at least ten years after the main action of the story (around 1975), but it drenches all those flashbacks with its allegorical significance. In this scene, Meridian faces down a tank in the town square that is barring a group of mostly black children from entering a circus wagon on a day not designated as "theirs" to allow them to view the "mummified white woman . . . Marilene O'Shay, One of the Twelve

Human Wonders of the World: Dead for Twenty-Five Years, Preserved in Life-like Condition."[46] This mummy can be read as a pointed satire on men whose treatment of women reduces them to the status of circus freaks. Likewise, Meridian's confrontation with the town's tank, "bought during the sixties when the townspeople who were white felt under attack from 'outside agitators'—those members of the black community who thought equal rights for all should extend to blacks"[47]—appears to be an anachronistic, melodramatic gesture for a relatively trivial end that seems to mock the civil rights movement and its heroic demonstrations so formative for Meridian and her friends. Why is Meridian willing to risk her life, or at least her health, to allow the children of Chicokema to see a mummy?

We learn of Marilene's fate from a flier entitled "The True Story of Marilene O'Shay," written and distributed by her husband Henry, who not only exhibits her but also narrates her experience for his own ends. Like "Truman Held," the nominal purveyor of masculine "truth" in this narrative, Henry can only tell his necessarily distorted version of his wife's demise. This is summarized by the four phrases emblazoned on the circus wagon's side: "Obedient Daughter . . . Devoted Wife . . . Adoring Mother . . . Gone Wrong"—a parody of the trope of the "fallen woman" of sensational Victorian era literature. According to Henry:

> Marilene had been an ideal woman [invocation of the cult of true womanhood], a "goddess" [put on a pedestal], who had been given "everything she *thought* she wanted" [his emphasis]. She had owned a washing machine, furs, her own car and a full-time housekeeper-cook [she was the "lady" in contrast with the woman, probably of color, who labored for her]. All she had to do, wrote Henry, was "lay back and be pleasured." But she . . . had gone outside the home to seek her "pleasuring,"

and so he shot her lover, strangled Marilene, and threw her body in the Great Salt Lake. Everyone, including the "'thorities," the "preacher," and "her ma," forgave Henry and condemned his wayward wife. When her body washed up on shore, Henry forgave her, and like the "newly dressed manikins behind sparkling glass panes" in the thriving shops on the white side of Chicokema,[48] he put her on display, cashing in on her now permanent obedience and passivity.

Deborah McDowell reads "the mummy woman" as "a metaphor for the preservation of dead, no longer viable traditions and institutions."[49] Like Marilene, segregation that had been legally dead for about as long is preserved in lifelike condition in this rural Jim Crow town where affluent white citizens can demand not to have to mingle with the children of poor workers. But Marilene serves a more complicated function with respect to

Walker's other concern, sexism, exemplifying the fate of "uppity" women, even pampered and privileged white ones, who actively seek "pleasure" or self-definition outside of narrowly defined patriarchal bounds. Though a victim of postwar, pre-Friedan gender conventions, Marilene's relevance twenty-five years later is as an example of continued male backlash against "women libbers." Meridian regards the mummy as a "fake" and does not go into the circus wagon because, she tells Truman, her former lover and movement coworker who has come to visit her, "I knew whatever the man was selling was irrelevant to me, useless."[50] When he asks why she expended so much energy on such a "meaningless action," she responds that it was important for the black children to discover the mummy's inauthenticity for themselves. She reports that the children think Marilene is made of "plastic," like the Barbie doll that had by that time saturated American kid culture. What they see, without waiting for "their day" or paying, are the effects of white affluence and privilege that turn women into domestic ornaments with no possibility of self-definition, and turn white men into socially acceptable murderers, necrophiliacs and con artists.

However, this mummy woman isn't as irrelevant and "useless" to Meridian as she thinks.[51] On the surface, Marilene and Meridian seem antithetical: Marilene has all the privileges of postwar middle-class affluence, while Meridian is forced to drop out of high school because of her pregnancy, gives up her child and her marriage, finally has her tubes tied after a second pregnancy and abortion, and lives a peripatetic and economically marginal life, first, as a college student and civil rights worker, and then, as a grassroots organizer, "someone [who] volunteers to suffer" for the people.[52] Despite these differences, Walker's text suggests that Meridian and Marilene are connected precisely as the mammy is to the mummy—through the social roles and cultural images that define them antithetically. First, their names echo each other, but with subtle differences. More importantly, Marilene's exhibition recapitulates the scandalous exhibition in Europe in the nineteenth century of African women, the most notorious of which was Sarah Bartmann, whose large buttocks earned her the title of the "Hottentot Venus." European interest in Bartmann essentially reduced her to her sexual parts, and when she died in Paris in 1815 at the age of twenty-five, her genitalia were dissected, preserved, and put on display at the French Academy.[53] Over the course of the nineteenth and into the twentieth century, according to Sander Gilman, black females come "not merely [to] represent the sexualized female, they also represent the female as the source of corruption and disease," an "other" to be controlled by white men.[54] Marilene is a white woman who tried to evade that control by refusing to "lay back." She was taken out of the kitchen and put on a pedestal, idealized as opposed to pathologized, fetishized (through her hair as we will see) as opposed to dismembered. While these treatments are by no means the same, they are, I would contend, different sides of the same coin.

Walker reinforces this link through another intriguing detail of the mummy. Henry tells in his "true account" how Marilene's body was "darkened" by its exposure to the salt water (an immersion in tears?), a phenomenon he attributes to her "sinfulness," continuing the nineteenth-century allegory of the fallen woman. Though he tries to "paint her original color from time to time, the paint always discolored,"[55] unlike Chico-kema's tank, which is painted white and decked out with red, white and blue ribbons to signify its metonymy for state-sanctioned power. Because Marilene's discoloration puts her "race" into question, it is her long red hair, Henry asserts, that confirms her whiteness, hair that he perpetually brushes and insists is still growing. However, his exhibition of the white woman successfully disciplined by culturally accepted gender violence is undermined by her unstable racial identity and association with black-ness. Henry's anxiety about the mummy's race suggests his commitment to white racial purity, which women's allegedly unbridled sexuality or irresistible sexual attractiveness to the dark races always threatens. The mummy's refusal or inability to retain its "original" white coloration sug-gests the artificiality of that identity. It also suggests a racial mixing or passing that the antithetical images of mammy and mummy are intended to refute. When white women refuse patriarchal definition, they can be said to "revert" to the cultural sign of female unruliness—the black woman. But this reversion underscores their common "othering" and serves to align white and black women as "all the same under the skin" and a threat to white masculine authority.

The mummy's fetishized hair, a conventional signifier of femininity, as-sociates her with the other significant white character in the novel, Lynn Rabinowitz, Truman's northern white Jewish wife who also becomes close to Meridian. Although hair is a major site for racial marking as well as an indication of spiritual status, its valuation shifts throughout the text. The Saxon College tradition of black "ladyhood" insists on long, straight-ened or marcelled hair. The "natural" or Afro that Meridian's radical friend Ann-Marion adopts is considered shocking. Both styles stand in uneasy relation to Lynn's long brown hair, hair Truman rhapsodized as "a song of lightness—untangled, glistening and free."[56] No wonder Lynn deluded herself into thinking that her long hair made her superior to black women: "As she swung it and felt it sweep the back of her waist, she imagined she possessed treasures they could never have."[57] But when the civil rights movement is replaced by Black Power, Truman stops ideal-izing Lynn, and begins obsessively painting pictures of "voluptuous black bodies, with . . . hair like a crown of thorns." Lynn mistakenly thinks she gave up Truman to Meridian, "with . . . her heroic nigger-woman hair"[58]—hair that, in the era of Black Power, is a sign of Lynn's deficiency. Sojourner Truth appears in the novel in the form of the "Sojourner Tree" that grows in the middle of the Saxon college campus Meridian attends, a symbol of black female strength and perseverance "whose heavy, flower-lit leaves hovered over it like the inverted peaks of a mother's half-straightened kinky hair."[59] This contradictory image links the motif of hair with the theme of redemptive, heroic maternity, which also applies to Meridian, whose hair has all but fallen out during her decade-long struggle to find a way to mother herself and the black community in a nonbiological, noncoercive way, and which is only at the moment of her confrontation with the mummy woman beginning to grow back.

Finally, Meridian's confrontation with de facto segregation also renders her passive, like Marilene, but only temporarily. After her "performance" in front of the tank, she falls down in a kind of paralysis, and four black men from the town pick her up, gently fold her arms and legs, carry her carefully, like a corpse, back to the bare house she occupies, and lay her in her dirty sleeping bag, her temporary resting place. A garrulous old black man, watching from the sidelines with Truman, also links the two female figures. He essentially exonerates Henry's violence when he says of Marilene, "This bitch was doing him wrong and that ain't right." Earlier, he had depersonalized and dismissed Meridian by calling her "that weird girl that strolled into town last year . . . who thinks she's God . . . or else she just ain't all there."[60] Truman agrees with the old man's affirmation of white male sexism and violent repression of women, foreshadowing Truman's perpetuation of a sexual double standard that is applied—and that he applies in the course of the novel—to all women, white and black.

Meridian's confrontation with the mummy woman occurs after she successfully "mothers" both Truman and Lynn who are separated and mourning the murder of their mixed race daughter, Camara. Her death, the text implies, is confirmation of the socially untenable nature of interracial love. Meridian escapes Marilene's fate by her refusal of marriage and through her renewed connection with southern black culture, which in the novel's final chapters is depicted as having absorbed some of the revolutionary ideals of the "movement." As opposed to Rich's idealized call for sisterhood, Meridian finally tells Lynn, "I tried very hard not to hate you. And I think I always succeeded."[61] Love and friendship, however, are another story. Lynn, who aestheticized black people and black culture and was fetishized in return by Truman, also struggles to escape the white affluence and sexual objectification that produce female mummification, but she is then bereft of home and community.

Before they go their separate ways, Walker depicts the two women to-

gether engaged in healing and nurturing activities: Meridian reads aloud
Margaret Walker's poetry while Lynn attempts to cornrow Meridian's
sparse hair. Still, "they hungered after more intricate and enduring patterns. Sometimes they talked, intimately, like sisters, and when they did
not they allowed the television to fill the silences."[62] Although these two
characters come together briefly over shared grief at the loss of innocent
life, they are stalled within fleeting and finally unsatisfying modes of relation. All that is unspeakable between them is "filled in" by the pervasive
national medium with its din of stereotypical images. It's as if black and
white women have reached some kind of limit, experiencing sisterhood
momentarily and in times of crisis, but unable to sustain the intimacy and
lapsing back into manufactured images. This impasse is still a far cry
from Rich's vision of loving identification. Yet, in *Meridian*'s final depic-
tion of interracial relations, Walker draws closer to Rich's conclusion: "If
then we begin to recognize what the separation of black and white
women means, it must become clear that it means separation from ourselves."[63]

NOTES

    1. Hortense Spillers, "Mama's Baby, Papa's Maybe: An American Grammar
Book," *Diacritics* 17, no. 2 (Summer 1987): 77.
    2. Diane Roberts, *The Myth of Aunt Jemima: Representations of Race and Religion*
(New York: Routledge, 1994), 2.
    3. Roberts, *The Myth of Aunt Jemima*, 6.
    4. Hazel Carby, *Reconstructing Womanhood: The Emergence of the Afro-American
Woman Novelist* (New York: Oxford University Press, 1987), 20–39.
    5. Peter Stallybrass and Allon White, *The Politics and Poetics of Transgression*
(London: Methuen, 1986), 5.
    6. Harriet Jacobs, *Incidents in the Life of a Slave Girl, Written by Herself*, ed. Jean
Fagan Yellin (Cambridge, Mass.: Harvard University Press, 1987).
    7. In 1832, William Lloyd Garrison adopted as the motto of the "Ladies De-
partment" of his abolitionist journal, *The Liberator*, the image of a kneeling, shack-
led and supplicating female slave with the words, "Am I Not a Woman and a
Sister?" This image was adapted by British abolitionists from a masculine version.
See Philip Laplansky, "Graphic Discord: Abolitionist and Antiabolitionist Images," in *The Abolitionist Sisterhood: Women's Political Culture in Antebellum
America*, ed. Jean Fagan Yellin and John C. Van Horne (Ithaca, N.Y.: Cornell University Press, 1994), 205–6.
    8. Karen Sánchez-Eppler, "Bodily Bonds: The Intersecting Rhetorics of Femi-
nism and Abolitionism," *Representations* 24 (1988): 31.
    9. Adrienne Rich, "Disloyal to Civilization: Feminism, Racism, Gynephobia,
1978," in *On Lies, Secrets, and Silence: Selected Prose, 1966–1978* (New York: Norton,
1979), 298.

10. Alice Walker, *Meridian* (New York: Pocket Books, 1976).

11. Adrienne Rich, *Of Woman Born: Motherhood as Experience and Institution*, 2nd ed. (New York: Norton, 1986).

12. Deborah Gray White points out, "Most of what we know about Mammy comes from memoirs written after the Civil War" that project an image that "is fully as misleading as that of Jezebel. Both images have just enough grounding in reality to lend credibility to stereotypes that would profoundly affect black women." *Ar'n't I a Woman? Female Slaves in the Plantation South* (New York: Norton, 1985), 47, 49.

13. M. M. Manring, *Slave in a Box: The Strange Career of Aunt Jemima* (Charlotteville: University of Virginia Press, 1998), 19–20.

14. W. E. B. Du Bois, *The Gift of Black Folk*, 188–89, quoted in Eugene Genovese, *Roll, Jordan, Roll: The World the Slaves Made* (New York: Random House, 1976), 356; Manring, *Slave in a Box*, 30. For an extended historical discussion of the Mammy's role and meaning, see Genovese, *Roll, Jordan, Roll*, 352–61.

15. Genovese, *Slave in a Box*, 360.

16. Elizabeth Fox-Genovese, *Within the Plantation Household: Black and White Women of the Old South* (Chapel Hill: University of North Carolina Press, 1988), 100, 292.

17. White, *Ar'n't I a Woman?* 56, 58.

18. Alice Walker, "Giving the Party: Aunt Jemima, Mammy, and the Goddess Within," *Ms.* 4, no. 6 (May/June 1994): 22.

19. Barbara Christian, *Black Feminist Criticism: Perspectives on Black Women Writers* (New York: Pergamon, 1985), 5.

20. Manring, *Slave in a Box*, 21.

21. Roberts, writing in 1994, remarks:
We in the United States have had at least three decades of powerful, passionate images of black women (and men) to complicate and challenge three hundred years of stereotypes, and yet the best-known black woman's face in the land looks out from a box of pancake mix.
(*The Myth of Aunt Jemima*, 1.) See also K. Sue Jewell, *From Mammy to Miss America and Beyond: Cultural Images and the Shaping of US Social Policy* (London: Routledge, 1993), 37–44, for an analysis of how the images of black women are used to justify discriminatory U.S. social policy.

22. Margaret Mitchell, *Gone with the Wind* (New York: Warner, 1964).

23. Mitchell, *Gone with the Wind*, 78*ff*.

24. Roberts, *The Myth of Aunt Jemima*, 1. This myth has been perpetuated through the production of household items in the shape of Mammy and her male counterpart, Uncle Mose, the eager-to-serve butler. See Kenneth Goings, *Mammy and Uncle Mose: Black Collectibles and American Stereotyping* (Bloomington: Indiana University Press, 1994).

25. This question is widely reprinted as "Ain't I a woman?" but appears as "Aren't I a woman?" in Gage's account and in the 1878 edition of Truth's autobiography. *The Narrative of Sojourner Truth, A Bondwoman of Olden Time*, compiled by Olive Gilbert (New York: Penguin, 1998), 133–34.

26. Nell Irvin Painter, *Sojourner Truth: A Life, A Symbol* (New York: Norton, 1996), 168.

27. Painter, *Sojourner Truth*, 171.

28. Sau-ling Wong, "Diverted Mothering: Representations of Caregivers of Color in the Age of 'Multiculturalism,'" in *Mothering: Ideology, Experience, and Agency*, ed. Evelyn Nakano Glenn, Grace Chang, and Linda Rennie Forcey (New York: Routledge, 1994), 69*ff*. For a history of the mammy image in film, see Donald Bogle, *Toms, Coons, Mulattoes, Mammies, & Bucks: An Interpretive History of Blacks in American Films* (New York: Continuum, 1991).

29. Rich, "Disloyal to Civilization," 298. For a discussion of the history and meaning of images of black and white women and their comparative empowerment, see Phyllis Palmer, "White Women/Black Women: The Dualism of Female Identity and Experience in the US," *Feminist Studies* 9, no. 1 (Spring 1983): 151–70. There has been an ongoing debate among feminist literary theorists about the effects of linking black women with embodiment and cultural agency; not surprisingly, many of them refer to Sojourner Truth. See, for example, Elizabeth Abel, "Black Writing, White Reading: Race and the Politics of Feminist Interpretation," *Critical Inquiry* 19 (Spring 1993): 470–98; and Deborah McDowell, "Transferences: Black Feminist Discourse: The 'Practice' of 'Theory'," in *Feminism beside Itself*, ed. Diane Elam and Robyn Wiegman (New York: Routledge, 1995), 93–118.

30. Rich, "Disloyal to Civilization."

31. Rich, "Disloyal to Civilization," 279–80.

32. Rich, "Disloyal to Civilization," 298.

33. Rich, "Disloyal to Civilization," 299.

34. Audre Lorde, "The Master's Tools Will Never Dismantle the Master's House," in *Sister Outsider: Essays and Speeches* (Freedom, Calif.: Crossing, 1984), 111. See also the long interview between Lorde and Rich, which Lorde reprints in *Sister Outsider*, 81–109. Although the interview takes place in 1979, it illuminates the thinking of both writers on the issues of racism in feminist theory and practice.

35. Rich, "Disloyal to Civilization," 307.

36. Adrienne Rich, "It Is the Lesbian in Us . . . ," (1976) in *On Lies, Secrets, and Silence: Selected Prose, 1966–1978* (New York: Norton, 1979), 199–200.

37. Rich, *Of Woman Born: Motherhood as Experience and Institution* (New York: Norton, 1986), 254.

38. Ann duCille, *Skin Trade* (Cambridge, Mass.: Harvard University Press, 1996), 108.

39. Rich, *Of Woman Born*, xxviii.

40. Rich, *Of Woman Born*, 255 note.

41. duCille, *Skin Trade*, 193, note 37.

42. Rich, "Disloyal to Civilization," 303.

43. Midge Wilson and Kathy Russell, *Divided Sisters: Bridging the Gap between Black Women and White Women* (New York: Anchor, 1996), 2.

44. Walker, *Meridian*, 91.

45. Walker, *Meridian*, 96–97.

46. Walker, *Meridian*, 19.

47. Walker, *Meridian*, 18.

48. Walker, *Meridian*, 19.

49. Deborah McDowell, "The Self in Bloom: Alice Walker's *Meridian*," in *CLA Journal* 3 (March 1981): 264.

50. Walker, *Meridian*, 26.

51. McDowell argues that in this scene Meridian, as an active social agent, "is in sharp contrastinction to the images presented of the mummy woman (which are, Walker suggests, images of all women)" and that she "can be said to triumph over tradition and authority" (265, 266). If the mummy represents "all women," then Meridian is not immune; furthermore, I argue that Walker includes details that suggest the resistant, subversive nature of the mummy in her connection with black women.

52. Walker, *Meridian*, 25.

53. Sander Gilman, "Black Bodies, White Bodies: Toward an Iconography of Female Sexuality in Later Nineteenth-Century Art, Medicine, and Literature," in *"Race," Writing, and Difference*, ed. Henry Louis Gates, *Critical Inquiry* 12, no. 1 (Autumn 1985): 213–18.

54. Gilman, "Black Bodies, White Bodies," 231.

55. Walker, *Meridian*, 20.

56. Walker, *Meridian*, 168.

57. Walker, *Meridian*, 166.

58. Walker, *Meridian*, 170.

59. Walker, *Meridian*, 48.

60. Walker, *Meridian*, 22.

61. Walker, *Meridian*, 175.

62. Walker, *Meridian*, 173.

63. Rich, "Disloyal to Civilization," 307.

Part III
Empowering Daughters

9

"I come from a long line of Uppity Irate Black Women": African-American Feminist Thought on Motherhood, the Motherline, and the Mother-Daughter Relationship

Andrea O'Reilly

"During the early stages of the contemporary women's liberation movement," bell hooks writes, "feminist analyses of motherhood reflected the race and class biases of participants."[1] "Some white middle-class, college-educated women argued," hooks continues:

> that motherhood [was] the locus of women's oppression. Had black women voiced their views on motherhood, it would not have been named a serious obstacle to our freedom as women. Racism, availability of jobs, lack of skills or education . . . would have been at the top of the list—but not motherhood.[2]

Feminist theory on motherhood, as hooks identifies, is racially codified. The aim of this chapter is to delineate the specificity of African-American feminist thought on motherhood in order to examine how maternal identification in black culture gives rise to daughters' empowerment. For the purpose of this discussion, I employ African-Canadian theorists Wanda Thomas Bernard and Candace Bernard's definition of empowerment:

> empowerment is naming, analyzing, and challenging oppression on an individual, collective, and/or structural level. Empowerment, which occurs through the development of critical consciousness, is gaining control, exercising choices, and engaging in collective social action.[3]

143

Identification with mothers and the motherline, I will argue, empowers daughters because of the particular ways motherhood in African-American culture grants mothers power and prominence. This chapter will first consider the connection-empowerment thesis in contemporary Anglo-American feminist theory; salient themes of black motherhood will then be examined to explicate how motherhood procures cultural significance and centrality. Finally, writings on the black mother-daughter relationship will be analyzed to determine whether, and in what ways, maternal identification and the motherline empower daughters. "I come from / a long line of / Uppity Irate Black Women" begins Kate Rushin's poem "Family Tree." "And [when] you ask me how come / I think I'm so cute" Rushin continues, "Nowadays / I cultivate / Being Uppity / it's something / my Gramon taught me."[4]

ANGLO-AMERICAN FEMINIST THEORY ON MOTHERS AND DAUGHTERS

Anglo-American feminist writers in the 1970s, most notably Nancy Chodorow, author of the influential *Reproduction of Mothering*, and Nancy Friday, author of the best-selling *My Mother/My Self*, argued that mother-daughter identification was ultimately determinantal to the daughter's attainment of autonomy: for Chodorow, writing from a psychoanalytical perspective, this was because mother-daughter identification resulted in daughters having "weak ego boundaries"; with Friday separation was required to enable the daughter to assume an adult sexual identity as a woman. The 1970s feminist view that problematizes, if not pathologizes, mother-daughter identification has now fallen out of favor among Anglo-American feminists. Indeed, most Anglo-American feminists, since at least the mid-1980s, regard mother-daughter connection and closeness as essential for female empowerment. Today, Anglo-American feminist writers challenge the normative view of mother-daughter attachment that scripts estrangement as both natural and inevitable. The received patriarchal view, or what Toni Morrison calls in another context the master narrative, is that this relationship, particularly in the daughter's adolescent years, is one of antagonism and animosity. The daughter must distance and differentiate herself from her mother if she is to assume an autonomous identity as an adult. The mother represents for the daughter, according to this received narrative, the epitome of patriarchal oppression that she seeks to transcend as she comes to womanhood, and yet the daughter's failings, as interpreted by herself and the culture at large, are said to be the fault of the mother. This is the patriarchal script of mother-daughter relation.

Mothers' and daughters' lives are shaped by these larger cultural narratives even as mothers and daughters live lives different from and in resistance to these assigned roles. Anglo-American feminist theory seeks to deconstruct this patriarchal narrative by first exposing this narration as precisely that: a narrative, an ideology, which by definition, is a construction, not a reflection of the actual lived reality of mothers and daughters, hence neither natural, nor inevitable. Second, feminists are concerned with how daughters and mothers may unravel the patriarchal script to write their own stories of motherhood and daughterhood. To this end, feminist theorists identify and challenge the various cultural practices and assumptions that divide mothers and daughters; they seek also to construct an alternative mother-daughter narrative scripted for empowerment as opposed to estrangement. Elsewhere, I have explored various cultural practices of estrangement—matrophobia, mother blame, cultural devaluation of motherhood, patriarchal institution of motherhood, fear of maternal power, and daughter-centricity—that disconnect daughters from their mothers and motherline.[5]

Adrienne Rich writes in *Of Woman Born: Motherhood as Experience and Institution,* "The loss of the daughter to the mother, the mother to the daughter, is the essential female tragedy."[6] For Anglo-American feminist theorists of the 1990s, this point held particular pertinence given the prominence of mother-daughter connection in their theory of empowerment. By the 1990s, girl power in adolescence became the mainstay of Anglo-American feminist literature on mothers and daughters, particularly as it crossed over into the pop-psychology market. Recent feminist research documents the loss of the female self in adolescence, investigates the various reasons for this self-effacement, and strategizes on ways that it may be resisted.[7] A strong mother-daughter connection, these writers agreed, is what makes possible a strong female self: thus, as they challenged the various patriarchal practices that undermine mother-daughter connection—mother blame, cultural devaluation, and so on—they simultaneously sought to create feminist principles and rituals that would strengthen the mother-daughter bond, the most notable of these being maternal storytelling and the motherline.

Recent feminist attention to maternal narrative may be attributed to the realization among writers on girls' empowerment that girls need to hear their mothers' stories in order of forge a strong female bond and to construct a female-defined identity.[8] The motherline, likewise, enables daughters to derive strength from their identities as women. Naomi Lowinsky explains:

When a woman today comes to understand her life story as a story from the Motherline, she gains female authority in a number of ways. First, her Moth-

erline grounds her in her feminine nature as she struggles with the many
possibilities now open to women. Second, she reclaims carnal knowledge of
her own body, its blood mysteries and their power. Third, as she makes the
journey back to her female roots, she will encounter ancestors who struggled
with similar difficulties in different historical times. This provides her with
a life-cycle perspective that softens her immediate situation. . . . Fourth, she
uncovers her connection to the archetypal mother and to the wisdom of the
ancient worldview, which holds that body and soul are one and all life is
interconnected. And finally, she reclaims her female perspective, from which
to consider how men are similar and how they are different.[9]

Writing about Lowinsky's motherline in her book *Motherless Daughters:
The Legacy of Loss,* Hope Edelman emphasizes that "motherline stories
ground a . . . daughter in a gender, a family, and a feminine history. They
transform the experience of her female ancestors into maps she can refer
to for warning or encouragement."[10] Motherline stories, made available
to daughters through the female oral tradition, reunite mothers and
daughters and reconnect them to their motherline thus making possible
the mother-daughter bond needed to effect change in the home and in
the larger patriarchal culture.

Feminist writers on daughters agree that mother-daughter connection
is vital for young women's empowerment. The perspective of this literature however is often daughter-centric: the mother's identity, particularly
as it is lived outside motherhood, is rarely, if at all, examined. Earlier,
feminist writers on the mother-daughter relationship, most notably
Judith Arcana and Adrienne Rich, recognized the importance of the
mother's empowerment for her own life and that of her daughter.
Mother-daughter connection empowers the daughters if and only if the
mothers with whom daughters identify are themselves living lives of
agency, authority, and autonomy. What daughters need, Rich argues:

[are] mothers who want their own freedom and ours. . . . The quality of the
mother's life–however embattled and unprotected–is her primary bequest to
her daughter, because a woman who can believe in herself, who is a fighter,
and who continues to struggle to create liveable space around her, is demonstrating to her daughter that these possibilities exist.[11]

This "courageous mothering" calls for the empowerment of daughters
and mothers and recognizes that the former is only possible with the
latter.

In patriarchal culture however, as noted by Anglo-American feminist
writer Paula Caplan, "women, to a disturbing degree . . . don't want to
be like our mothers. Why *should* we want to be like them, we might ask,
since so much of what they do is ignored or devalued?"[12] This marks the

theoretical impasse of Anglo-American maternal thought: as mother-daughter connection and the motherline are celebrated as sites of female power, feminist writers recognize that mothers and mothering are culturally devalued, if not demonized. The connection-empowerment trajectory thus works if and only if the mother with whom the daughter identifies is, in Rich's words, "trying to expand the limits of her life. To *refuse to be a victim:* and then to go on from there."[13] Too often, however, in the dominant patriarchal culture the mother models not agency but, again in Rich's words, "the restrictions and degradations of female existence."[14] Rejection, rather than emulation of the maternal role, is thus for these daughters the route to emancipation. Anglo-American feminist writers, since the early 1990s as they became increasingly cognizant of this disparity between theory and practice, began to link the daughter's self-esteem to that of her mother; the confidence, tenacity, self-respect, determination, and autonomy we desire in daughters now depends on mothers developing in and for themselves these very same traits. "If we want girls to grow into free women, brave and strong," as Judith Arcana concludes, "we must be those women ourselves."[15]

AFRICAN-AMERICAN MOTHERING

The Anglo-American feminist emphasis on modeling and mentoring is quite recent and emerges from the connection-empowerment thesis of the new mother and adolescent daughter literature. In contrast, African-American feminist theory on motherhood and the mother-daughter relation takes as a given the connection-empowerment trajectory and foregrounds it as central to both black and female emancipation in America. In African-American culture the daughter's empowerment derives from maternal identification because motherhood is valued in, and central to, black culture. African-American mothering is distinct from Anglo-American motherhood in theory and practice; this section will detail five points of difference and explore how the cultural specificity of black mothering effects empowerment through maternal connection.

The Afrocentric model/practice of mothering, according to Patricia Hill Collins, differs from Eurocentric ideology in three important ways:

First, the assumption that mothering occurs within the confines of private, nuclear family households where the mother has almost total responsibility for child-rearing is less applicable to Black families. While the ideal of the cult of true womanhood has been held up to Black women for emulation, racial oppression has denied Black families sufficient resources to support private, nuclear family households. Second, strict sex-role segregation, with separate male and female spheres of influences within the family, has been less commonly found in African American families than in White middle-class ones. Finally, the assumption that motherhood and economic dependency on men are linked and that to be a "good" mother one must stay at home, making motherhood a full-time "occupation" is similarly uncharacteristic of African-American families.[16]

African-American mothering, in contrast to these formulations, is defined and experienced by a different, quite distinct, cluster of expectations, assumptions, and conventions that Collins organizes under two separate themes, the first of which is "Other mothers and Woman-Centred networks." Collins writes:

> Biological mothers or blood mothers are expected to care for their children. But African and African-American communities have also recognized that investing one person with full responsibility for mothering a child may not be wise or possible. As a result, "Other mothers," women who assist blood-mothers by sharing mothering responsibilities, traditionally have been central to the institution of Black motherhood.[17]

Carol Stack's early, but important, book *All Our Kin: Strategies in a Black Community* emphasizes how crucial and central extended kin and community are for poor urban blacks. "Black families in The Flats and the non-kin they regard as kin," Stack writes in her conclusion:

> have evolved patterns of co-residence, kinship-based exchange networks linking multiple domestic units, elastic household boundaries, lifelong bonds to three-generation households, social controls against the formation of marriages that could endanger the network of kin, the domestic authority of women, and limitations on the role of the husband or male friend within a woman's kin network.[18]

"The centrality of women in African-American extended families," as Nina Jenkins concludes in "Black Women and the Meaning of Motherhood," "is well known."[19]

Black women's role of community othermothers redefines motherhood as social activism. Collins explains:

> Black women's experiences as othermothers have provided a foundation for Black women's social activism. Black women's feelings of responsibility for nurturing the children in their extended family networks have stimulated a more generalized ethic of care where Black women feel accountable to all the Black community's children.[20]

In *Black Feminist Thought* Collins develops this idea further:

Such power is transformative in that Black women's relationships with children and other vulnerable community members is not intended to dominate or control. Rather, its purpose is to bring people along, to—in the words of late-nineteenth-century Black feminists—"uplift the race" so that vulnerable members of the community will be able to attain the self-reliance and independence essential for resistance.[21]

Collins argues that this construction of mothering as social activism empowers black women because motherhood operates, in her words, as "a symbol of power." "A substantial portion of Black women's status in African American communities," she writes, "stems not only from their role as mothers in their own families but from their contributions as community Other mothers to Black community development as well."[22] "More than a personal act," write Bernard and Bernard:

> black motherhood is very political. Black mothers and grandmothers are considered the "guardians of the generations." Black mothers have historically been charged with the responsibility of providing education, social, and political awareness, in addition to unconditional love, nurturance, socialization, and values to their children, and the children in their communities.[23]

Black motherhood, as Jenkins observes, "is a site where [black women] can develop a belief in their own empowerment. Black women can see motherhood as providing a base for self actualization, for acquiring status in the Black community and as a catalyst for social activism."[24] Othermothering and social activism accord black women community and authority and make the role of motherhood a prestigious and powerful one.

Anglo-American feminist theorist Miriam Johnson in *Strong Mothers, Weak Wives* argues that the wife's role and not the mother's role occasions women's secondary status in a patriarchal culture. In contrast, matrifocal cultures, such as African-American culture, according to Johnson, emphasize women's mothering and are characterized by greater gender equality. "In matrifocal societies," Johnson writes, "women play roles of cultural and social significance and define themselves less as wives than as mothers."[25] Matrifocality, Johnson continues, however, does not refer to domestic maternal dominance so much as it does to the relative cultural prestige of the image of mother, a role that is culturally elaborated and valued. Mothers are also structurally central in that mother as a status "has some degree of control over the kin's unit economic resources and is critically involved in kin-related decision making processes." It is not the absence of males (males may be quite present) but the centrality of women as mothers and sisters that makes a society matrifocal, and this matrifocal emphasis is accompanied by a minimum of differentiation between women and men.[26]

The wife identity, according to Collins, is less prevalent in African-American culture because women assume an economic role and experience gender equality in the family unit. She writes:

> African-American women have long integrated their activities as economic providers into their mothering relationships. In contrast to the cult of true womanhood, in which work is defined as being in opposition to and incompatible with motherhood, work for Black women has been an important and valued dimensions of Afrocentric definitions of Black motherhood.[27]

"Whether they wanted to or not," Collins continues, "the majority of African-American women had to work and could not afford the luxury of motherhood as a non economically productive, female 'occupation.'"[28] Thus, black women, at least among the urban poor, do not assume the wife role, which Johnson identified as that which structures women's oppression. Moreover, in African-American culture motherhood, not marriage, emerges as the rite of passage into womanhood. As Joyce Ladner emphasizes in *Tomorrow's Tomorrow:*

> If there was one common standard for becoming a woman that was accepted by the majority of the people in the community, it was the time when girls gave birth to their first child. This line of demarcation was extremely clear and separated the girls from the women.[29]

In African-American culture, motherhood is the pinnacle of womanhood. The emphasis on motherhood over wifedom and black women's role as economic provider means that the wife role, as described by Johnson, is less operative in the African-American community.

The fourth way that African-American mothering differs from the dominant model is the way in which nurturance of family is defined and experienced as a political enterprise. In African-American culture, as theorist bell hooks has observed, the black family, or what she terms "homeplace," operates as a site of resistance. She explains:

> Historically, African-American people believed that the construction of a homeplace, however fragile and tenuous (the slave hut, the wooden shack), had a radical political dimension. Despite the brutal reality of racial apartheid, of domination, one's homeplace was one site where one could freely confront the issue of humanization, where one could resist. Black women resisted by making homes where all black people could strive to be subjects, not objects, where one could be affirmed in our minds and hearts despite poverty, hardship, and deprivation, where we could restore to ourselves the dignity denied to us on the outside in the public world.[30]

hooks emphasizes that when she talks about homeplace she is not speaking merely of black women providing services for their families; rather, she refers to the creation of a safe place where, in her words, "black people could affirm one another and by so doing heal many of the wounds inflicted by racist domination . . . [a place where they] had the opportunity to grow and develop, to nurture [their] spirits."[31] In a racist culture that deems black children inferior, unworthy, and unlovable, maternal love of black children is an act of resistance; in loving her children the mother instills in them a loved sense of self and high self-esteem, enabling them to defy and subvert racist discourses that naturalize racial inferiority and commodify blacks as other and object. African-Americans, hooks emphasizes, "have long recognized the subversive value of homeplace and homeplace has always been central to the liberation struggle."[32] This view of mothering differs radically from the dominant discourse of motherhood that configures home as politically neutral space and views nurturance as no more than the natural calling of mothers.

Mother love is thus at the heart of black resistance and emancipation. The self-love made possible through mother love is sustained through ancestral memory. Various African-American writers, most notably Toni Morrison, argue that the very survival of African-American culture depends on the preservation of black culture and history. Morrison writes, "When you kill the ancestor you kill yourself. I want to point out the dangers, to show that nice things don't always happen to the totally self reliant if there is not historical connection."[33] If black children are to survive, Morrison argues, they must know the stories, legends, and myths of their ancestors. In African-American culture women are, in Trudier Harris's words, "the keepers of the tradition, the culture bearers."[34] Black women, Karla Holloway continues, "carry the voice of the mother—they are the progenitors, the assurance of the line. . . . As carriers of the voice [black women] carry wisdom—mother wit. They teach the children to survive and remember."[35] In African-American culture mothers embody and carry ancestral memory; the motherline is the way by which the ancient path is followed and passed on generationally.

Anglo-American writer Naomi Lowinsky argued, as we saw earlier, that women today are disconnected from their motherline and have lost, as a consequence, the authenticity and authority of their womanhood. For Lowinsky, female empowerment becomes possible only in and through reconnection to the motherline. In contrast, the motherline in African-American society remains integral both to women's self-definition and to the community as a whole because of the cultural significance of ancestral memory and women's role as "tradition keepers." The maternal function of culture bearer coalesces with the mother-love-as-resistance theme discussed earlier; with both, mothering is experienced and viewed as a deeply political and cultural enterprise on which the resistance and emancipation of black Americans depends. These two maternal functions, alongside black women's work as othermothers, economic providers, and social activists, accord mothers and their mothering cultural prominence and veneration. It would seem therefore that the empowerment-through-connection thesis of Anglo-American theory holds true in practice in the instance of African-American culture: daughters obtain power in and through maternal identification because mothers and mothering are esteemed and regarded as fundamental to black culture. Recent African-American women's writings on the mother-daughter relation confirm this contention.

AFRICAN-AMERICAN MOTHERS AND DAUGHTERS

Gloria Joseph and Jill Lewis in their early but important work *Common Differences: Conflicts in Black and White Feminist Perspectives* contrast Anglo-American and African-American women's experiences of motherhood and daughterhood. Joseph argues that respect for the mother was a central and organizing theme of the mother-daughter relationships examined.[36] She also found that female socialization centered on the teaching of survival skills and an insistence on independence:

> What was startlingly evident, as revealed in the mother/daughter questionnaire, was the teaching of survival skills to females for their survival in and for the survival of the Black community. Intra-group survival skills were given more importance and credence than survival skills for dealing with White society at large. There is a tremendous amount of teaching transmitted by Black mothers to their daughters that enables them to survive, exist, succeed, and be important to and for the Black communities. . . . Black daughters are actually "taught" to hold the Black community together.[37]

The independence that mothers insist upon for their daughters is to be achieved through education and effort.[38] This may be contrasted to the dominant narrative of Anglo-American feminine achievement that scripts marriage as the avenue through which women will "get ahead." The African-American mothers' insistence on independence for their daughters includes a critique of marriage, particularly the dependency inherent in the wife role. These mothers recognize with Miriam Johnson that it is the wife role and not the mother role that organizes women's secondary status. Candace Bernard comments in "Passing the Torch":

> Through Mom's guidance and direction , I learned the value of hard work, self determination, goal setting, and shared responsibility. . . . I experienced

empowerment through Mom's ability to survive in a climate that was not conducive to survival.[39]

The daughter adds, "It is indeed empowering to know that I have come from such a long line of strong Black women. . . . I feel honored that . . . I am able to carry on the struggle you began a generation ago."[40]

Contemporary African-American women's writing also celebrates mothers as mentors and role models. Readers of black women's literature have long observed a deeply rooted matrilineal tradition in which daughters think back through their mothers. In Marianne Hirsch's words, "[there is], in much of contemporary black women's writing, a public celebration of maternal presence."[41] In a 1980 article, appropriately entitled "I Sign My Mother's Name," Mary Helen Washington speaks of a "generational continuity" among African-American women in which "a mother serves as the female precursor who passes on the authority of authorship to her daughter and provides a model for the black woman's literary presence in this society."[42] "For black women writers," as Dolana Mogadime observes in "A Daughter's Praise Poem for Her Mother," "the idea of thinking back through our mothers is rooted in the notion of revisiting and learning about maternal knowledge and female-centered networks as expressions of African continuities in contemporary society."[43] Respect and gratitude for "women who made a way out of no way" is repeated time and time again in the recent collection of writings on black mothers and daughters, appropriately entitled *Double Stitch: Black Women Write about Mothers and Daughters*.[44]

In an introductory section to this collection, Beverly Guy-Sheftall writes:

> In section after section, daughters acknowledge how their mothers provided road maps and patterns, a template which enables them to create and define themselves. . . . Though daughters must forge an identity which is separate from the mothers, they frequently acknowledge that a part of themselves is truly their mother's child.[45]

Margaret Walker in her poem "Lineage" pays tribute to her grandmothers who "were strong . . . full of sturdiness and singing."[46]

Judy Scales-Trent writes, "My mother opened the door for me . . . and set me free."[47] The first stanza of Irma McClaurin's poem "The Power of Names" reads:

> I slip my mother's name like a glove and wonder if I will become like her absolutely. Years number the times I have worn her pain as a child, as a teenager, as a woman—my second skin—as she sat, silver head bowed silent hedging the storm.[48]

In her moving autobiographical narrative, *Pushed Back to Strength: A Black Woman's Journey,* some of which is excerpted in *Double Stitch,* Gloria Wade-Gayles argues that in the segregated South of the forties "surviving meant being black, and being black meant believing in our humanity, and retaining it, in a world that denied we had it in the first place."[49] The survival of black culture and black selfhood was sustained by the motherline. "The men in my family were buttresses and protectors," writes Wade-Gayles, "but it was the women who gave meaning to the expression 'pushed back to strength.'"[50] Whether named mentor, role model, guide, adviser, wise woman or advocate, the mother represents for the daughter a sturdy bridge on which to cross over on. Even the author Renita Weems, who was abandoned by her alcoholic mother, writes, "Though not sturdy as others, she is my bridge. When I needed to get across she steadied herself long enough for me to run across safely."[51]

Alice Walker's classic essay "In Search of Our Mothers' Gardens" is a moving tribute to her African-American foremothers in which Walker delineates a theory of creative identity that juxtaposes the male paradigm of literary achievement that demands separation and individuation.[52] As Dannabang Kuwabong observes about Afro-Caribbean women's writing, but applicable, I would argue, to all black female diaspora literature, "the mother-daughter relationship is central to the development of identity and voice."[53] Black female subjectivity generally, and creativity specifically, are formed, nurtured, and sustained through women's identification with, and connection to, their motherline. As Sylvia Hamilton, noted documentary writer and director, commented in *Black Mother, Black Daughter,* "[Our foremothers] created a path for us . . . we are bound to something larger than ourselves. . . . I am moved by the example of their lives."[54]

CONCLUSION

African-American daughters seek and hold connection with mothers and the motherline; they achieve empowerment through this identification because motherhood is valued by and central to African-American culture. In her recent book *Not Our Kind of Girl: Unraveling the Myths of Black Teenage Motherhood,* Elaine Bell Kaplan proposes a "poverty of relationship" thesis to account for the high incidence of black unwed teenage pregnancy. "[T]eenage mothers," she writes, "describe being disconnected from primary family relations, abandoned by their school and by the men in their lives . . . at the time of adolescence, when it is most important that they experience positive relationships."[55] The absence of relationships in the adolescent girl's life, Kaplan argues, results from the loss of black neighborhood and community occasioned by the economic restructuring of the 1970s. In the 1950s and 1960s a strong sense of family and community prevailed in black neighborhoods; there was also a low incidence of unwed teenage pregnancy. Whether the two are causally related, as Kaplan maintains, her argument explicates, albeit inadvertently, the connection-empowerment thesis advanced in this chapter. Disconnection, a word Kaplan herself uses, is at the core of the adolescent girl's aloneness and at the center of the community's despair. As African-American women celebrate the power acquired through connection to a strong mother and a strong motherline, Kaplan's words remind us that the very survival of African-American culture may depend on them.

NOTES

This research was funded in part by a Social Science and Humanities Research Council of Canada (SSHRC) grant.

1. bell hooks, "Revolutionary Parenting," in *Feminist Theory: From Margin to Center* (Boston: South End Press, 1984), 133. For an excellent discussion of second-wave feminism and motherhood, see Laura Unmansky, *Motherhood Reconceived: Feminism and the Legacies of the Sixties* (New York: New York University Press, 1996).

2. hooks, "Revolutionary Parenting," 133.

3. Wanda Thomas Bernard and Candace Bernard. "Passing the Torch: A Mother and Daughter Reflect on Their Experiences Across Generations," *Canadian Woman Studies* 18, nos. 2 & 3 (Summer/Fall 1998): 46.

4. "Family Tree," in *Double Stitch: Black Women Write about Mothers and Daughters,* ed. Patricia Bell-Scott et al. (New York: Harper Perennial, 1993), 176, 177. Reprinted with permission.

5. Adrienne Rich, in *Of Woman Born: Motherhood as Experience and Institution* (New York: Norton, 1986), defines matrophobia as "the fear not of one's mother or of motherhood but of becoming one's mother" (235, emphasis in original). *Daughter-centricity* is a term used by Maureen Reddy and Brenda Daly to describe "a daughter's perspective [that] pays attention mostly to the effects of current conditions of mothering on children's progression into adulthood"(2). Introduction to *Narrating Mothers: Theorizing Maternal Subjectivities,* ed. Brenda Daly and Maureen Reddy (Knoxville: The University of Tennessee Press, 1991), 1–18. For a examination of how these cultural practices, among others, disconnect and devalue daughters and mothers, see my article " 'Across the Divide': Contemporary Anglo-American Feminist Theory on the Mother-Daughter Relationship," in *Redefining Motherhood: Changing Identities and Patterns,* ed. Sharon Abbey and Andrea O'Reilly (Toronto: Second Story Press, 1998), 69–91.

6. Rich, *Of Woman Born,* 237.

7. See, for example, Lyn Mikel Brown and Carol Gilligan, *Meeting at the Crossroads: Women's Psychology and Girls' Development* (Cambridge, Mass.: Harvard,

1992); Carol Gilligan, *In a Different Voice: Psychological Theory and Women's Develop-ment* (Cambridge, Mass.: Harvard University Press, 1982); Mary Pipher, *Reviving Ophelia: Saving the Selves of Adolescent Girls* (New York: Grosset/Putnam, 1994); Virginia Beane Rutter, *Celebrating Girls: Nurturing and Empowering Our Daughters* (Berkeley, Calif.: Conari, 1996).

8. Elizabeth deBold, Marie Wilson, and Idelisse Malave in *Mother-Daughter Revolution: From Good Girls to Great Women* (New York: Bantam, 1994) argue that the compromise of female selfhood in adolescence may be resisted or, at the very least negotiated, when the mother connects with her daughter through story. The mother, in recalling and sharing with her daughter her own narrative of adoles-cence, gives her daughter strategies of resistance and hence constructs an alterna-tive script of coming into womanhood.

9. Naomi Lowinsky, *Stories from the Motherline: Reclaiming the Mother-Daughter Bond, Finding Our Female Souls* (Los Angeles: Tarcher, 1992), 13.

10. Hope Edelman, *Motherless Daughters: The Legacy of Loss* (New York: Delta, 1994), 201.

11. Rich, *Of Woman Born,* 247.

12. Paula Caplan, *Don't Blame Mother: Mending the Mother-Daughter Relationship* (New York: Harper & Row, 1989), 31.

13. Rich, *Of Woman Born,* 246.

14. Rich, *Of Woman Born,* 235.

15. Judith Pilders Arcana, *Our Mothers' Daughters* (Berkeley, Calif.: Shameless Hussy Press, 1979), 33.

16. Patricia Hill Collins, "The Meaning of Motherhood in Black Culture and Black Mother-Daughter Relationships," in *Double Stitch,* 43–44.

17. Collins, "The Meaning of Motherhood," 47.

18. Carol Stack, *All Our Kin* (New York: Basic Books, 1974), 124. Childbearing and children are valued by members of this community, and black women in The Flats, Stack continues, "unlike many other societies, . . . feel few if any restrictions about childbearing. Unmarried black women, young and old, are eligible to bear children, and frequently women bear their first children when they are quite young" (47). Many of these teenage mothers, however, do not raise their first born; this responsibility is left to the mother, aunt, or elder sister with whom the biological mother resides. The child thus may have both a "mama," the woman "who raised him up," and the biological mother who birthed him. The mama, in Stack's terminology, is the "sponsor" of the child's personal kinship network; the network is thus matrilineal and matrifocal.

19. Nina Jenkins, "Black Women and the Meaning of Motherhood," 206.

20. Collins, "The Meaning of Motherhood," 49.

21. Patricia Hill Collins, *Black Feminist Thought: Knowledge, Consciousness, and the Politics of Empowerment* (Boston: Unwin Hyman, 1990), 132.

22. Collins, "The Meaning of Motherhood," 51.

23. Bernard and Bernard, "Passing the Torch," 47.

24. Jenkins, "Black Women and the Meaning of Motherhood," 206.

25. Miriam Johnson, *Strong Mothers, Weak Wives* (Los Angeles: University of California Press, 1988), 226.

26. Johnson, *Strong Mothers, Weak Wives*, 226.

27. Collins, "The Meaning of Motherhood," 48.

28. Collins, "The Meaning of Motherhood," 49.

29. Joyce Ladner, *Tomorrow's Tomorrow: The Black Woman* (New York: Doubleday, 1971), 216. Ladner goes on to argue:

> This sharp change in status occurs for a variety of reasons. [It] demonstrat[es] the procreative powers that the girls possess. Children are highly valued and a strong emphasis is placed on one's being able to give birth. The ultimate test of womanhood, then, is one's ability to bring forth life. This value underlying childbearing is much akin to the traditional way in which the same behavior has been perceived in African culture. So strong is the tradition that women must bear children in West African societies and barren females are often pitied and in some cases their husbands are free to have children by other women. The ability to have children also symbolizes (for these girls) maturity that they feel cannot be gained in any other way. (216)

In the dominant culture, marriage, not motherhood, is what ushers girls into womanhood. The elaborate, ritualized (and I may add costly) traditions of matrimony—engagement parties, bridal showers, wedding ceremonies, receptions, honeymoons, and so forth—bear testimony to the emphasis on marriage in Anglo-American culture.

30. bell hooks, "Homeplace," in *Yearning: Race, Gender, and Cultural Politics* (Boston: South End Press, 1990), 42.

31. hooks, "Homeplace," 42.

32. hooks, "Homeplace," 42. She goes on to argue:

> [The] liberatory struggle has been seriously undermined by contemporary efforts to change the subversive homeplace into a site of patriarchal domination of black women by black men, where we abuse one another for not conforming to sexist norms. This shift in perspective, where homeplace is not viewed as a political site, has had a negative impact on the construction of black female identity and political consciousness. Masses of black women, many of whom were not formally educated, had in the past been able to play a vital role in black liberation struggle. In the contemporary situation, as the paradigm for domesticity in black life mirrored white bourgeois norms (where home is conceptualized as politically neutral space), black people began to overlook and devalue the importance of black female labor in teaching critical consciousness in domestic space. Many black women, irrespective of class status, have responded to this crisis in meaning by imitating leisure-class sexist notions of women's roles, focusing their lives on meaningless compulsive consumerism. (47)

33. Toni Morrison, "Rootedness: The Ancestor as Foundation," in *Black Women Writers (1950–1980)*, ed. Mari Evans (New York: Doubleday, 1984), 344.

34. Trudier Harris, *Fiction and Folklore: The Novels of Toni Morrison* (Knoxville: University of Tennessee Press, 1991), 41.

35. Karla Holloway and Stephanie Demetrakopoulos, *New Dimensions in Spiri-*

tuality: A Biracial and Bicultural Reading of the Novels of Toni Morrison (New York: Greenwood, 1987), 123.

36. Gloria Joseph and Jill Lewis, *Common Differences: Conflicts in Black and White Feminist Perspectives* (Boston: South End Press, 1981). Joseph's research—a 1979–1980 American survey—revealed that the majority of black daughters (94.5 percent) said that they respected their mothers. Joseph's research identified different issues and trends in the Anglo-American mother-daughter relationship. Joseph found a greater belief in romance among Anglo-American mothers, as expressed in the commonly offered advice "marry for love." Joseph discovered further that "the ways in which the White daughters said they feared their mothers disclosed an area that was rarely, if ever, mentioned by the Black daughters. The response was, 'I fear I might be like her. I want to be independent of her'" (125). Here, the Anglo-American daughters bespeak matrophopia, first defined by Adrienne Rich in *Of Woman Born*. White women were included in the survey, but because of the small number of respondents, Joseph writes, "it was not possible to conduct a comparative study between the White subjects and the Black ones" (125). Joseph discovered in her analysis that class was an important variable to the degree that working-class white mothers gave responses more similar to the black mothers' responses (125).

37. Joseph and Lewis, *Common Differences*, 106.

38. "87.5% of the black daughters felt that the best way to get ahead was through their own effort, or through education, or using both in combination" (Joseph and Lewis, 107).

39. Bernard and Bernard, "Passing the Torch," 48.

40. Bernard and Bernard, "Passing the Torch," 48, 49.

41. Marianne Hirsch, *The Mother/Daughter Plot: Narrative, Psychoanalysis, Feminism* (Bloomington: Indiana University Press, 1989), 177.

42. Mary Helen Washington, "I Sign My Mother's Name: Alice Walker, Dorothy West, Paule Marshall," in *Mothering the Mind: Twelve Studies of Writers and Their Silent Partners*, ed. Ruth Perry and Martine Watson Brownley (New York: Holmes & Meier, 1984), 147.

43. Mogadime, Dolana. "A Daughter's Praise Poem for Her Mother: Historicizing Community Activism and Racial Uplift among South Africa Women," *Canadian Woman Studies* 18, nos. 2 & 3 (Summer/Fall 1998): 87.

44. Bell-Scott et al., eds., *Double Stitch*.

45. Bell-Scott et al., eds., *Double Stitch*, 61.

46. Margaret Walker, "Lineage," in *Double Stitch*, ed. Bell-Scott et al., 175. Reprinted with permission.

47. Judy Scales-Trent, "On That Dark and Moon-Less Night," in *Double Stitch*, ed. Bell-Scott et al., 213. Reprinted with permission.

48. Irma McClaurin, "The Power of Names," in *Double Stitch*, ed. Bell-Scott et al., 63. Reprinted with permission.

49. Gloria Wade-Gayles, *Pushed Back to Strength: A Black Woman's Journey Home* (Boston: Beacon, 1993), 6. Reprinted with permission.

50. Wade-Gayles, *Pushed Back to Strength*, 13. Reprinted with permission.

51. Renita Weems, "Hush. Mama's Gotta Go Bye-Bye," in *Double Stitch*, ed. Bell-Scott et al., 129.

52. Alice Walker, "In Search of Our Mothers' Gardens," in *Double Stitch*, ed. Bell-Scott et al. For example, Harold Bloom's theory of the anxiety of influence modeled on the Oedipal narrative posits that the young male writer (son) must kill his literary predecessor (the Father) to cultivate his own unique individual voice (avoid castration). See Harold Bloom, *The Anxiety of Influence: A Theory of Poetry* (New York: Oxford University Press, 1973). Walker's essay advances a specific feminine mode of creativity, what may be termed the security of influence model. This paradigm of "security of influence" may also be observed in Anglo-American women's writing. Anglo-American women writers often attribute their ability to write to a female tradition of writing; this tradition gave them authority to voice their artistic talents and shaped the development of this voice. I would suggest, however, that the motherline figures far more prominently in African-American women's writing. In her essay "Speaking in Tongues: Diologics, Dialectics, and Black Women's Literary Tradition," in *Reading Black, Reading Feminist*, ed. Henry Louis Gates (Toronto: Meridian, 1990), Mae Gwendolyn Henderson argues that the literary traditions of white and black women differ significantly. Unlike Gilbert and Gubar's "anxiety of authorship" model informed by the white woman writer's sense of "dis-ease" within a "white patriarchal tradition," writes Henderson, "black women's [tradition of writing] is generated less by neurotic anxiety of dis-ease than by an emancipatory impulse" (138). The model of "anxiety of authorship" among white women identified by Henderson and studied by Gilbert and Gubar may be alleviated when white women identify with literary sisters and/or foremothers. In this identification with literary foremothers the tradition of white women writers is similar to that of black women. See Sandra Gilbert and Susan Gubar, *The Madwoman in the Attic: The Woman Writer and the Nineteenth-Century Literary Imagination* (New Haven, Conn.: Yale University Press, 1979).

53. Dannabang Kuwabong, "Reading the Gospel of Bakes' Daughters' Representation of Mothers in the Poetry of Claire Harris and Lorna Goodson," *Canadian Woman Studies* 18, nos. 2 & 3 (Summer/Fall 1998): 132.

54. From the NFB film *Black Mother, Black Daughter*, dir. Sylvia Hamilton and Claire Prieta (NFB Film Atlantic Studio, 1990).

55. Elaine Bell Kaplan, *Not Our Kind of Girl: Unraveling the Myths of Black Teenage Motherhood* (Berkeley: University of California Press, 1997), 11.

10

Mothers as Moral Educators: Teaching Language and Nurturing Souls

Deborah Orr

Mothers in the patriarchal nuclear family are powerful educators of their children although their work is almost entirely erased by theorists in all areas, certainly in moral theory. The effect of this erasure has been especially pernicious in the construction of moral theory, on the one hand, and in the individual's self-understanding as a moral being, on the other. Thus, I argue that the theoretical restoration of the maternal presence will create the condition for a more adequate moral theory, enrich maternal practice and the moral lives of girls and women by helping create a more adequate self-understanding, and open a space for the growth of an ethos developed out of spiritual eroticism. In this chapter I argue further that the work of Carol Gilligan in moral psychology and Ludwig Wittgenstein in the philosophy of language help move us theoretically toward a restoration of the mother to her rightful place as moral educator, as well as toward a reconceptualization of morality as style of life, a holistic ethos, rather than as a matter of simple problem solving as the dominant patriarchal tradition in ethics would have it. The work of Audre Lorde and her philosophical predecessor, Diotima of Mantinea, are used to help flesh out the notion of a spiritual erotics that guides the practice of the morally mature woman by forming her vision of the good as loving and generative activity, a vision that she seeks to instantiate on all levels of her life, from the most intimately personal to the broadly social and political.

In what follows, I speak in very general terms about the role of mothers in developing their daughters' most basic language games and consequently their beliefs and behaviors. I do not wish, in doing so, to imply either a romanticized or an essentialized view of mothers. A mother's work is, of course, mediated by her culture and society and influenced by those with whom both she and her daughter come into contact. Space permits my doing little more than acknowledging these factors here, but it seems to me that the risks attendant upon this approach are justified by our need, on both the personal and cultural levels, to develop a fuller appreciation of a mother's role in her daughter's moral development. This chapter is a gesture in that direction.

TEACHING AND LEARNING MORAL LANGUAGE-GAMES

Carol Gilligan's *In a Different Voice* has been a major influence in shaping the form of contemporary feminist moral theory. At the same time it has been widely criticized for its essentialism; its white, heterosexual, and middle-class North American bias; and for its potential to keep women locked into an idealized and sentimentalized morality of self-sacrifice. These criticisms, and others, are to the point and must be addressed by Gilligan and her supporters. In spite of this, Gilligan's work, I believe, points to a new and rich understanding of the importance of mothering for moral life as well as an expanded understanding of the form that moral life takes in contemporary North America.

In pointing out the empirical existence of an ethic of care alongside of the dominant patriarchal traditions' ethic of rights, Gilligan's work provides us with an impetus to conceptualize morality as a family of gendered language-games. In making this claim I am drawing on the work of Wittgenstein, who argued that language can profitably be understood as "language-games"—that is, speech woven into lived experience. This culture-lived experience is socially constructed not only along the axes of gender, race, and class but also along those of sexual orientation, ability, ethnicity, age, and others, and thus there exists a large family of moral language-games inflected by these variables. My focus in this chapter is narrow, the axis of gender, although the philosophical considerations I bring to bear can usefully be extended to explore the other dimensions that I must ignore here. I draw on both empirical research and theory to make the fairly uncontroversial point that in contemporary North America, girls are socialized to some form or other of femininity and a feminine ego style, which puts a premium on such qualities as empathy, caring for others, and the maintenance of relationships. As Gilligan's work theorized, the connection between biological sex and moral voice—or language-game, to use Wittgenstein's term—is constructed through the intermediate variable of socially constructed gender. Thus, as primary teachers of gender identity, mothers are also teaching their daughters an ethical style. Furthermore, I argue that these considerations encourage the reconceptualization of moral life and the moral domain, an extension of its boundaries beyond the range of choices and actions in the public sphere that is the terrain of the dominant moral discourse. In the conception developed in this chapter, the range of the moral is isomorphic with one's life in all of its aspects. It is what Wittgenstein calls a "form-of-life"—that is, a way of life—which involves and to some degree is shaped by the use of language, rather than being simply a matter of engaging in solving moral problems, on the model of math problems, as the dominant patriarchal tradition in ethics would have it. In this connection it is important to notice, as I have argued elsewhere,[1] that the logic of the feminine ethical style, which Gilligan[2] has called an ethic of care and responsibility and which I am calling "feminine" here because she has found that it is contingently connected with girls and women, is characterized by a narrative structure, and that moral thinking frequently takes place in the context of "moral talk" with others. With the notion of moral talk I mean to stress the importance of both talking to and listening to others in an attempt to understand a moral situation in all of its complexity and creatively respond to it. This contrasts radically with the solipsistic nature and more formalized argumentative structure of what is, at least in theory, the dominant style, designated the ethic of rights and justice by Gilligan.

Philosophically, however, the importance of mothers and mothering goes well beyond these considerations. Annette Baier[3] has argued that even the best modern liberal theorists, among whom she counts John Rawls, take for granted parenting (read "mothering") and its effects in producing moral agents. Here again Wittgenstein's work throws philosophical light. In his study of language-games Wittgenstein showed that the acquisition of primary language-games grows out of primitive, pre-, and nonlinguistic behaviors, especially our interactions with others. It is mothers who are largely the ones charged with the teaching of these primitive language-games to children through their interactions with their children in daily life. I argue that these considerations show that mothers are largely responsible for the teaching that shapes morality on a primitive level, in part by shaping concepts of self and others—that is, the concept of the human soul, and modes of interaction between them. They also show the degree to which human life and language are an irreducibly social affair, for language is not learned in solipsistic solitude but in the course of the lives a mother and her children share. That being the case, the concept of the moral self and the moral other which emerges from Wittgenstein's work is what Seyla Benhabib has called "concrete"—embodied, socially and historically embedded.[4] It is not the disembodied and abstracted "generalized" ego of modern liberal theory, from Descartes to Rawls.

Speaking of the "ritual of rebirth" in Descartes' *Meditations*, Naomi
Scheman holds that its "central achievement" is "the denial of the
mother."[5] It is only through this denial that the illusion of the autonomous and isolated willing and choosing ego of liberal ethics can be maintained, for the acknowledgment of the role of the mother necessarily
brings with it an acknowledgment of how deeply and unavoidably social
and connected human life is in all of its aspects—material, emotional,
mental, and spiritual. Restoring the role of the mother bursts the bubble
that is this ego and so makes room for flesh-and-blood moral beings who
have attained a degree of moral maturity through the efforts of mothers.
I want to turn now to Wittgenstein's *Philosophical Investigations*[6] to highlight six important points that emerge from that work relevant to our understanding of the moral life and the role of the mother in the nurturance
of the moral person.

First, for Wittgenstein, language, including moral uses of language, is
acquired and used by a human being in the course of living her life and
developing into the person she becomes. Its acquisition and use are intimately tied up with her growth and development and her interactions
with others, most especially at an early age with her mother or mother
surrogate. The process of maturation is crucial to the acquisition and use
of language-games. For instance, an infant could not sensibly use the
word *commitment* as she would not have the level of personal development necessary for her to employ that concept; thus, she could not play
the language-games of commitment. Similarly, the word *love* used by a
child would have a quite different sense than the same word used by an
adult: the contexts of lived experience in which it is used, the experiences
of the child's and the adult's lives, are qualitatively different. Here we can
distinguish two distinct language-games of love with family resemblances that tie them together.

In this connection we must stress that, for Wittgenstein, language is acquired and used by a "person," an embodied and socially embedded
soul, and not by a "subject" or an "ego" in the technical theoretical senses
of modern and postmodern philosophy or of psychoanalytic theory in
any of its various manifestations, such as the Chodorowdian or Lacanian
forms that are currently so important in theorizing both femininity and
masculinity and their associated moralities. While these latter theoretical
approaches foreground gender, Wittgenstein in his work was oblivious
to gender and this has proved to be a drawback in that he did not explore
language-games as gendered entities. But his approach also has its
strengths; his work on the language-games of childhood and adulthood
is not contaminated by the founding assumptions of essential female dif

ference and inferiority that ground modernist and postmodernist theories of language and of the subject.

Second, Wittgenstein's work critiques and rejects the imposition of binary categories on the person, such as inner/outer, mind/body, reason/emotion, which produce metaphysical dualisms, and it rejects the essentialism so often tied up with the deployment of those categories. This is important in that these binarisms have been widely employed to metaphysically ground femininity and women's purported moral and intellectual inferiority, and in the dismissal of women's moral endeavors as mere "good life" concerns appropriately confined to the domestic sphere. What emerges from Wittgenstein's work in place of dualistic and essentialized conceptions is a nonmetaphysical and holistic picture of the human soul that is sourced in day-to-day lived experience and relationships with others. This logically primitive concept of the soul is the host on which the binarisms that structure philosophical and psychoanalytic theories are parasitic and without which they could not emerge.

These binarisms also ground and enable the "linguistic alienation" that is the medium for patriarchal morality. This paradigm of morality, theorized rationalistically in the modern period primarily in a range of consequentalist and deontological forms, is what is held to be true moral activity, undertaken by men in the cultural domain of social, political, and economic life. I will return to the notion of linguistic alienation in points five and six later to argue that the notion of the linguistically alienated self that this paradigm of morality involves, what Benhabib calls "the abstract self" and which is both the moral agent and the moral object of masculinist ethics, is an incoherent notion.

Third, Wittgenstein's work on the language of everyday activities challenges and destroys the credibility of the privatized, autonomous, and self-contained Cartesian ego that is the holder of rights as well as the container for individual thought, desire, and emotion. It is this conception of the human being as Cartesian ego that functions both in much modernist ethical theory as well as in this culture's endemic concept of romantic love. In its place a picture emerges from Wittgenstein's work of the person who is radically open to others and their experiences and who is fluid, changing, and growing as new language-games are developed and incorporated into one's life.

Fourth, Wittgenstein notes that the concept of the soul is used as a linguistic marker of the human. Here, the conception of the human person, or human soul, is holistic. It is an embodied person who thinks, feels, plans, desires, loves, and hates. It is also a person embedded in her particular cultural and historical matrix, and this most especially through her participation in the language-games available to her. This is closely akin to Benhabib's delineation of the "concrete" self. About this self Wittgenstein says, "My attitude toward him [sic] is an attitude towards a soul. I am not of the opinion that he has a soul."[7] In this he captures the point that this is a natural although socially shaped attitude toward another and is not the product of ratiocination.

My fifth Wittgensteinian point is that the abstract self that forms a large part of the cultural ideal of masculinity and that is to function in patriarchal culture's moral undertakings is parasitic on the concrete self developed during childhood and largely in the domestic sphere. In point six I will argue further that the concept of the abstract self is also a product of linguistic alienation. Here I wish to make the point that this abstract self is incoherent and, logically, cannot do the job assigned to it by moral theory.

To say that one concept is parasitic on another is to make the point that it cannot function well, if indeed it can function at all, in logical isolation from the concept(s) on which it depends. In other words, in certain language-games some concepts are logically prior to others. An example of this relationship, which Wittgenstein treats at length in his work, is the relationship between the concepts of doubt and certainty: we cannot sensibly doubt something unless we have certainty about relevant related matters, unless we can play that particular language-game without doubt. For instance, it makes no sense to say that a baby doubts that $12 + 12 = 24$ if she cannot do simple arithmetic. Doubt only functions in a language-game and depends on things that we logically cannot doubt, about which we have logical certainty. Doubt about the product of a sum is parasitic on the ability to play the games of simple math without doubt. Wittgenstein shows in *Philosophical Investigations* that the concrete self, in Benhabib's sense, is logically primary and in some sense natural in that it is an outgrowth of primitive, pre-, and nonlinguistic ways of being in the world with others. The theoretical creation of the Cartesian ego with its dependency on binarisms such as inner/outer and mind/body is only possible after the groundwork of a wide range of everyday uses of language has been laid, including both the language of personhood and the language used to form those binarisms. For Wittgenstein it is a point of logic that we can only play the games of metaphysics and theory because we have mastered the more primitive games that are the homes of the words that theory and metaphysics use. Further, dualistic conceptions of the person, what Gilbert Ryle calls the myth of the ghost in the machine,[8] have a certain plausibility for us because they reflect the deep or conceptual grammar of natural language. But "sensations are inner" makes a point of logic; it demarcates the boundary of a language-game and tells us what logical type of things sensations are. It is a philosophical mistake to think that it expresses an ontological truth, but it is a mistake that philosophers are inclined to make because conceptual grammar gives this philosophical view an air of naturalness. Furthermore, it is a mistake that has become deeply embedded in culture because of its usefulness in, among other things, grounding power politics. The Cartesian ego, then, can be seen to be an abstraction from the natural-language concept of a human soul and depends for its formation on severing certain parts of that concept (rational function) from its conceptual surroundings (the body, emotion).

Wittgenstein went further, to show that this conception of the privatized, Cartesian ego is incoherent; it results in, first, a radical solipsism and, finally, in the reduction of language to nonsense. Thus, it becomes logically impossible to think or decide anything since language cannot be used with sense. It follows that ethical theories founded on such an incoherent conception of the ego cannot do their work of determining the good for oneself and others and instantiating that determination in moral acts.

My sixth and final Wittgensteinian point is that such an abstract Cartesian concept of the self can only be developed through a process of linguistic alienation. To develop my notion of linguistic alienation, I draw upon that feature of Wittgenstein's concept of a language-game that foregrounds the use of speech in the context of the experiences and activities of the person. Because using language is bound up with the way in which we live and act, the development and discursive use of the Cartesian ego involves more than simply ignoring or overriding the original uses of language; it involves the failure, or even the inability, to participate in the activities in which they function. In the case of the concept of the person, this means a failure, refusal, or inability to respond to her as a human soul, a failure of understanding, of care, and ultimately of humanity. It is this failure, this linguist alienation, that undergirds the moral theories of modern patriarchal culture.

On the basis of the foregoing, we can see that Wittgenstein's investigation of the language of everyday interactions, of the "private" or "domestic" sphere, the place in which many of our most intimate and personal interactions take place, shows that the concept of the human soul employed there is holistic and not dualistic. The language of the human soul is also nonhierarchical with regard to sex and aspects of the self such as mind and body in that this culture's concept of hierarchy is developed out of its polarization of human reality into mutually exclusive categories (male/female, reason/emotion, etc.) that are parasitic on the logically more primitive concept of the soul. The language that we learn from birth, through the teaching of mothers, has the concept of the soul, the concept of an embodied person with emotions, desires, thoughts, and values, at its core. Part of the process of maturation involves the participation in ever more mature and sophisticated language-games involving human souls, our own and others, and these games are also learned to a great extent "in the home." It is this rich concept of personhood that must be suppressed in order to participate in the moral discourse of the dominant patriarchal tradition in ethics—ethics as decision procedure in which persons are reduced to place holders in a moral calculus.

Furthermore, the concept of the "concrete" person that mothers live out in their own lives in the home and nurture in their children, especially in their daughters, is both richer, and richer in potential for the formation of the moral life, than the concept of the "abstract" self. The concept of the person as a concrete self is implicated in what Carol Gilligan calls the ethics of care and responsibility. In what follows, I want to flesh out some features of that morality and the direction it could possibly take were it to be extended into what is now the public sphere, the realm of culture, and especially into its formal institutional manifestations.

ETHICS AND THE SPIRITUAL EROTIC

Earlier I drew distinctions between the concept of a person as a human soul and the abstract subject or ego of patriarchal discourse, and also between moral talk (the ethic of care) and moral argumentation (the ethic of rights). I now wish to draw a distinction between morality as ethos, as a complete way of life and living, which, I argue, more completely engages the human soul, and the rationalistic ethical paradigm constructed by the dominant moral discourse.[9] I argue that on this conception of ethics as ethos, taking oneself and others seriously as flesh-and-blood souls involves a spiritual erotics such as that developed by Audre Lorde and by Andrea Nye in her work on Diotima of Mantinea.

In her essay "Uses of the Erotic: The Erotic as Power," Audre Lorde, who has been called "the founding mother of the spirituality of eroticism" by Susan Cahill,[10] extends the notion of the erotic beyond the narrow, objectified sexuality that term usually connotes in patriarchal culture. The erotic is rooted, Lorde says, in our "spiritual plane,"[11] and it is the source of our deepest, nonrational knowledge.[12] Importantly for my concerns here, she identifies the erotic with "an internal sense of satisfaction to which, once we have experienced it, we know we can aspire . . . in honor and self-respect we can require no less of ourselves."[13] In her essay Lorde describes the ways in which the erotic colors all of the activities she undertakes, from painting a fence, to writing a poem, to making love. She holds that the erotic provides a kind of internal guide or compass in all we do, be our undertaking physical, emotional, psychic, or intellectual,[14] be it in the "private," domestic sphere of mothers and children, or in the "public," political and social sphere. We know from how we feel about it if we are doing well or ill. Guided by the erotic, Lorde says:

The aim of each thing which we do is to make our lives and the lives of our children richer and more possible. Within the celebration of the erotic in all our endeavors, my work becomes a conscious decision—a longed-for bed which I enter gratefully and from which I rise up empowered.[15]

Clearly, for Lorde the erotic is a generative, although not necessarily procreational, principle at the center of life. The erotic, she holds, is love in the sense of creativity in all of its forms,[16] and it promotes human flourishing and proliferation. Since she writes as a black lesbian feminist, she focuses on love between women, and she does clearly identify the erotic as the power of women that,[17] I hold, is a limitation that cannot be sustained by the concept of the human soul I developed earlier in this chapter.

This limitation is unfortunate on a practical level in that, if the possibility for positive change not only on the personal but also on the social and political levels lies in the erotic, and if the erotic inheres only in women, then we seem bound for a separatist culture, dictated by an unbridgeable ontological gulf between men and women. We must notice and take account as well of the "natural" hierarchy built into Lorde's conception, a hierarchy, built on dualistic thinking and essentialism, which carries with it all of the potential for intersexual conflict and inequality that is built into our current state of affairs.

The natural language concept of the soul that I have argued Wittgenstein's philosophy has uncovered at the heart of our linguistic practices does not carry with it Lorde's naturalized hierarchy. At its most primitive level the soul is unsexed and ungendered, and this opens up the possibility that the goods that flow from the erotic can be available to both sexes. In this respect Wittgenstein's natural language concept of the soul is closer to that which Andrea Nye has revealed in Diotima of Mantinea's speech in Plato's *Symposium,* and so I will conclude with a brief discussion of Diotima's spiritual erotics as it relates to the concerns of this essay.[18]

Over several papers Andrea Nye[19] argues that Diotima's philosophy, to be properly understood, must be wrested free of the Platonic metaphysics and gynophobic bias in which it has been embedded by generations of male philosophers, beginning with Plato. What emerges from this reading is a concept of the human soul strikingly similar to that revealed by Wittgenstein's investigations, as well as a concept of spiritual erotics with a close family resemblance to Lorde's, although severed of Lorde's exclusive connection with women. As the human soul matures, Diotima argues, it outgrows its romantic, privatized, and obsessive love of the particular other and expands its conception of the beauty which is worthy of love to include the "beauty of the soul,"[20] and "beauty as it exists in activities and institutions"[21] and in the sciences,[22] until finally, with gaze fixed on "the vast ocean of beauty,"[23] it will "bring forth in the abundance of his [sic] love of wisdom many beautiful and magnificent sentiments and ideas,"[24] and finally will catch sight of eternal beauty.[25]

Socrates quotes Diotima as teaching that:

> [w]hen a man [sic with the masculine form throughout], starting from this sensible world and making his way upward by a right use of his feeling of love for boys, begins to catch sight of that beauty, he is very near his goal. This is the right way of approaching or being initiated into the mysteries of love, to begin with examples of beauty in this world, and using them as steps to ascent continually with that absolute beauty as one's aim, from one instance of physical beauty to two and from two to all, then from physical beauty to moral beauty, and from moral beauty to the beauty of knowledge, until from knowledge of various kinds one arrives at the supreme knowledge whose sole object is that absolute beauty, and knows at last what absolute beauty is.[26]

This, Diotima continues, is "the region where a man's life should be spent, in the contemplation of absolute beauty."[27]

It is only with the prior assumption of Plato's dualistic and hierarchical metaphysics that passages such as these can be read as an articulation of the philosophical process of intellectual ascent to a vision of Platonic forms. If we simply use language in a nontheoretical fashion, as Wittgenstein shows we do in ordinary conversation and as Nye maintains Diotima does in her speech, then the lover's progress will be "not vertical, from lower to higher, but lateral, from narrow sexual relations to an exclusive concern with one's own family, to 'better' (not 'higher'), more inclusive relationships."[28] The "vast ocean of beauty" on which the lover gazes in erotic desire, in "the creative desire which is of the soul,"[29] will hold within it not only beautiful bodies but also beautiful souls, ideas, and institutions; it will issue in not only physical progeny but also spiritual progeny in the form of beautiful ideas and deeds. And, as the generative activity of Lorde's erotic woman is guided by an inner principle, so Diotima's lover is led by a generative impulse at the center of life,[30] an impulse to create the beautiful: "The generic concept embraces every desire for good and for happiness; that is precisely what almighty and all-ensnaring love is,"[31] argues Diotima.

The Diotimian lover is far from either the Platonic deserter of the realm of Becoming, or the stable, autonomous but alienated ego of modern moral theory which is his descendant. Rather, this person, this soul, is enmeshed in her world and society and is ever-changing, open to the process of birth, growth, death, and decay in both flesh and character. In Diotima's words:

Even during the period for which any living being is said to live and to retain his [*sic* throughout] identity—as a man, for example, is called the same man from boyhood to old age—he does not in fact retain the same attributes, although he is called the same person; he is always becoming a new being and undergoing a process of loss and reparation, which affects his hair, his flesh, his bones, his blood, and his whole body. And not only his body, but his soul as well. No man's character, habits, opinions, desires, pleasures, pains, and fears remain always the same; new ones come into existence and old ones disappear.[32]

Such a lover will not remain content with the narrowness and restrictions of modern culture's notion of romantic love for long. That privatized relationship, cut off from all others but the beloved, neglectful of work, oblivious to social and political issues, that characterizes the notion of romantic love would have difficulty even gaining a foothold with her. What I am suggesting is not that such a lover would necessarily be sexually promiscuous but rather that her erotic, loving activity would permeate all aspects of her life and extend well beyond any single relationship. Any form of love that restricted or prohibited this would be no love at all to her. A Diotimian lover would find ways to give birth to beautiful forms in all areas of her life, in social and political institutions as well as in her personal relationships and home. That is, like Lorde's erotic woman, a Diotimian lover would be concerned to create culture and society, her life and love would be inherently political. But, in contrast to Lorde's positioning of the erotic in women, with a Wittgensteinian notion of the soul a Diotimian lover could be either female or male.

In conclusion, and to return to my initial concern with mothers and mothering, I have argued that nondichotomized and nonhierarchalized primary uses of language, the concept of the person as a human soul, and the possibility of a spiritual erotics are built into the natural language that mothers teach their children. As Wittgenstein has shown, these language-games grow out of the behaviors and concerns of flesh-and-blood persons in living relationships with others. Thus, mothers teach language-games that could develop into the mature ethos described by Audre Lorde and by Andrea Nye in her work on Diotima, a spiritual erotics of generative love. Modern Western culture encourages males to "go beyond" these games that mothers teach, but that "beyond" is into a sterile realm of alienation and dehumanization. It is into the polis conceived as a marketplace where all human relationships are structured on an exchange model and morality becomes, in the words of Annette Baier, "traffic rules for self-assertors."[33] On this model much of what is human about human life—relationship, care, nurturance, development, generativity, and, in addition, a much diminished erotic—is relegated to the private, domestic realm of women, and especially mothering women, and children. This dichotomization means, among other things, that the qualities of the fully human soul, which Nye claims Diotima identified but which were appropriated by and recast for the use of men at that party Socrates attended so long ago, cannot be brought to bear on the pressing social and political issues that face us today.

The power and the ethical import of mothering lie in the ability of actual mothers to nurture complete human souls and to teach both their daughters and their sons to insist on the expression of their full humanity in all areas of their lives.

NOTES

1. Deborah Orr, "On Logic and Moral Voice," *Informal Logic* 17, no. 3 (1995): 347–63.

2. Carol Gilligan, *In a Different Voice* (Cambridge, Mass.: Harvard University Press, 1982).

3. Annette C. Baier, "What Do Women Want in a Moral Theory?" in *An Ethic of Care: Feminist and Interdisciplinary Perspectives*, ed. Mary Jeanne Larrabee (New York and London: Routledge, 1993), 19–32.

4. Seyla Benhabib, *Situating the Self: Gender, Community and Postmodernism in Contemporary Ethics* (New York: Routledge, 1992).

5. Naomi Scheman, "From Hamlet to Maggie Verver: The History and Politics of the Knowing Subject," in *Engenderings: Constructions of Knowledge, Authority, and Privilege* (New York: Routledge, 1993), 106–25.

6. Ludwig Wittgenstein, *Philosophical Investigations*, trans. G. E. M. Anscombe (Oxford: Blackwell, 1968).

7. Wittgenstein, *Philosophical Investigations*, 178.

8. Gilbert Ryle, *The Concept of Mind* (Harmondsworth, England: Penguin, 1973), 13–25.

9. Kathryn Pyne Parson, "Nietzsche and Moral Change," in *Nietzsche: A Collection of Critical Essays*, ed. Robert Solomon (Garden City, N.Y.: Anchor, 1973), 169–93. Parson distinguishes four features of the ethic-of-rights paradigm: (1) a focus on notions of obligation, (2) the centrality of moral principles, (3) the justification of principle by argument, and (4) the [deductive] justification of acts by principles (169 *ff*).

10. Susan Cahill, ed., *Wise Women: Over 2000 Years of Spiritual Writing by Women* (New York: Norton, 1996), 239.

11. Audre Lorde, "Uses of the Erotic: The Erotic as Power," in *Sister Outsider: Essays and Speeches* (Freedom, Calif.: Crossing Press, 1984), 53.

12. Lorde, "Uses of the Erotic," 53.

13. Lorde, "Uses of the Erotic," 54.

14. Lorde, "Uses of the Erotic," 54.

15. Lorde, "Uses of the Erotic," 55.

16. Lorde, "Uses of the Erotic," 55.

17. Lorde, "Uses of the Erotic," 55.

18. Andrea Nye, "The Hidden Host: Irigaray and Diotima at Plato's Symposium," *Hypatia* 3, no. 3 (Winter 1989): 47. It is very interesting that a related notion of love as a generative life force is articulated by Eryximachus, a doctor and thus the person at Agathon's dinner party whose work with the lives and bodies of actual people would most closely approximate that of mothers. In his speech in *The Symposium* (Plato, 53 *f.*), Eryximachus holds, in part, that

> my professional experience as a doctor has shown me that love does not operate only in men's souls and has not only beautiful boys as its object, but that it has many other objects and other spheres of action, the bodies of all animals, for example, and plants which grow in the earth, and practically all existing things; in fact love is a great and wonderful god whose influence extends everywhere, and embraces the worlds of gods and men alike.

19. Nye, "The Hidden Host," 45–60; "The Subject of Love: Diotima and Her Critics," *Journal of Value Inquiry* 24 (1990): 135–53; "Rethinking Male and Female: The Pre-Hellenic Philosophy of Moral Opinion," *History of European Ideas* 9, no. 3, (1998): 261–80.

20. Plato, *The Symposium*, trans. Walter Hamilton (Harmondsworth, England: Penguin, 1981), 92.

21. Plato, *The Symposium*, 93.

22. Plato, *The Symposium*, 93.

23. Plato, *The Symposium*, 93.

24. Plato, *The Symposium*, 93.

25. Plato, *The Symposium*, 93–94.

26. Plato, *The Symposium*, 94.

27. Plato, *The Symposium*, 94.

28. Nye, "The Hidden Host," 48.

29. Plato, *The Symposium*, 90.

30. See n. 18.

31. Plato, *The Symposium*, 31.

32. Plato, *The Symposium*, 88–89.

33. Baier, "What Do Women Want in a Moral Theory?" 31.

11

The Global Self-Esteem of an African-American Adolescent Female and Her Relationship with Her Mother

Barbara Turnage

Like all children, the developing African-American girl needs a secure and consistent environment to form the foundation for a positive global self-esteem.[1] Self-esteem consists of two components: feeling that one is lovable and feeling that one is competent.[2] Self-esteem can be viewed as an individual's attitude about herself, as well as her estimate of how capable, worthwhile, and successful she feels she is as a person.[3] Self-esteem exists on a continuum, and a person's self-esteem level can appear anywhere along this continuum, from high to low self-esteem.[4] An individual with high self-esteem, as defined by Rosenberg, "feels that [she/he] is a person of worth; [she/he] respects [her-/himself] for what [she/he] is, but [she/he] does not stand in awe of [her-/himself] nor does [she/he] expect others to stand in awe of [her/him]."[5] This individual communicates, to the world, an attitude of being "good enough."[6] Joseph identified high self-esteem, for adolescents, as protective armor.[7]

At the opposite end of high self-esteem is low self-esteem. An individual with low self-esteem is viewed to exhibit behaviors that reflect "self-rejection, self-dissatisfaction, [and] self-contempt."[8] Unlike an individual with high self-esteem, this individual does not respect nor enjoy her current self. Although she may wish otherwise, she finds her self-picture to be disagreeable.[9]

A variety of factors influence a person's overall or global self-esteem level.[10] In reference to adolescents' self-esteem, Wade and his colleagues, based on a review of the literature, identified five factors. They are "physical and sexual development, sexual activity, physical and sexual attrac-

175

tiveness, interpersonal relationships, and competency."[11] These authors concluded, using a data set of 1,153 adolescents who were tested at age eleven and again at age seventeen (336 of these adolescents were African-American, or 29 percent), that "predictors of self-esteem for Black respondents do not resemble those of White respondents."[12] The authors further noted that, based on gender, the factors also differed for the African-American respondents.[13] As Wade and his colleagues demonstrated, knowing the factors that influence European-American males' and/or females' and African-American males' self-esteem will not help predict the factors that influence African-American females' level of self-esteem.[14] For example, physical attractiveness influenced the self-esteem of both African-American and European-American females in Wade and his associates'[15] study; however, the standards of beauty differed. The European-American females were more influenced by media-imposed standards of beauty than the African-American females. Of particular importance to an African-American female's global self-esteem level are the levels of her ethnic identity,[16] appearance evaluation,[17] and trust of mother (attachment).[18]

The purpose of this investigation is to add another dimension to the scholarly discussion of the African-American mother-daughter relationship. Specifically, this research will investigate interrelationships between the daughter's global self-esteem, her ethnic identity, appearance evaluation, and the daughter's trust of her mother (secure attachment).

FACTOR 1: ETHNIC IDENTITY

The first of the three factors, ethnic identity, is derived from membership in a social group.[19] Historically in the United States, African-oriented features (darker skin-tones, thick lips, broad noses, kinky hair, etc.) have been devalued and ridiculed.[20] Unfortunately, this practice continues. However, today's African-American female who possesses African-oriented features has at her disposal a variety of self-esteem-enhancing materials.[21] The most significant is her mother.[22]

Many African-American mothers have been charged with the task of providing an environment in which their daughters can become emotionally and spiritually sound, happy, healthy, and productive African-American women.[23] This enormous task is made more difficult because of America's racist and sexist history. African-American mothers who choose to play this role must be willing to prepare their daughters to live as black women.[24]

There is no room, for many African-American mothers, to forget what it means to confront racial and sexist barriers. Also, in the day-to-day lives of black women, racism and sexism can lead to various forms of prejudice and discrimination.[25] Grier and Cobbs contend that "a parent's essential and fundamental purpose, beyond assuring the child's survival, is to provide an interpretation of the society to the child."[26] Thus, an African-American mother may work to communicate to her daughter how these experiences and their consequences may affect her psychological well-being.[27] Through information she receives from her mother, and personal experiences, the daughter learns of life's pitfalls on a daily basis. Sadly, through each experience, she learns to prepare herself for the next. On occasions, lessons learned through experience (personal or example) are not enough protection. Her mother, along with her father and significant family and nonfamily members, teaches her that life isn't fair, and sometimes it just is that way.

Under these circumstances, ethnic group identification, "together with the value and emotional significance attached to membership,"[28] can have either a positive or negative impact on the African-American girl's global self-esteem. During adolescence and into adulthood, "concerns about ethnicity shift from learning one's ethnic label to understanding the significance of one's group membership."[29]

FACTOR 2: APPEARANCE EVALUATION

While learning what it means to be an African-American female, the adolescent further exposes her unfolding self-esteem to public scrutiny. As a result, by identifying herself as a black woman, she will most likely incur all of the negative (and positive) connotations associated with both her ethnic identification and her gender identification.[30] For example, an adolescent may, inside her home, be told that her hair is attractive and versatile, while outside her home she experiences ridicule from non-African-American peers based on her hairstyles.[31] The conflicting nature of the messages may lead her to question the relevance of the information received from either inside or outside of her home. Depending on how she evaluates her appearance, she may discontinue her expression of her ethnic identity through the wearing of ethnic-oriented hairstyles—that is, if she chooses conformity. The ridicule invoked by her peers may weaken her global self-esteem level and spur her to seek solace in their acceptance (to conform). However, if her global self-esteem level includes an appearance evaluation that was established based on her ethnic heritage, she may choose to continue expressing her African-American pride through her hairstyles.

Concerning the significance of peer-related conformity, Makkar and Strube report that black women who possessed high self-esteem, and high African self-consciousness, were more likely to judge their physical appearance in accordance with members of their own ethnic group.[32] The women in Makkar and Strube's study, ages seventeen to twenty-two years, consistently chose other black women as reference points when asked questions about their appearance evaluation (body image). Many of these reference points were inside of their immediate family.[33]

Based on her personal experiences, one would expect an African-American mother to encourage her daughter to develop an appearance evaluation based on African-American beauty standards.[34] A person's appearance evaluation (body image) is her opinion of her body and is impacted by her shape, age, size, gender, self-esteem level, culture, ethnicity, and historical time. According to Singh, "the female body shape is determined by both the amount of fat and its' distribution."[35] Both body-fat distribution (body shape) and overall weight (body size) may jointly determine the perception of ideal female body shape. Thus, it is not, necessarily, the amount of fat (how much the person weighs), that determines how one looks, but the fat combined with the elements mentioned here (shape, age, size, etc.). Rucker and Cash add the element of culture as another determining factor.[36] They state that "cultures purvey gender-specific standards for physical attractiveness, body weight, and body shape."[37] From their point of view, "cultural standards shape the individual's body-image experiences and his/her adjustment behaviors."[38]

FACTOR 3: TRUST OF MOTHER

Many African-American women during adolescence struggled with the task of filtering out nonobtainable images of womanhood.[39] Based on these firsthand experiences, these women may possess the ability to identify and dismantle inappropriate images of womanhood that are directed at their daughters. An African-American mother may present obtainable images of womanhood into her parenting practices.[40]

Based on the emotional bond that developed between the mother and daughter during the daughter's early years of life, a level of trust was established.[41] That is, the daughter develops a level of trust in regard to her mother's ability/willingness to soothe and protect her. In her role as mediator,[42] an African-American mother signals to her daughter that she is willing to serve as a secure base from which her daughter can explore and experience the world.[43] As her daughter's mediator, an African-American mother also signals to her daughter that she wishes to take an active role in her daughter's life. She teaches her daughter to "stay the course" when times get hard, that she is worthy of love and respect, that she has the right to dream and accomplish her dreams, and that others' opinions of her should be secondary (if at all) to her opinion of herself. For her daughter to achieve a positive global self-esteem, an African-American mother must not only verbally encourage her daughter, she must model the image of womanhood she wishes her daughter to obtain.

To ensure her daughter's global self-esteem survives the onslaught of negative stimuli directed at African-American females, an African-American mother must be prepared to mediate the harm attached to these stimuli.[44] Regardless of the situation, an African-American female needs to be sure that her mother will either assist her efforts to alleviate the problem or take care of the problem herself. Knowing that her mother is willing and able to assist her efforts to develop renews the trust that was developed early in the daughter's life. This trust helps the daughter tackle the most insidious stress. Without her mother, an African-American adolescent female may be left unprotected.

By instilling a positive global self-esteem in her daughter, an African-American mother works to mediate the dangerous societal forces identified earlier. This can occur through an African-American mother encouraging her daughter to develop an African-American ethnic identity, providing her daughter with an appearance evaluation that is reflective of her daughter's ethnic heritage and the enhancement of a trusting mother-daughter relationship, and teaching her daughter effective coping strategies. For the reasons already stated, the global self-esteem of an African-American girl is "the armor that protects [her] from the dragons of life."[45] These dragons may be early withdrawal from high school, early pregnancy, drug usage, and/or crime.

METHODOLOGY

This section will present the two research hypotheses, information about study participants, study procedures, and study instruments. The sampling method this exploratory, cross-sectional study used was convenience. For the sake of clarity the term *predictor variable* will be used when addressing the three independent variables—Ethnic Identity achievement, Appearance Evaluation, and Trust of Mother.

HYPOTHESES

Hypothesis 1 addresses the relationship between global self-esteem and the predictor variables. That is, self-esteem will be positively correlated with Ethnic Identity Achievement, Appearance Evaluation, and Trust of Mother.

The second hypothesis addresses the amount of variance that could be explained by the predictor variables. That is, an African-American adolescent female's global self-esteem level can be predicted by levels of Ethnic Identity Achievement, Appearance Evaluation, and Trust of Mother.

SUBJECTS

Data for this study were collected from 105 African-American females recruited from a Catholic, all-girls high school in an urban area. The participants were twelfth graders between the ages of sixteen and eighteen (mean age, 16.83). Of the 105 participants, 24 (23 percent) were sixteen, 75 (71 percent) were seventeen, and 6 (6 percent) were eighteen (see table 11.1).

Overall, half (51 percent) of these young women lived with both of their biological parents, while 39 percent of them lived with their biological mother only. Of the remaining 10 percent, 7 percent lived with their mother and a stepfather, 2 percent lived with their grandmother, and 1 percent lived with another family member.

One hundred three of the participants responded to the question concerning their mother's education (see table 11.1). Forty-eight percent of the participants reported their mothers receiving some type of college degree. Of this 48 percent, 7 percent were reported to have obtained an associate degree, 29 percent had obtained a bachelor's degree, and 12 percent had obtained a graduate or professional degree. Only 3 percent of the mothers had obtained less than a high school education (one mother had less than nine years of schooling). There was a significant correlation ($r = .338, p = .000$) between mothers' education and fathers' education.

PROCEDURES

Data was collected on two separate days. Participants were surveyed in their religion class on either Monday or Tuesday. The research packet consisted of four instruments—one self-esteem (HARE Self-Esteem Scale), one ethnic identity achievement (My Ethnicity), one appearance evaluation (My Body), one attachment to mother (My Mother). Research instruments were counterbalanced to protect the data from order effects by reducing the possibility of missing data and nonrandom error. The counterbalance procedure consisted of arranging the odd-numbered packets with the self-esteem instrument first (the format presented earlier), while the even-numbered packets had the attachment to mother instrument first.

Table 11.1 Participant's Parent's Education and Employment

Parents' Level of Education	Participant's Age in Years						
	16		17		18		Sum
	Mother	Father	Mother	Father	Mother	Father	
High School and Below	7% (7)	7% (7)	11% (11)	19% (19)	4% (4)	3% (3)	25% (51)
Some College and Associate	7% (7)	8% (8)	30% (31)	30% (30)	1% (1)	2% (2)	39% (79)
College Degree and Above	10% (10)	8% (8)	30% (31)	21% (21)	1% (1)	1% (1)	36% (72)
Total	**23% (24)**	**23% (23)**	**71% (73)**	**71% (70)**	**6% (6)**	**6% (6)**	**100%**
Work Outside of Home	21	23	67	59	4	5	

INSTRUMENTS

The participants completed four instruments. The HARE General and Area-Specific (School, Peer, and Home) Self-Esteem Scale[46] (HARE) was used to measure participants' global self-esteem. The HARE is a thirty-item self-administered instrument. The seven-item Ethnic Identity Achievement subscale of Phinney's[47] Multigroup Ethnic Identity Measure was used to measure participants' ethnic identity. To measure participants' appearance evaluation, the seven-item Appearance Evaluation subscale of Cash's Multidimensional Body-Self Relations Questionnaire[48] was used. Trust of mother was measured by the ten-item Trust subscale of the Parent Inventory of the Inventory of Parent and Peer Attachment.[49] Chronbach alphas for this study's instruments study ranged from .81 to .95.

RESULTS

This section will discuss the results of a stepwise multiple regression and a test of correlation (Pearson Product Moment). The stepwise multiple regression was run to test hypothesis 1: An African-American adolescent female's global self-esteem level can be predicted by levels of ethnic identity achievement, appearance evaluation, trust of her mother, and coping. This hypothesis was supported. Ethnic identity achievement, appearance evaluation, and trust of mother together explained 43 percent of the variance in global self-esteem (see table 11.2).

The correlation analysis was used to test hypothesis 2: Self-esteem will be positively correlated with ethnic identity achievement, appearance evaluation, and trust of mother. This hypothesis was also supported. The results of a test of correlation revealed that ethnic identity achievement, appearance evaluation, and trust of mother was significantly ($p = .000$) correlated to self-esteem (see table 11.3).

Table 11.2   Results of Stepwise Regression with Predictor Variables on Self-Esteem

	Global Self-Esteem	
Variable	Beta	Alpha
Ethnic Identity Achievement	.19	.021
Appearance Evaluation	.32	.000
Trust of Mother	.40	.000

Table 11.3   Results of Correlation Analysis between Global Self-Esteem
and the Predictor Variables

Variables	Global Self-Esteem	Ethnic Identity Achievement	Appearance Evaluation	Trust of Mother
Global Self-Esteem	—			
Ethnic Identity Achievement	.40[a]	—		
Appearance Evaluation	.46[a]	.31[b]	—	
Trust of Mother	.52[a]	.26[c]	.19[d]	—

[a] Significant at the 0.000 level (2-tailed).
[b] Significant at the 0.001 level (2-tailed).
[c] Significant at the 0.01 level (2-tailed).
[d] Significant at the 0.05 level (2-tailed).

DISCUSSION

The results of the statistical tests performed revealed that, of the three predictor variables, the Trust of Mother variable was key when predicting global self-esteem. The strength of the relationship between Trust of Mother and global self-esteem truly reflected nonshared variance ($r = .52, p = .000$). This variable, Trust of Mother, was the first predictor variable to be entered in the stepwise regression analysis where it alone explained 27 percent of the variance in global self-esteem. Adding Ethnic Identity Achievement and Appearance Evaluation only increased the explained variance by 16 percent (3 percent and 13 percent, respectively).

The second variable to be entered in the stepwise regression analysis was Appearance Evaluation. The strength of the beta weight for Appearance Evaluation, combined with the amount of variance it explains, is boosted by the presence of Ethnic Identity Achievement. The significance of these two variables clearly illustrates the critical role attributed to the evaluation of one's appearance from an ethnic position. Without a doubt, possessing an ethnic- (African-American-) oriented Appearance Evaluation contributed to how these young women felt about themselves. In particular, a positive African-oriented body image (Appearance Evaluation) for this sample had a direct bearing on their global self-esteem (correlation between Appearance Evaluation and global self-esteem: $r = .46$, $p = .000$).

CONCLUSION

As this study suggests, the major contributors to its participants' global self-esteem, in relation to this study's predictor variables, were (1) trust of their African-American mothers and (2) their acceptance of their appearance based on an understanding and an embracing of their African-American heritage. The participants were 105 African-American adolescent females who attend a Catholic all-girls high school in an urban area. The mean age of the participants was 16.83, and the age range was from sixteen to eighteen.

This study demonstrates that African-American mothers play an important role in their daughters' self-esteem development. That is, the young women in this study who had high self-esteem also trusted their mothers to be there for them. A second important finding was the acknowledgment of an African ancestry. This theme resounded throughout all of the statistical tests that were performed. For the young women in this study, Ethnic Identity Achievement was the only predictor variable that was significantly correlated with all of the study variables (see table 11.2).

African-American mothers have been charged with the task of providing an environment in which their daughters can become emotionally and spiritually sound, happy, healthy, and productive African-American women. To accomplish this task, during their daughters' developmental years, many African-American mothers mediate their daughters' exposure to external environments.[50] These African-American mothers, in raising their daughters to respect their ethnicity, have experienced America's disgust for difference. For an adolescent African-American female, knowledge of her African heritage helps her define her body image and structures her expectations.

The information provided by these young women, although not generalizable, delivers a clear message in reference to their mothers. The significance of this message cannot be overstated. The relationship between these African-American young women and their mothers instilled in them the knowledge that they are competent and lovable. Based on their trust in their mothers, these young women believed, when confronted with difficult situations, that they could rely on their mother's assistance. Thus, as they grow into black womanhood, they grow with the knowledge that they can accomplish their goals and that they are worthy of love and respect.

NOTES

1. Beverly A. Greene, "What Has Gone Before: The Legacy of Racism and Sexism in the Lives of Black Mothers and Daughters," *Women and Therapy* 9, nos. 1 & 2 (1990): 207–30; Beverly A. Greene, "Sturdy Bridges: The Role of African-

American Mothers in the Socialization of African-American Children,'' *Women and Therapy* 10, nos. 1 & 2 (1990): 205–25.

2. W. B. Swann, *Self-traps* (New York: Freemand, 1996).

3. Jeffrey Bogan, ''The Assessment of Self-Esteem: A Cautionary Note,'' *Australian Psychologist* 23, no. 3 (1988): 383–89.

4. Earle Silber and Jean S. Tippett, ''Self-Esteem: Clinical Assessment and Measurement Validation,'' *Psychological Reports* 16 (1965): 1017–71.

5. Morris Rosenberg, *Society and the Adolescent Self-Image* (Princeton, N.J.: Princeton University Press, 1965), 31.

6. Rosenberg, *Society and the Adolescent Self-Image*, 31.

7. Joanne M. Joseph, *The Resilient Child: Preparing Today's Youth for Tomorrow's World* (New York: Plenum, 1994).

8. Rosenberg, *Society and the Adolescent Self-Image*, 31.

9. Rosenberg, *Society and the Adolescent Self-Image*, 31.

10. Bruce R. Hare, ''Self-Perception and Academic Achievement: Variations in a Desegregated Setting,'' *American Journal of Psychiatry* 137, no. 6 (1980): 683–89; C. Mruk, *Self-Esteem Research, Theory, and Practice* (New York: Springer, 1995).

11. T. J. Wade, V. Thompson, A. Tashakkori, and E. Valente, ''A Longitudinal Analysis of Sex by Race Differences in Predictors of Adolescent Self-Esteem,'' *Personality Individual Differences* 10, No. 7 (1989): 717, 727.

12. Wade et al., ''A Longitudinal Analysis of Sex,'' 717, 727.

13. Wade et al., ''A Longitudinal Analysis of Sex,'' 717, 727.

14. T. J. Wade, ''Race and Sex Differences in Adolescent Self-Perceptions of Physical Attractiveness and Level of Self-Esteem During Early and Late Adolescence,'' *Personality Individual Differences* 12, no. 12 (1991): 1319–24.

15. Wade et al., ''A Longitudinal Analysis of Sex,'' 717, 727.

16. Jean S. Phinney, ''The Multigroup Ethnic Identity Measure: A New Scale for Use with Diverse Groups,'' *Journal of Adolescent Research* 7, no. 2 (1992): 156–76.

17. Jalmeen K. Makkar and Michael J. Strube, ''Black Women's Self-Perceptions of Attractiveness Following Exposure to White versus Black Beauty Standards: The Moderating Role of Racial Identity and Self-Esteem,'' *Journal of Applied Social Psychology* 25, no. 17 (1995): 1547–66.

18. Howard C. Stevenson, Jr., ''Validation of the Scale of Racial Socialization for African-American Adolescents: Steps toward Multidimensionality,'' *Journal of Black Psychology* 20, no. 4 (1994): 445–68.

19. Phinney, ''The Multigroup Ethnic Identity Measure,'' 156–76.

20. Selena Bond and Thomas F. Cash, ''Black Beauty: Skin Color and Body Images among African-American College Women,'' *Journal of Applied Social Psychology* 22, no. 11 (1992) 874–88.

21. Vivian Church, *Colors around Me* (Chicago: Afro-American, 1971/1993); Deborah Easton, *Color Me Proud* (Milwaukee: Identity Toys, 1994).

22. S. Hammer, *Daughters and Mothers: Mothers and Daughters* (New York: Quadrangle/New York Times, 1976); Deborah Plummer, ''Patterns of Racial Identity Development of African-American Adolescent Males and Females,'' *Journal of Black Psychology* 21, no. 2 (1995): 168–80.

23. Greene, ''What Has Gone Before,'' 207–30; Greene, ''Sturdy Bridges,'' 205–25.

24. Patricia Hill Collins, *Black Feminist Thought: Knowledge, Consciousness and the Politics of Empowerment* (New York: Routledge, 1991).

25. Carlton T. Pyant and Barbara J. Yanico, "Relationship of Racial Identity and Gender-Role Attitudes of Black Women's Psychological Well-Being," *Journal of Counseling Psychology* 38, no. 3 (1991): 315–22.

26. W. H. Grier and P. M. Cobbs, *Black Rage*, 2d ed. (New York: Basic Books, 1992).

27. Pyant et al., "Relationship of Racial Identity and Gender-Role Attitudes," 315–22.

28. Phinney, "The Multigroup Ethnic Identity Measure," 156–76.

29. Phinney, "The Multigroup Ethnic Identity Measure," 156–76.

30. Althea Smith and Abigail J. Stewart, "Approaches to Studying Racism and Sexism in Black Women's Lives," *Journal of Social Issues* 39, no. 3 (1983): 1–15.

31. Makkar et al., "Black Women's Self-Perceptions of Attractiveness," 1547–66.

32. M. B. Lykes, "Discrimination and Coping in the Lives of Black Women: Analyses of Oral History Data," *Journal of Social Issues* 39, no. 3 (1983): 79–100.

33. Lykes, "Discrimination and Coping in the Lives of Black Women," 79–100.

34. Greene, "What Has Gone Before," 207–30; Greene, "Sturdy Bridges," 205–25.

35. Devendra Singh, "Body Fat Distribution and Perception of Desirable Female Body Shape by Young Black Men and Women," *International Journal of Eating Disorders* 16, no. 3 (1994): 289–94.

36. Clifford E. Rucker and Thomas F. Cash, "Body Images, Body Size-Perceptions, and Eating Behaviors among African-American and White College Women," *International Journal of Eating Disorders* 12, no. 3 (1992): 292.

37. Rucker et al., "Body Images, Body Size-Perceptions," 292.

38. Rucker et al., "Body Images, Body Size-Perceptions," 292.

39. Daisy L. Bates, "I Did Not Really Understand What It Meant to Be a Negro," in *Black Women in White America: A Documentary History*, ed. G. Lerner (New York: Vintage Books, 1973), 306–8.

40. Greene, "What Has Gone Before," 207–30; Greene, "Sturdy Bridges," 205–25.

41. John Bowlby, "Attachment and Loss: Retrospect and Prospect," *American Journal of Orthopsychiatry* 52, no. 4 (1982), 664–78; V. L. Colin, *Human Attachment* (Philadelphia: Temple University Press, 1996); Robert Karen, "Becoming Attached," *Atlantic Monthly* (February 1990), 35–70.

42. Vetta L. Sanders Thompson, "Socialization to Race and Its Relationship to Racial Identification among African-Americans," *Journal of Black Psychology* 20, no. 2 (1994): 175–88.

43. Bowlby, "Attachment and Loss," 635–70.

44. Greene, "What Has Gone Before," 207–30; Greene, "Sturdy Bridges," 205–25.

45. Judith McKay, "Building Self-Esteem in Children," in *Self-Esteem*, ed. Matthew McKay and Patrick Fanning (Oakland, Calif.: New Harbinger, 1987), 327–73.

46. Hare, "Self-Perception and Academic Achievement," 683–89; Mruk, *Self-Esteem Research*.

47. Phinney, "The Multigroup Ethnic Identity Measure," 156–76.

48. Thomas F. Cash, *The Multidimentional Body-Self Relations Questionnaire Manual* (Norfolk, Va.: Old Dominion University, 1994).

49. Gay C. Armsden and Mark T. Greenberg, "The Inventory of Parent and Peer Attachment: Individual Differences and Their Relationship to Psychological Well-Being in Adolescence," *Journal of Youth and Adolescence* 16, no. 5 (1987): 427–54.

50. Greene, "What Has Gone Before," 207–30; Greene, "Sturdy Bridges," 205–25.

12

Educated Mothers as a Tool for Change: Possibilities and Constraints

Sue Marie Wright

Based on studies of women's education and social conditions in eighteen nations (representing North America, Latin America, Asia, the Middle East, Sub-Saharan Africa, and Western Europe), this chapter focuses on several common themes. These themes include the effects of culture and economic development on women's access to education, women's use of education as a resource, and the process of accelerated social change in terms of women's equality. This cross-cultural study suggests that generational change is a gendered process in which mothers and the mother-daughter link are of paramount significance for increasing women's equality. Three points are particularly salient in this argument: (1) women invest more of their income and time in children than men do; (2) women invest resources in daughters and sons more equitably than men, who spend much more time and effort on their sons; and (3) better-educated mothers gain greater influence over their children, especially daughters, than less-educated mothers. Overall, then, formal schooling would appear to foster women's equality. However, closer inspection of historical processes uncovers a paradox: while formal schooling may empower women in the process of raising their daughters, it also constrains mothering practices and perpetuates women's inequality. Working through this paradox helps advance a critique of education and its implications for the mother-daughter line.

Given the caveat that Western-style education represents something of an urban and elite phenomenon and that the advantages trickle down from elite, urban families to the masses, formal education is generally understood as a process that fosters progress. More specifically, women's education has been linked to progress through increasing women's resources and their influence in the family and the community. But how does women's education shape mothering, and do educated mothers' interactions with daughters contribute to social change? Until recently, most studies have focused on the impact of father's education on their children's success. Studies that do examine mothers' contributions to daughters' achievements or explore the process by which mother-daughter interactions contribute to accelerated social change generally focus on a single country or culture. In addition, the variety of approaches (e.g., ethnographies, interviews, questionnaires) makes direct comparisons of results and generalizations about education and the process of mothering difficult.

Despite these limitations, use of comparative historical methods illuminates processes whereby educated women foster social change through mothering. Information gathered here suggests that formal education reshapes the process of women's socialization, including increased expectations for advancement and willingness to question authority; educated mothers, then, transfer these skills and expectations to their daughters. Therefore, each succeeding generation of educated women appears to be able to take better advantage of the successes of preceding generations and to become more empowered.

On the other hand, although the documented effects of women's education appear overwhelmingly positive, closer inspection of developments in education and women's equality across nations and cultures raises a nagging suspicion that the story of women's education is more complex and less positive than the spin it has generally been given. Insights gained from a comparative historical approach prompt new questions. For instance, how does education impact women when it is part of a system of colonization? How does education affect women when it establishes and supports hierarchy? And in what ways is education limited as a tool for women's progress?

"PROGRESS" FOR WOMEN

Accelerated social change refers to broad, long-standing social patterns that shift rapidly and in a sustained way. While social change may take place slowly and with little notice for some time, in the case of accelerated social change, new patterns emerge and gain momentum, driving change forward relatively quickly and in a noticeable way. Aspects of rapid social change that scholars have begun to research cross-culturally include the increase in nuclear family households, the increase in more egalitarian marriages, increased participation by women in paid employment outside the household, and decreased fertility.[1]

In the case of family structure, the focus has been on the shift from traditional extended family households with rigidly defined gender roles to nuclear households with more "jointness," that is, where husband and wife share space and roles.[2] Jointness represents a greater degree of empowerment for women and relatively more equality between husband and wife. Several studies suggest that this change is driven by wives who insist on participating in family decision-making with their husbands rather than allowing the extended family and/or the husbands to control decisions.[3] As this example suggests, a number of changes may be related and contribute to the process of accelerated social change.

WOMEN'S EDUCATION AND SOCIAL CHANGE

Most research supports increasing levels of formal education as a major factor in many instances of accelerated social change.[4] Some scholars see the increase in educational equality signaling the decline of the patriarchal structure. Mass education, which reduces children's contribution to productive labor and increases the overall costs of children's dependence, reverses the flow of wealth within families. When the flow of wealth between generations is reversed, traditional authority is challenged and cultural change is accelerated.[5]

While increasing levels of formal education accelerate cultural change, increasing levels of formal education for women appear to have a more profound impact on social conditions than the rising level of education in general. Research consistently shows women's increased participation in education to be highly correlated with lowered fertility, greater labor-force participation, and the growing power of women within marriage.[6] Women's education also appears to be linked to the current shift toward nuclear households and greater levels of equality between husbands and wives. Initiation into the educational system and opportunities for respected work can provide women with a legitimate identity outside of family roles. Even in cultures where the intent is to keep women under the control of men (especially husbands' control), educational and occupational privileges for a few women can become legitimate educational and occupational opportunities for women in general.[7]

In the transformation of Mexican society since 1960, women's schooling has proved to be a key factor. In this case, as in others, women's education is associated with both reduced mortality and fertility, when other socioeconomic factors are controlled.[8] In fact, women's education appears more strongly related to both health and reproductive outcomes than any other household-level factor.[9] More specifically, women's education directly affects the way that mothers use medical services. In turn, greater utilization of medical services positively impacts both maternal and child health[10] and helps reshape women's preferences toward smaller families.[11]

With the exception of a few cross-cultural statistical studies,[12] however, most research that includes mothers' education as a variable or focuses on the process of mothering are limited to a single country or culture, and their authors take a variety of approaches.[13] Fortunately, comparative historical methods are designed to draw on a variety of sources for data in uncovering commonalities in social processes among diverse regions, nations, classes, and cultures. As such, comparative historical analysis offers a way to make the most of available information on mothering and, perhaps, shed new light on the connections between education, mothering, and social change.[14]

In trying to better understand the impact of education (as an institution) on mothering, then, I have drawn on cross-national statistical studies, comparative analyses, and case studies of eighteen nations representing a range of cultural groups and stages of development.[15] Cross-national statistical analysis highlights correlations between levels of education for women and different outcome measures. While these correlations should not be confused with causality, they can point the researcher in the direction of interesting questions about what happens inside "the black box." Comparative analysis provides more information about the development of education for women in specific areas. Case studies, which focus on descriptive analysis of women's daily lives, provide the best source of information on parenting practices and aspirations for daughters.

GENERATIONAL CHANGE AS A GENDERED PROCESS: THE MOTHER-DAUGHTER LINK

Women's education effectively generates a number of social benefits through providing women with extra income, increasing women's knowledge and awareness (especially of health practices and family planning), and affording them extra leverage in the family, particularly in the decisions that involve their children. Increased education for women generally results in increased income, since more-educated women are more likely to work in the paid sector and to have better jobs and higher incomes than women with less education. Moreover, women channel much of this income into their children. Women's investment in their children is almost universal, and mothers channel more of their income into expenditures on children than do men.[16]

The impact of women's education on social conditions is decidedly more complex, however, than simply increased income and occupational status. The knowledge and the awareness that education promotes can shape women's experiences in a number of ways. First, schools serve to resocialize girls, giving them a place to acquire "new motives, identities, skills, and models for interpersonal behavior."[17] For example, schools provide girls with the opportunity to climb "a ladder of ranked statuses" through academic performance. Such socialization to status advancement means that the longer a girl attends school, the more she will desire advancement through learning.

Second, advancement through the ranks means that women as well as men gain the ability to access new information through literacy, to reason through new information, and to argue for their point of understanding and how it fits in with their existing knowledge schema. As such, schooling promotes critical thinking in girls, as well as boys. But critical thinking creates questions, and these questions often challenge authority since the act of questioning itself can be seen as a challenge.

In turn, the ability to challenge authority fosters autonomy and means that women are more likely to make decisions on their own. For example, while girls may still be instructed in domestic skills in school, if the culture does not value these skills (as in the United States and many other societies), the girl now has the option of using those skills that are valued (productive labor vs. reproductive labor). She has the resources to be more choosy in a mate, even if the culture pressures her to marry (as most still do). She may be more likely to work and save before marriage, perhaps delaying marriage as a result. Women's older age at marriage can provide increased status in relation to her husband (not always the case, but often); her education imparts skills that can be used as a resource to gain influence in the relationship; her wages, if she works, can serve as yet another resource; and her literacy can enable her to access information that may challenge the inequality that exists between husbands and wives and between men and women in general.

Educated women may use their sense of autonomy to challenge male authority in the husband-wife relationship, thus producing more egalitarian relationships between couples. Increased autonomy also affects women's relationships with their children. For instance, education increases access to information and the ability to use information gathered from the media to make decisions about fertility and health care. Moreover, where women have access to information and rights to act independently, they tend to seek early medical treatment for their children.[18]

Third, educated mothers are also more likely to see their role as one of "teacher" to their young children and to engage their children in verbal interaction, starting in early infancy. Educated mothers talk more to their children than noneducated mothers. Children of educated mothers,

therefore, have an easier time succeeding in formal education and bureau-
cratic advancement.

As "teachers," educated mothers gain an increasing level of influence
over their children. They transfer cultural resources and instill aspirations
and expectations in their children through role modeling, in addition to
transferring economic resources. And in transferring cultural capital in
the home, mothers may well be more influential than fathers because they
spend more time with children than fathers do.[19] While both parents may
affect the schooling of their children by molding occupational aspirations
and socioeconomic expectations, "mothers engage in school-related activities with children more often than do fathers" and educated mothers appear to exert more pressure on their children to do well in school.[20]

Educated mothers, therefore, are likely to have a stronger impact on the
aspirations and expectations of their children. Case studies suggest that
better-educated mothers take more interest in their children's academic
achievements and are more instrumental in selecting schools for their
children than less educated mothers.[21] If, through the process of cultural
socialization, the mother's cultural resources are more important than the
father's, then the mother's education should have a stronger effect than
the father's. Moreover, as a society begins to value women's economic
roles and occupational status, mothers may become an increasingly important role model of socioeconomic achievement for their children, particularly for their daughters.

While fathers may provide the most important source of communication about work and occupations and serve as the primary role model for
future occupational status for boys,[22] mothers are more likely to serve as
an educational and occupational role model for daughters and to wield
more influence over daughters' decisions. In the United States, daughters
of employed mothers have been shown to name their mother as someone
they want to resemble most later in life more often than sons.[23] Other
studies show that mothers' earnings appear to increase the completed education of daughters, but not of sons[24]; and mothers' educational levels
and career roles strongly predict daughters' educational and career
goals.[25] The relationship between a women's education and her daughter's situation is reflected in the hopes of literate women in India that their
daughters will complete secondary school.[26] Mothers' aspirations and influence over their daughters' futures are also reflected in studies of educated Iraqi women. Despite the degree of male control in this culture,
these mothers report treating sons and daughters more equally, including
plans for university education. Moreover, some of these mothers plan to
forego arranged marriages for their daughters and express the hope that
their daughters' husbands will contribute to household and child care
duties.[27]

Thus, women's education has a significant impact on the mothering of daughters. For instance, educated mothers may encourage both daughters and sons to question and to succeed,[28] but mothers appear especially likely to influence daughters. Educated mothers may worry about their daughters becoming stigmatized for not conforming to expected gender norms (not married, not circumcised, etc.) but still use new information to challenge various form of sexist oppression. And while the ability to question and to challenge generally becomes available to boys as they grow older, educated mothers appear to make this resource more readily available and acceptable for girls; the ability to question and challenge inequality has future consequences both for the individual women and for women as a whole.

In being socialized by an educated mother, a girl may grow to accept the fact that she can challenge both parental and male authority. And while a girl's challenge to a father may not get her very far, she may quickly enlist her mother as a behind-the-scenes ally. Daughters of educated mothers may also be more likely to challenge male peers. Although male peers may not appreciate such challenging behavior, they may eventually accept it. Males who do not accept critical verbal behavior (challenges) will either be less likely to accept the woman in marriage or she less likely to accept him. Eventually, when she does marry, she will be more likely to choose someone who accepts (more or less) her nontraditional behavior, who may approve women working, who will agree with her choices about fertility, and so forth. The daughter's daughters, therefore, will be more likely to grow up in a household where the father accepts female autonomy and respects women's contributions.

LIMITS AND CONSTRAINTS

The scenario depicted here underscores the contribution of educated mothers in furthering women's equality; however, occasional hints about negative outcomes exist. For example, note that increased education and status for Ghanaian women may threaten male power, and educated women's older age at marriage may limit marital options.[29] Although increasing levels of education are generally related to increases in monogamous marriage, in Ghana, the most highly educated women exhibit the highest incidence of polygamous marriage, often as the second wife. Marginalized in this way through marriage, educated Ghanaian women are unlikely to wield much influence.

Thus, when we begin to look more closely at the historical processes of development, including education, a paradox emerges. Education (i.e., the Western model of formal schooling) may increase women's autonomy and equality as part of the accelerated social change it triggers. In many instances, however, Western colonialization has also brought about or contributed to the degree of inequality that women experience. In many of the more egalitarian cultures (e.g., West African, Native American), colonialization and development has undercut women's autonomy and their value to the community.[30] Western colonialization has systematically reduced women's economic production, forcing them into a position of greater dependence on men. As a result, the women come to be defined by domesticity. Even in the Western industrialized nations, where women have gained autonomy and equality largely through increased access to education, education has not produced gender parity across institutions (or, for that matter, even within education). Women in these countries often lack political rights, equal political representation, work equity, marital equity, and so forth.

In looking more closely at the process of education, then, we must start by understanding that when we speak of education we are referring to the Western idea of education: formal schooling in a hierarchical setting focused on literacy, math, and science skills. In this educational process, the child is routinely removed from the family system for an extended period during most days.[31] In the formal education system, the teacher is seen as the expert (the person with the knowledge) and the student must be able to prove that they have mastered the required (valued) knowledge. The ability to show mastery of such knowledge (literacy, verbal skills, quantitative skills, logic/reasoning skills) and the hidden curriculum (conformity, timeliness, ranks) leads to advancement.

At least in theory, such advancement and the attached status is ungendered. But when we problematize the concepts of "education" and "success"—that is, when we critique the way these concepts are shaped by our history and social systems and in turn impact our everyday experiences in invisible ways—Western education emerges as part of a patriarchal order, and its hidden curriculum, which is gendered, must be explored.[32] As part of an elite, Western, male-dominated system, education allows women to succeed but only on the terms already set down by men—through individual competition where the rewards for those who succeed come at the expense of others. As part of an established system of power and privilege, current systems of education do not challenge but, rather, support male domination and ultimately shape the discourse on change.

Numerous examples exist that illustrate this process. For instance, foot binding in China was ended within two decades through Western education and political pressure that presented foot binding as barbaric.[33] However, while Western ideology and power were used to liberate Chinese women's feet, they were not used to liberate Chinese women from the more usual forms of male oppression.

Another example of the use of Western education and accelerated social change may be seen in the current debates on female genital mutilation (FGM).[34] Eliminating the physical and mental damage perpetuated
on thousands of women who experience female genital mutilation is
likely to be shaped by Western medical discourse rather than any attempt
at female liberation, sexual or otherwise. We can see that this emerging
discourse will be shaped by relations of ruling inside Western industrialized nations, where medical institutions wield power and national aid societies are able to raise and contribute money through the auspices of
health improvement. Such powers may well be able to convince local
elites of the medical and health benefits of eliminating FGM (lowered
mortality rates for young girls, fewer complications at childbirth, and better long-term health for women). Moreover, such information will likely
be disseminated through educational channels, including the transfer of
knowledge and changes to traditions through educated mothers. Like the
campaign against foot binding, this effort promises to be effective, and
any effort that reduces such suffering will be laudable. But we can see that
such an effort will not (and, in fact, cannot) really be focused on women's
autonomy or equality.

Perhaps more importantly, the discourse available, which is shaped by
patriarchal power, leaves us only with the options of romanticizing or
blaming mothers when it comes to their influence on daughters. If we ro-
manticize mothers, we cannot believe that they would want to inflict pain
or deprivation on their daughters. But this seems empirically insupport-
able. Chinese mothers willingly inflicted the pain of bound feet on their
daughters, if partly out of fear that their daughters would reproach them
later in life if they were not marriageable. Somolian mothers see FGM as
a rite of passage, as a cultural identifier, as necessary to ensure their
daughter's ability to marry, despite their intimate knowledge of the pain
and limitations FGM entails. On a less dramatic note, we might also recall
that mothers in the United States expose their daughters to many painful
(or possibly painful) experiences in the name of beauty: curling and per-
ming hair; tweezing eyebrows; waxing, shaving, or chemically removing
hair from legs and underarms; dieting; and so forth.

The point here is that in many cases women's suffering is understood
as necessary and even valued in the name of appearance and marriage-
ability (or, more broadly, competition for men). But to blame mothers is
not to understand women's place in the system either. While mothering
entails protecting children and fostering their growth, it also means socializing children to fit into an existing social world. Therefore, when
mothering occurs in a male-dominated society, mothers must socialize
their daughter to fit into this system.

Therefore, while women's education contributes greatly to their equality and may be passed on to their daughters in a way that produces rapid social change in terms of gender equality, education alone will not ensure gender equity. Rather women must be involved in development, especially education, in ways that ensure their economic and ideological autonomy. But to do this, we, as women, as mothers, and as daughters, must understand how our vision and strategies are shaped by relations of ruling. We must not be content to teach women to "succeed" in the current system of education anymore than we should be content with ending FGM. Instead, we must strive to provide women in all cultures with real choices.

NOTES

1. For instance, F. M. T. Uribe, R. A. LeVine and S. E. LeVine, "Maternal Behavior in a Mexican Community: The Changing Environment of Children," in *Cross-Cultural Roots of Minority Child Development*, ed. P. Greenfield and R. Cocking (Hillsdale, N.J.: Erlbaum, 1994), examine a "demographic transition of major proportions," where Mexico's mortality rate for children under five dropped from 140 per 1,000 to 51 per 1,000 and total fertility declined from 6.8 to 3.4 in just three decades (43).

2. A. C. Smock, *Women's Education in Developing Countries* (New York: Praeger, 1981).

3. For example, S. Cochrane, "The Relationship between Education and Fertility," in *Women, Education, and Modernization of the Family in West Africa*, ed. H. Ware (Miami: Austrian National University Press, 1981); and S. Kaldate, "Educated Women: Equality and Role Conflict," in *Women in India: Equality, Social Justice, and Development*, ed. L. Devasia and V. V. Devasia (New Delhi: Indian Social Institute, 1990).

4. The spread of education worldwide from 1965 to 1986 has been dramatic; the rate of growth for girls' enrollment, however, has outpaced that of boys. See L. H. Summers, "Best Third World Investment? Girls' Education," *The Oregonian* (May 10, 1993); and B. London, "School-Enrollment Rates and Trends, Gender, and Fertility: A Cross-National Analysis," *Sociology of Education* 65 (1992): 306–16.

5. London, "School-Enrollment Rates and Trends, Gender, and Fertility," 306–16; J. Caldwell, "Routes to Low Mortality in Poor Countries," *Population and Development Review* 12 (1986): 171–220.

6. For studies on education as it relates to fertility see Caldwell, "Routes to Low Mortality," 171–220; Cochrane, "The Relationship"; D. Koening, "Education and Fertility among Cameroonian Working Women" in *Women, Education, and Modernization of the Family in West Africa*, ed. Ware; London, "School-Enrollment Rates and Trends, Gender, and Fertility," 306–16; C. Oppong and K. Abu, "Seven Roles of Women: Impact of Education, Migration, and Employment on Ghanaian Mothers," *Women, Work, and Development* 13 (Geneva: International Labor Office, 1987); I. O. Orubuloye, "Education and Socio-Demographic Change in Nigeria: The Western Nigerian Experience," in *Women, Education, and Modernization of the*

Family in West Africa, ed. Ware. For studies on education as it relates to labor-force participation see, for example, A. Benavot, "Education, Gender, and Economic Development: A Cross-National Study," *Sociology of Education* 62 (1989): 14–32; A. W. Brown and H. R. Barrett, "Female Education in Sub-Saharan Africa: The Key to Development?" *Comparative Education* 27, no. 3 (1991): 275–85; R. P. Devadas, G. Ramathilagam, and K. Arulselvam, "Equality of Women through Education and Employment and Challenges to Social Justice," in *Women in India,* ed. Devasia and Devasia; N. Hijab, *Womanpower: The Arab Debate on Women at Work* (New York: Cambridge University Press, 1988); S. Jayaweera, "Education of Girls and Women in the Context of an Economically Developing Society," in *Women at the Cross-roads: A Sri Lankan Perspective,* ed. S. Kiribamune and V. Samarasinghe (New Delhi: Vikas, 1990); Kaldate, "Educated Women"; Oppong and Abu, "Seven Roles of Women"; A. C. Smock and N. H. Youssef, "Egypt: From Seclusion to Limited Participation," in *Women: Roles and Status in Eight Countries,* ed. J. Z. Giele and A. C. Smock (New York: Wiley, 1977); N. H. Youssef, "Differential Labor Force Participation of Women in Latin American and Middle Eastern Countries: The Influence of Family Characteristics," *Social Forces* 51 (1972): 135–53. For studies on education as it relates to marital power, see S. al-Khayyat, *Honor and Shame: Women in Modern Iraq* (London: Saqi, 1990); H. Ballmer and P. C. Cozby, "Family Environments of Women Who Return to College," *Sex Roles* 7 (1981): 1019–26; M. Blais and A. Z. Pulido, "Family, Social Life, and Leisure: Cultural Differences among University Students in Caracas and in Montreal," *McGill Journal of Education* 27 (1992): 150–64; Devadas et al., "Equality of Women"; Kaldate, "Educated Women"; S. Kelly, *The Prize and the Price: The Changing World of Women Who Return to Study* (North Ryde, Australia: Methuen Haynes, 1987); Oppong and Abu, "Seven Roles of Women"; G. N. Ramu, "Indian Husbands: Their Role Perceptions and Performance in Single- and Dual-Earner Families," *Journal of Marriage and the Family* 49 (1987): 903–15; C. Safilios-Rothschild, "Macro- and Micro-Examinations of Family Power and Love," *Journal of Marriage and the Family* 38 (1976): 355–61; R. L. Warner, "Social Organization, Spousal Resources, and Marital Power: A Cross-Cultural Study," *Journal of Marriage and the Family* 48 (1986): 121–28; D. M. Zuckerman, "Family Background, Sex-Role Attitude, and Life Goals of Technical College and University Students," *Sex Roles* 7 (1981): 1109–26.

7. S. M. Clark and S. M. Wright, "Gender, Education, and the Family: A Cross-Cultural Comparison of Women with Postsecondary Education," in *The Young Leaders Forum on the Challenges of the 21st Century: Conference Report* (Beijing: Ryoichi Sasakawa Young Leaders Fellowship Fund, 1994).

8. R. A. LeVine, S. E. LeVine, A. Richman, F. M. T. Uribe, C. S. Correa, and P. M. Miller, "Women's Schooling and Child Care in Demographic Transition: A Mexican Case Study," *Population and Development Review* 17 (1991): 459–496.

9. Uribe et al., "Maternal Behavior in a Mexican Community."

10. Caldwell, "Routes to Low Mortality in Poor Countries," 171–220, in a cross-national comparison, finds the same type of relationship between women's schooling and health and reproductive outcome. In this study, developing countries with "superior achievements" in health improvement, all maintain relatively high rates of girls' school attendance. Conversely, the poorest health achievers all

have extremely low rates of girls' schooling. Countries making "superior achievements" in health improvements include Sri Lanka, Burma, and the state of Kerala in southern India where education of girls is on par with boys. The poorest health achievers include Saudia Arabia, Iran, and Libya.

11. This observed shift in attitudes and behaviors of Mexican women has taken place in just two decades in a culture where the men generally "want more children than their wives and tend to dominate in reproductive decision making" (Uribe et al., "Maternal Behavior in a Mexican Community," 48).

12. Caldwell, "Routes to Low Mortality in Poor Countries," 171–220.

13. For studies that include mothers' education as a variable, see, for example, E. G. Menaghan and T. L. Parcel, "Determining Children's Home Environments: The Impact of Maternal Characteristics and Current Occupational and Family Conditions," *Journal of Marriage and the Family* 53 (1991): 417–31; M. Kalmijn, "Mother's Occupational Status and Children's Schooling," *American Sociological Review* 59 (1994): 257–75; Uribe et al., "Maternal Behavior in a Mexican Community"; K. Sanders, "Mothers and Daughters in the Netherlands: The Influence of the Mother's Social Background on Daughters' Labor Market Participation after They Have Children," *European Journal of Women's Studies* 4 (1997): 165–81. For studies that explore the impact of education on the process of mothering, see, for example, al-Khayyat, *Honor and Shame;* Kaldate, "Educated Women"; Kelly, *The Prize and the Price;* L. Lenero-Otero, *Investigation of the Family in Mexico* (Mexico City: Galve, 1968).

14. T. Skocpol, *Vision and Method in Historical Sociology* (New York: Cambridge University Press, 1984) argues that comparative historical methods have been developed as a means of "understanding the nature and effects of large-scale structures and fundamental processes of change" (4).

15. Countries include the United States, Canada, Australia, Italy, Greece, Mexico, Puerto Rico, Venezuela, Japan, Sri Lanka, India, Iraq, Saudi Arabia, Egypt, Ghana, Nigeria, and Cameroon.

16. Summers, "Best Third World Investment?"

17. Uribe et al., "Maternal Behavior in a Mexican Community."

18. According to Caldwell, in "Routes to Low Mortality," greater female autonomy

renders it more likely that a mother will make her own decision that something must be done when she identifies a child as sick (it also seems to lead her to make that identification at an earlier time), that she will venture outside the home to seek help, that she will struggle for adequate treatment with doctors and nurses, and that she will understand the advice and take responsibility for carrying it out. (202)

19. A. Leibowitz, "Home Investments in Children," *Journal of Political Economy* 82 (1974): S111–31; R. J. Murnane, R. A. Maynard, and J. C. Ohls, "Home Resources and Children's Achievement," *Review of Economics and Statistics* 63 (1981): 369–77.

20. Kalmijn, "Mother's Occupational Status," 260.

21. For example, Lenero-Otero, *Investigation of the Family in Mexico;* H. S. A.

Rawaf, and C. Simmons, "The Education of Women in Saudi Arabia," *Comparative Education* 27 (1991): 287–95.

22. It is understood that when the father is the primary breadwinner, he probably also serves as the central model of socioeconomic achievement. However, according to Kalmijn, in "Mother's Occupational Status," historically, "this was probably more true for sons than for daughters, simply because men were more focused on an occupational career than were women. . . . For girls, fathers and mothers appear to be equally important role models" (261).

23. L. W. Hoffman, "Effects of Maternal Employment on the Child: A Review of the Research," *Developmental Psychology* 10 (1974): 204–28.

24. M. S. Hill and G. J. Duncan, "Parental Family Income and Socioeconomical Attainment of Children," *Social Science Research* 16 (1987): 39–73.

25. P. K. Knaub, "Growing Up in a Dual-Career Family: The Children's Perceptions," *Family Relations* 35 (1986): 431–37; Zuckerman, "Family Background," 1109–26. In fact, in the United States, mothers may be the most influential parent for both young men and young women.

26. Smock, *Women's Education in Developing Countries*.

27. Al-Khayyat, *Honor and Shame*.

28. Mothers, if not fathers, seem to accept challenges to parental authority as part of the socialization process, even when they find them embarrassing, a nuisance, and so on.

29. Oppong and Abu, "Seven Roles of Women."

30. R. Clark, "Multinational Corporate Investment and Women's Participation in Higher Education in Noncore Nations," *Sociology of Education* 65 (1992): 37–47.

31. In boarding schools (whether optional, as in elite communities, or forced, as in Native American communities), the child is removed from the family almost completely.

32. My most grateful appreciation goes to Dorothy Smith and her work on institutional ethnography in *The Everyday World as Problematic: A Feminist Sociology* (Boston: Northeastern University Press, 1987). My participation in a workshop on institutional ethnography at Ontario Institute for Studies in Education (OISE) in Toronto in 1997 created the catalyst for beginning to think about the process of women's education and social change in new ways.

33. G. Smits, *Footbinding: Issues of Sex and Power* (forthcoming).

34. Beverley B. Mack, "Islam and Female Genital Mutilation (FGM): Female Circumcision and Infibulation," paper presented at the American Sociological Association Annual Meetings, Toronto, 1997.

13

Telling Our Stories: Feminist Mothers and Daughters

Christina Baker

> Most of what has been, or is, between mothers, daughters, and in motherhood, in daughterhood, has never been recorded, nor written with comprehension in our own voices, out of our own lives and truths.
>
> —Tillie Olsen[1]

As we interviewed feminist mothers and daughters for our book *The Conversation Begins*, my daughter and I asked each mother and daughter pair to talk about their own relationship as they attempted to live their feminism. During our interviews with more than twenty-five pioneers of feminism's second wave and their now-grown daughters, two questions were uppermost in our minds: First, had these feminist mothers passed down a feminist legacy to their daughters? Second, what were the costs for mothers and daughters of combining motherhood with a passionate commitment to a broader life? The answer to our first question—had feminist mothers passed down a feminist legacy to their daughters?—was a simple yes. Although not all the daughters are activists like their mothers, all are practicing feminists.

Feminist mothers are world changers; they believe in justice. When Tillie Olsen's daughter Julie came home from school one day quoting the old chestnut, "I complained because I had no shoes until I met a man who had no feet," Tillie responded, "Then I hope you complained twice as hard because both conditions are lousy and neither should be tolerated."[2] Journalist Barbara Ehrenreich says that after her children were born she wanted to change the world for them: "I felt I wouldn't be a good mother if I wasn't stopping nuclear war while making a nutritional dinner." But she adds, "You have to be a superparent to raise children and make the world safe for them at the same time."[3]

Feminist mothers conveyed confidence as well as principles to their daughters. Attorney Lori Smeal, daughter of Eleanor Smeal, twice president of the National Organization of Women and current president of the Feminist Majority, learned she was "capable of doing any job . . . capable of anything."[4] Nina Beck, physical therapist and daughter of author and professor Evelyn Torton Beck, says, "I was told that if I wanted to be a rocket scientist, nothing would stand in my way. In fact, I think I was expected to be a rocket scientist."[5] Kirsten Wilson, a performance artist, has drawn great strength from the knowledge that her mother, Ms. Foundation president Marie Wilson, loves the rebel in her—"the part that is inappropriate, that is too loud, that says the wrong things." Knowing she is worthy in her mother's eyes means Kirsten can "dare to be different."[6] For daughters of feminists, the idea of equality handed down by their mothers is securely in place.

Answers, however, to our second question—what were the personal costs of combining motherhood and activism?—were more complicated and sometimes troubling. Motherhood is a topic which the women's movement has addressed, when it has done so at all, with ambivalence. Since Betty Friedan's clarion call in *The Feminine Mystique* for women to leave the "comfortable concentration camp of the home and find added fulfillment in careers,"[7] women have struggled to combine motherhood and feminism, often in lonely silence. Second-wave pioneer and author Alix Kates Shulman recalls motherhood as "one of the great explosive divides"[8] in the women's movement. Barbara Seaman, founder of the women's health movement, remembers "a lot of debate about whether you could be a mother and a feminist."[9] *Ms.* magazine cofounder Letty Cottin Pogrebin wrote in 1973 that a discussion of motherhood would "shake sisterhood to its roots."[10]

The reason is apparent. Feminist motherhood complicates the role of the emancipated woman. In *The Second Shift,* Arlie Hochschild tells us that "feminism is infinitely easier when you take motherhood out, but then it speaks to fewer women."[11] Bearing and nurturing children remain a fact of life for more than 90 percent of women worldwide. Two decades after Adrienne Rich lamented in *Of Woman Born* that motherhood remained a "crucial, still relatively unexplored, area for feminist theory,"[12] the discussion remains in its early stages.

Despite the second wave's silence on the subject, motherhood and feminism have always been inextricably linked. Tillie Olsen, in her mideighties when we interviewed her, declares:

> Motherhood remains central in my life;—more than illuminator, instructor of my feminism—touchstone for sustenance, hope, connectedness, self

knowledge; human understanding, beauty, and anguish; yes, and well-spring, passionate source for all I am, do, write.[13]

In reality, the experiences of pregnancy and giving birth led many women to feminism. Congresswoman Patsy Mink, who learned in 1976 that she had been issued diethylstilbestrol (DES) two decades earlier as part of an experimental study, led the fight for gender equity in Congress. Barbara Seaman, enraged upon learning that her infant's illness was caused by a routinely administered laxative that had traveled through her breast milk, used her anger to found the National Women's Health Network. Barbara Ehrenreich became radicalized after her doctor, impatient to leave for vacation, introduced the speed-up drug oxytocin into her otherwise normal labor.

Motherhood for feminists remains fraught with problems. "Mothering is so unsupported in our society that every attempt to raise a child is a complex juggling act,"[14] says Shulman. Early childhood specialist Julie Olsen Edwards, who says that mothering is "the hardest thing I have ever done,"[15] still grieves over the things she couldn't do for her children in a political climate that "wages war on children" and where often families have to "go it alone."[16] Marie Wilson agrees: "Mothering should be joyous work, but trying to raise children in isolation is crazy. Children need to connect to caring adults, lots of them." Wilson adds, "We live in a culture that neither appreciates nor rewards parenting, a culture where the difficulty and hard work of constantly being responsible for another life is enormously denied."[17]

Mother-blame still permeates much of our culture. For many women, says Barbara Seaman, "the way you spell mother is G-U-I-L-T." A manuscript that Seaman began writing years ago, entitled "The American Mother: Whatever You Do, It's Wrong," remains unfinished because she felt "too guilty" as a mother.[18] To remain credible, the women's movement must tackle in earnest the question of how to further the advancement of women and at the same time create conditions that guarantee the adequate nurturing of children.

History reminds us that women have always worked outside the home. Prior to 1940, most middle-class women did so before rather than after marriage. My own mother, for example, had no choice but to resign her teaching position when she married in 1928; married women were not allowed to teach in North Carolina. During World War II, women demonstrated their competence at jobs normally held by men. Although most women returned home immediately after the war, they began to reenter the workforce after their childbearing years.

As the century turns, motherhood is no longer the assumed way of life and calling it was at midcentury; rather, mothering competes with career and personal growth as a source of a woman's identity. In 1996, 77 percent of all married women with school-age children were employed or looking for work. For those with preschool-age children, the figure was 63 percent—five times what it was in 1950. In addition, more than a quarter of all children live in single-parent families with mothers who work full-time. Society, however, has not yet caught up with this cultural redefinition. Neither employers nor government nor many men recognize that mothers need support if they are to balance what Andrew J. Cherlin calls "their double burden."

Not surprisingly, the gravest health crisis currently facing mothers, according to Seaman, is exhaustion.[19] Despite progress over the past two decades, employed women continue to do between 70 and 80 percent of all housework including most of the repetitive chores, laboring from dawn to dusk and beyond. In addition to the "second shift" identified by Arlie Hochschild—that of housework, parenting, and emotion work—most women undertake a "third shift."[20] Routinely ignored by policymakers and analysts, this shift involves the maintenance of community—caring for relatives and friends outside the home by keeping in touch through letters, phone calls, visits, and invitations.

All told, women who work outside the home devote thirty-five more hours per week than their male partners, the equivalent of an extra month each year, to the second and third shifts. Women have reduced the amount of time they spent doing housework in the past two decades (take-out food sales have increased, while floor-wax sales have gone down), but husbands and male partners have been slow to pick up the slack. While men have increased the amount of social time they spend with their children, mothers still do more than 80 percent of the day-to-day physical care. Letty Cottin Pogrebin says that her daughter, television producer Abigail Pogrebin, is honest about the fact that "you can't be a superwoman without help. Something is going to slip or drop."[21] Those 14 percent to 20 percent of mothers who can afford to hire outside help do so.

Second-wave feminists who tell their stories in *The Conversation Begins* testify to their personal struggles with these issues. In 1969, Shulman, mother of two, saw that the only way toward true equality in marriage was genuine "task sharing." Her defiant manifesto, "A Marriage Agreement," proposed that men and women play equal roles in taking care of their children and their households. After *Life* and *Redbook* published the "Agreement," Shulman was flooded with letters asking how she got her husband to agree. Twenty-five years later, she says, "The answer is, either he agrees or the marriage is over; but I never said so outright. Despite our best efforts, our agreement didn't work very well. I wanted [my husband] to take responsibility; he wanted to escape."[22]

For some men, escape took the form of rationalization. Eager to get back to work after her daughter, Nguyen, was born, Miriam Ching Louie, a grassroots activist, remembers arguing with her husband, Belvin. "We have to figure out if it's worth your going to work because of the cost of child care," he said. "Maybe it's not worth it." Finally, Louie asked, "How come the price of a baby-sitter is deducted from my salary? How come the cost of the sitter is not deducted from both our salaries?" And she returned to work.[23]

The few fortunate women for whom motherhood and feminism did not clash cite supportive partners as the reason. Patsy Mink says, "A supportive husband made it easier. Because I spent so much of my time organizing and attending meetings, John played a large role in raising Wendy. . . . One of us was there all the time."[24] Smeal's husband made it "immensely easier to do what I did—and probably made it possible. He was always supportive . . . able to be fully present when I wasn't around."[25] Deborah Wolf acknowledges the strong framework of support provided by her husband: "Leonard helped enormously. He was more nurturing than I, and in many respects he was a model feminist father."[26] Ehrenreich's husband did "more than half the childrearing." While she worked, he took care of daughter Rosa, and even after their divorce, he came over to cook dinner three nights a week for the children.[27] Yolande Moses, president of City College of New York, notes that her husband has been the primary parent "two-thirds of the time." She also had helpful assistance from a sister and mother, but the efforts of the husband were crucial. "That's how I've been able to do it," Moses concludes.[28]

Some daughters of these feminists thought of their attentive fathers as equal if not prime caregivers in the home. About her father, attorney Lori Smeal says, "He was an unusual father; not only was he always there for my brother and me, he also helped out at home by cleaning, doing laundry, and cooking."[29] Writer Naomi Wolf observes that her parents' egalitarian relationship gave her "a skewed sense of what was normal. I thought the whole world was going to be like that bubble of tolerance and progression I grew up in and was astonished to find it wasn't true."[30] Rosa Ehrenreich, an attorney, says, "Dad was around the whole time I was growing up." Even after her parents' divorce, she says, "We occasionally had bizarre situations where Mom would be out of town, Dad would come over to make dinner, and my stepfather, my brother, and I would join him at the table."[31] Shana Moses Bawek, a college student, underscores the point: "My father has been the primary parent. I would not be the same person if my father hadn't been around as much as he was."[32] College student Nguyen Louie felt closer to her father "because he did things with me."[33]

Whether or not they had supportive husbands, all our feminist mothers needed some form of mother substitute to help them through. Seaman, insisting that her housekeeper, Ann P. Wilson, be included in the photographs of mothers and daughters in *The Conversation Begins,* says candidly, "Behind every mother you ever heard of there usually stands another woman who propped her up." She adds, "If we don't do more to provide affordable child care and other assistance to mothers, the slow ascent of women toward equality will stall and our children will be in major trouble."[34] Most mothers cannot choose not to work, but until quality child care is available and affordable for all, equality for women remains elusive.

Some mothers were astonishingly candid in retrospect about the conflict between being active in the world and being present for their daughters. Full-time activist Elizabeth Martinez says that she was often not available to her daughter, Tessa, adding that she was there for her only in emergencies or on occasions like graduation.[35] Evelyn Torton Beck recalls being "so preoccupied with discovering her own capabilities" that she wasn't fully present for her children. Beck sometimes wonders "if daughters have a particular way of getting lost when their mothers are trying to find themselves, especially if the daughter is the firstborn."[36] Helen Rodriguez-Trias, an international leader of the women's health movement, regrets "not being more attentive, not taking more time with the kids."[37]

The daughters spell out their responses clearly. Rodriguez-Trias's daughter, nutritionist Laura Brainen-Rodriguez, says, "I was resentful that my mother was gone so much. I always felt she wanted to be the mother of the world, but not my mother."[38] Her sister, psychiatrist JoEllen Brainen-Rodriguez, adds, "I have missed having [my mother] present for me. I told her, 'I want you to be a grandparent to your grandchildren.' I still wish she were more present for me, which is evidence of how powerful childhood longings are."[39] Teacher Shira Seaman says, "I often felt that I had to compete with my mother's work. I felt that other people got her attention and I didn't. She was preoccupied, and I sometimes felt abandoned."[40]

Daughters admit to having sometimes felt abandoned by their feminist mothers. Lauralee Brown, a singer, says her mother, Paula Gunn Allen, was often absent: "I never seemed to be able to get enough attention from her. She had a studio and was painting and writing poetry. . . . To get her attention was really difficult."[41] Rainy Dawn Ortiz remembers that her mother, poet and singer Joy Harjo, was away on trips a lot: "I know it was part of her career, but it was rough at times. There were times I wished she had been there to help me or could have seen what I was going through."[42]

Daughters' attitudes ranged from resentment to resignation. Kianga Stroud, a student and daughter of activist Nkenge Toure, says, "We were latchkey kids. A lot of times I wished my mother had been at home. I resented her for being away at meetings. I felt neglected, and I missed her."[43] Shana Moses Bawek says of her mother, "The way I see it, she's trying to be perfect, to have a good job and be a mom who is present all the time, but that's impossible. You can't be in two places at once. . . . I like my mother best when she is just being my mom."[44]

Mothers usually found it easier to integrate one child into their lives. Television anchorwoman Carol Jenkins says, "Elizabeth became my little partner. I took her everywhere I could, including work. She simply became part of my working life. When I did the news, she would stretch out under the anchor's desk and color."[45] Shamita Das Dasgupta, professor and author, carried her daughter with her to classes and demonstrations—wherever she went. "Sayantani was part of me, like my arm," she says. "I couldn't stick my role as a feminist in one compartment and my role as a mother and wife in another." Das Dasgupta believes strongly that you "cannot give quality time if you don't spend quantity time with a child."[46]

Third-wave daughters are beginning to speak out about the next hurdle for feminism: finding a balance between family and career. Abigail Pogrebin says clearly what many pioneers of the second wave are only beginning to admit publicly:

> Women having kids right now are having a tough time. It's not clear how to handle all the demands or the conflicting pulls. There should be some room for addressing the pitfalls of the career–family balancing act—especially for my generation. . . . Maybe it's not possible to have a husband, kids, career, and toned body all at the same time. There are costs, and I don't think it's terrible to acknowledge that.[47]

Mothering one's own daughters as feminists especially requires rigorous personal honesty. Marie Wilson, a mother of five, notes:

> It is important to tell the truth, that we not pretend to live in these we-can-have-it-all pictures. There are costs. . . . That we abandoned our children in some ways while we did the work to save them in others is real. It is important not to gloss things over or to slip into the trap that because we are feminists we were perfect mothers who raised perfectly feminist daughters. We learn most from each other when we are honest about our own lives.[48]

Shulman says, "How you parent involves not just your political commitment or ideology but your whole sociological and psychic makeup."[49] Although feminism influences our mothering, it is only a part of the picture.

The way we parent our children stems in large measure from our own personal experiences. Feminists must address the causes and effects of dysfunction in our own lives if we wish to change the world. Paula Gunn Allen points the way:

> If I can unsnarl the dreadful historical tangle of intergenerational dysfunction, then my children will not have to continue the cycle; we can all let go of it and do something else. That is a legacy I would like to leave my children and grandchildren.[50]

Allen's daughter, Lauralee Brown, now in her midforties, has arrived at a place of understanding:

> In the sixties and seventies my mother tried to instill in me a self-assurance she didn't have herself at the time. I'd tell my friends, "She's got me believing and behaving in ways that she doesn't even truly believe or behave in yet." She helped forge the way by not breaking down, by going through therapy, and enriching her own knowledge. I know that any action she took and any choices she made when I was growing up were the best she could do. . . . Certainly some of it was painful for me and I didn't understand it, but she has made every effort to heal that. . . . She has gone through a lot of recovery and therapy to be a good mother.[51]

That effort was echoed in the experience of other feminist mothers and daughters we interviewed. Forging a new relationship with her daughter, Tessa, Elizabeth Martinez found that "all sorts of emotions and complications" required attention. The night her mother died, Elizabeth went back to her apartment with Tessa, and there they talked until dawn. "Tessa told me about things that had been difficult for her in our relationship, things she had not said before," recalled Elizabeth. "At some point I had the sense just to listen. I didn't even feel defensive, and was glad she talked."[52]

The conversation has begun as we learn from feminist pioneers who have gone before. In the past, mothers everywhere offered their daughters the best love they knew. Today feminism informs and strengthens the mother-daughter bond as we—mothers and daughters together—continue to expand our vision of social justice and deepen our self-knowledge. Therein lies the healing of ourselves, each other, and the world. May the conversation continue.

NOTES

1. Tillie Olsen, *Mother to Daughter, Daughter to Mother* (New York: Feminist Press, 1984), 275.

2. Christina Looper Baker and Christina Baker Kline, *The Conversation Begins: Mothers and Daughters Talk about Living Feminism* (New York: Bantam, 1996), 21.

3. Baker and Kline, *The Conversation Begins*, 253.
4. Baker and Kline, *The Conversation Begins*, 199.
5. Baker and Kline, *The Conversation Begins*, 112.
6. Baker and Kline, *The Conversation Begins*, 229.
7. Betty Friedan, *The Feminine Mystique* (New York: Dell, 1963), 266.
8. Baker and Kline, *The Conversation Begins*, 91.
9. Baker and Kline, *The Conversation Begins*, 135.
10. Quoted in Baker and Kline, *The Conversation Begins*, xv.
11. Quoted in Baker and Kline, *The Conversation Begins*, xv.
12. Adrienne Rich, *Of Woman Born* (New York: Norton, 1976), xvii.
13. Baker and Kline, *The Conversation Begins*, 19.
14. Baker and Kline, *The Conversation Begins*, 95.
15. Baker and Kline, *The Conversation Begins*, 27.
16. Baker and Kline, *The Conversation Begins*, 28.
17. Baker and Kline, *The Conversation Begins*, 223.
18. Baker and Kline, *The Conversation Begins*, 123.
19. Baker and Kline, *The Conversation Begins*, 126.
20. Arlie Hochschild, *The Second Shift* (New York: Avon, 1989).
21. Baker and Kline, *The Conversation Begins*, 183.
22. Baker and Kline, *The Conversation Begins*, 93.
23. Baker and Kline, *The Conversation Begins*, 338.
24. Baker and Kline, *The Conversation Begins*, 52.
25. Baker and Kline, *The Conversation Begins*, 196–97.
26. Baker and Kline, *The Conversation Begins*, 144.
27. Baker and Kline, *The Conversation Begins*, 255–56.
28. Baker and Kline, *The Conversation Begins*, 303.
29. Baker and Kline, *The Conversation Begins*, 201.
30. Baker and Kline, *The Conversation Begins*, 150.
31. Baker and Kline, *The Conversation Begins*, 260–61.
32. Baker and Kline, *The Conversation Begins*, 310–11.
33. Baker and Kline, *The Conversation Begins*, 343.
34. Baker and Kline, *The Conversation Begins*, 126.
35. Baker and Kline, *The Conversation Begins*, 38.
36. Baker and Kline, *The Conversation Begins*, 108.
37. Baker and Kline, *The Conversation Begins*, 71.
38. Baker and Kline, *The Conversation Begins*, 79.
39. Baker and Kline, *The Conversation Begins*, 77–78.
40. Baker and Kline, *The Conversation Begins*, 134.
41. Baker and Kline, *The Conversation Begins*, 216.
42. Baker and Kline, *The Conversation Begins*, 380–81.
43. Baker and Kline, *The Conversation Begins*, 365.
44. Baker and Kline, *The Conversation Begins*, 311, 315.
45. Baker and Kline, *The Conversation Begins*, 269.
46. Baker and Kline, *The Conversation Begins*, 318.
47. Baker and Kline, *The Conversation Begins*, 179, 181.

48. Baker and Kline, *The Conversation Begins,* 228.
49. Baker and Kline, *The Conversation Begins,* 95.
50. Baker and Kline, *The Conversation Begins,* 212.
51. Baker and Kline, *The Conversation Begins,* 218–19.
52. Baker and Kline, *The Conversation Begins,* 39.

14

Biting the Hand That Feeds You: Feminism as the "Bad Mother"

Astrid Henry

In her introduction to *Daughters of Feminists*, Rose Glickman writes:

> In a profound sense all women roughly between the ages of eighteen and
> thirty-five, whether they embrace or reject feminism, are the daughters of
> feminism, heir to its struggles, failures, and successes; inheritors, willy-nilly,
> of the heroic phase of the modern women's movement.[1]

Here Glickman describes feminism as a mother figure, giving birth, as it
were, to a generation of women whose lives will be radically different
than those of the women who came before them. The question becomes,
then, how will these "daughters" treat their "mother feminism"? By examining the writing of so-called third-wave writers, such as Katie Roiphe,
Rebecca Walker, Rene Denfeld, and Naomi Wolf, it becomes clear that the
mother-daughter relation has become a central trope in depicting the relationship between the second and third waves of U.S. feminism. What
complicates this generational structure, however, is that there appears to
be two "mothers" in this writing: relationships to biological, or "real,"
mothers seem to coexist alongside relationships to this "mother feminism."

First a note about my terminology. Although I am skeptical as to
whether what is being called "the third wave" actually constitutes a new
wave of feminism, I use the term both as a kind of shorthand for a generational difference, based on chronological age, and to represent the desire
of those who embrace this term to signal a "new" feminism, one that is
distinct from the second wave. I am aware, however, that in using the
term I am helping reify it.[2]

The term *third wave* has been attributed to Rebecca Walker, daughter of second-wave feminist Alice Walker, who first used it in a 1992 *Ms.* essay; later that same year, Walker cofounded a national organization called Third Wave devoted to young women's activism. In her 1992 essay "Becoming the Third Wave," Walker uses the term to emphasize both that feminism is not dead and that a new generation of feminists are beginning to mobilize. As she states, "I am not a postfeminism feminist. I am the Third Wave."[3] In defining herself as not postfeminist, Walker insists that she has not moved beyond the space created by the second wave; she is not beyond feminism. Yet her naming of herself as "the Third Wave" suggests that she is, in fact, charting new territory, relying on the connotation of progress suggested by the term. The bravado behind her claim "I am the Third Wave" would further seem to suggest a breaking away from second-wave feminism—the feminism of her mother—even as it disavows this break.

If this third-wave writing is any indication, it would seem that feminism is experienced quite differently by those who come to it a generation after the second wave. When we come to feminism, we are confronting a social and political movement and theory that already exists. Third-wave feminists do not bring feminism into being; we do not create feminism from scratch. Our response to feminism, then, will invariably involve a whole set of issues that second-wave feminists did not have to confront. This is not to imply, of course, that second-wave feminists "invented" feminism. However, their experience of becoming feminists and developing a women's movement had a sense of newness, discovery, and rebellion about it that cannot be said of the third wave. The newness, discovery, and particularly the rebellion offered by third-wave writers lies somewhere else than in the act of making feminism. They lie in the confrontation with it.

As many third-wave commentators have noted, for women of our generation "feminism is our birthright."[4] Given this unique and historically unprecedented relationship to feminism, women in their twenties and thirties inevitably experienced feminism in very different ways than did women of our mothers' generation. Particularly for those of us who were raised by feminist parents to be feminists, feminism is a given, handed to us at birth. It is not something we need to seek out or fight for. "I didn't spend much time thinking about feminism," Katie Roiphe writes in *The Morning After*. "It was something assumed, something deep in my foundations."[5] Roiphe's description of feminism as that which is "deep in her foundations"—like Rebecca Walker's statement that feminism "has always been so close to home"—suggests that feminism is indeed "our birthright," a kind of genetic inheritance, passed down at birth.[6]

To understand feminism as something we inherit rather than create on our own has significant consequences for the way we take on the cause of feminism, and identify as feminists. As one third-wave writer notes, we often experience feminism as "a sense of entitlement."[7] Women in their twenties and early thirties, according to one commentator, have been "raised with a sense of entitlement, they had working mothers and women's studies. They took *Roe v. Wade,* the Pill, and affirmative action for granted. . . . They assumed they would have it all."[8] This sense of entitlement has meant that for women of my generation, feminism is no longer the volatile issue that it was for our mothers; it is not, as Roiphe puts it, something we need to "spend much time thinking about."[9] In the generational shift from second to third wave, then, we have seen feminism transform from a controversial political ideology that had to be actively chosen to one that is often taken for granted and not given much thought.

For women of my generation becoming a feminist is, therefore, no longer the process that it once was.[10] We rarely come to feminism in the same way that our mothers' generation did. As Barbara Findlen writes in *Listen Up: Voices from the Next Feminist Generation,* "My feminism wasn't shaped by antiwar or civil rights activism; I was not a victim of the problem that had no name."[11] We don't need to get to feminism through some means—whether consciousness-raising, activism, or reevaluating our personal relationships—because feminism is already there for us.[12] We don't need to create feminism; it already exists. We don't need to become feminists; we already are. "So when I was very young I thought of feminism as something like a train you could catch and ride to someplace better," Roiphe writes. "My grandmother missed it, but my mother caught it."[13] If feminism is indeed like a train heading toward "someplace better," it may be that for third-wave feminists the train has already reached its destination. While Roiphe's grandmother missed the train and her mother caught it, Roiphe herself may not need to take the trip at all. If she is already "someplace better," is there anywhere for her to go?

Because women of my generation often do not experience feminism as a process—that is, as something we actively choose or help to create—we have a much more ambivalent identification with it. Even for those of us who see ourselves as aligned with second-wave feminism, our sense of owning feminism can still feel tenuous. We own feminism in the sense that it is our birthright, yet in other ways it is not ours. It belongs to another generation, another group of women: second-wave feminists. They were the ones who went through the heady experience of creating feminism; we just get to reap the benefits.

To get a sense of how different feminism felt for second-wave feminists, one need only look at Gloria Steinem's introduction to Walker's *To Be Real.* She writes, "Because I entered when feminism had to be chosen and even reinvented, I experienced almost everything about it as an unmitigated and joyful freedom—and I still do."[14] When one compares

Steinem's "unmitigated and joyful freedom" with the depressing sense of confinement and curbed independence found in some third-wave texts, it is clear that there has been a definite generational shift in the way that women experience feminism. Perhaps the third-wave criticism that feminism feels constricting—as opposed to feeling like unmitigated freedom—should be read as a lament for what we missed out on: entering feminism when it had to be chosen and reinvented. We don't go through this process, and so feminism feels different to us.

It may be that the third-wave "reinvention" of feminism is an attempt to gain access to the heady and wonderful feelings we were denied by accident of birth. Even the naming of a new wave seems to suggest a desire for a new beginning, one which will give women of my generation our own origins. One might see the resistance to contemporary feminism espoused by Denfeld, Roiphe, and Wolf as a sign of their opposition to merely inheriting the feminism of the previous generation. In other words, they don't want feminism handed down to them; they want to (re)create it for themselves. Paradoxically, these third-wave writers attempt to recreate the "joyful freedom" of the feminist past by breaking away from feminism. While Steinem achieved this sense of freedom through the identification with feminism, for some third-wave writers it would seem that freedom can only come through disidentification.

There are, however, other methods of re-creating or transforming feminism than repudiating the past. The desire to break free from the previous generation seems indicative of a particular kind of feminism, one that is more interested in claiming the spotlight than it is in maintaining connections, particularly when those connections are difficult. This method of relating to the past seems particularly foreign to me as someone working within academic feminism. In my feminist world, feminisms are critiqued, dismissed, and often trashed, to be sure, but it is rare that one sees an academic feminist completely repudiate all that came before her in order to proclaim herself the harbinger of something new. Not only would this be considered sloppy research, but it would go against a fundamental principle of academic writing: namely that however original one's own thoughts and ideas, they are invariably indebted to the thoughts and ideas which came before them. In other words, ideas are built on other ideas. I would argue that within most academic feminism a lineage is maintained between ideas and between thinkers, even when that connection is made through critique rather than praise.

In the work of Denfeld, Roiphe, and Wolf, however, there is relatively little articulation of such a lineage. Rather, what I am calling the academic model of maintaining connections is replaced by something closer to disavowal or rejection. Perhaps the explanation for this disavowal can be explained, in part, by the fact that they are writing popular books aimed at a mass audience. Since this audience is not going to hold their work to academic standards, they are able to present themselves as vanguards of a new movement without having to do the more difficult work of unraveling the various feminisms that led us to this present moment.

The third wave's tendency to make a clean break with the past rather than maintain a sense of connection may be inevitable given the way in which they describe their relationship to feminism and the previous generation of feminists. Conceiving of feminism as a "birthright" passed from mother to daughter undoubtedly influences their understanding of and relationship to it. It may be that something inherited from one's mother will be rejected, no matter what it is. It may be that a "birthright," bound up as it is with one's mother, is unable to produce individuality. To identify with one's mother—with her feminism, with being like her—may ultimately produce rebellion, a desire to "move away," as Denfeld calls for.[15]

In fact, I would argue that the excessive focus on individualism in the work of Denfeld, Roiphe, and Wolf is more than just a sign of their preference for liberal feminism. In their descriptions of what this individuality is in opposition to, one gets the sense that, for them, individuality is a way of resisting the group identity implied by the terms *feminists* and *women*.[16] Beyond simply disidentifying with these two identity categories, it may be that this resistance also suggests a desire to break away from their mothers, both real and figurative. In *Fire with Fire*, for example, Wolf describes power feminism, the feminism she advocates, as that which "encourages a woman to claim her individual voice rather than merging her voice in a collective identity."[17] Wolf gives us a clue as to what individuality represents for many third-wave feminists: it is the antithesis of "merging her voice in a collective identity." What is to be resisted is staying (sub)merged in collectivity. Wolf's description suggests that to retain—or even to gain—one's identity and autonomy, one must "unmerge," move away, break free.

In psychoanalytic terms, the notion that one achieves autonomy and individuality through making a "clean break" from the mother has traditionally been ascribed to the male experience. As part of the individuation process, girls must also separate from their mothers, but because of the gender identification between a girl and her mother, this process is often more difficult, more confusing, and less clear. It has been argued that the inability to make such a clean break from the mother—which is, of course, itself an impossible fantasy—causes women to experience their identity as relational. That is, self-identity is always interconnected with the identity of the other, causing girls and women to have less investment in the defensive clean-break model of autonomy exhibited by many boys and men.[18] While this theory has been adopted by many feminists to

stress the positive psychological traits produced by such identity formation, in general, it has not been able to account for the more "negative"—or perhaps less idealized—aspects of the female individuation
process.[19] In particular, feelings such as ambivalence and even outright
hostility toward the mother have gone relatively unexplored.

In the third wave's relationship to the second wave, I believe we see
signs of the difficulty that individuation poses for women, particularly in
the face of a powerful mother figure: in this case, feminism. In both their
retaining of the identity "feminist" and in the rare moments when they
champion second-wave feminism, the desire to maintain a connection to
their mothers' generation—and often their real mothers—is apparent.
Like the shared gender identity between mother and daughter, they are
not easily able to extricate themselves from the shared identity of "feminist." In their more frequent attempts to radically break free from the
feminism of the past, however, their desire for autonomy and their own
individual identity is exposed. They want a shared connection through
feminism, but they want their freedom and individuality too.[20]

Calling feminism a birthright reveals the way that familial metaphors,
specifically the mother-daughter relation, seem to serve as an effective
shorthand for larger and more complicated conflicts and differences
among and between various versions of feminism.[21] This is particularly
evident in discussions of the current generational structure between
second- and third-wave feminists, based as it is on an age difference that
is the equivalent of one generation. When the mother-daughter trope is
relied on to describe generational conflicts between feminists, feminism
often appears as "an embittered, puritanical mother," to quote one commentator.[22] Thinking of feminism as a mother, let alone a "puritanical"
one, profoundly shapes the kinds of relationships that will be possible
between that feminism and the successive generation of feminists. Can
anything passed down from mother to daughter be revolutionary, or will
it, by necessity, be something to be resisted and dismissed? What does it
mean to write as a daughter in the face of "mother feminism"? What is
at stake for third-wave "daughters" in maintaining a connection to their
second-wave "mothers" through such conflict or rebellion? Finally, what
are alternative models for struggling with feminism and feminist history
than those offered by rebelling against mother feminism?

Given feminism's tendency to ebb and flow as a political movement, it
may be that feminist generational conflict will inevitably be mapped onto
the mother-daughter relation, which has its own set of dynamics surrounding change, progress, and regression. One generation, whether
feminist or familial, may reject the past, the next may carry on its tradition. One generation may be conservative, the next radical. A woman's
relationship to feminism, then, may invariably be bound up with her rela-

tionship to her mother and her mother's generation of women. A first-wave feminist writing in 1871, according to historian Carroll Smith-Rosenberg, "experienced her feminism as a revolt against her mother's ways."[23] A young antifeminist woman interviewed for a 1982 article on "the postfeminist generation" said, "My feelings about feminism are at least partially a reaction to my [feminist] mother."[24] Feminism may be embraced as either a "revolt" against one's mother or as a way of identifying with her, while the same may be true of the rejection of feminism.

The authors that I have examined here—Rene Denfeld, Katie Roiphe, Rebecca Walker, and Naomi Wolf—all were raised by feminist mothers.[25] These "real" mothers are unequivocally described in positive terms in their texts.[26] What they bequeath these women is desired and praised.[27] These are the "good mothers" of third-wave feminism. However, relationships to these real mothers coexist alongside relationships to "mother feminism": a "mother" who more often than not is described as confining, regulating, and puritanical. What this mother feminism bequeaths is unwanted, and these third-wave writers seem to reject what she has to offer. She is the "bad mother" of these texts.

In Roiphe's *The Morning After*, for example, these two relationships are represented by two central figures in the text. The first is Roiphe's biological mother, Anne Roiphe, herself a well-known feminist author, who represents Roiphe's notion of "good feminism": equality feminism that advocates sexual liberation and is against censorship. As such, she is the "good mother" of Roiphe's text.[28] The other figure is Catherine MacKinnon, who plays an equally pivotal role in *The Morning After* as the dour feminist who "looks like someone's aunt" but acts as the strict, prohibitive voice of contemporary feminism and all that is wrong with it.[29] The different relationships that Roiphe has to these two women is representative of the relation between the third and second waves as described in much third-wave writing. In other words, while these writers frequently represent their relationships to their own mothers as being positive, especially when those mothers are feminists, there is nevertheless the sense in which feminism itself—whether embodied in a figure such as MacKinnon or not—has come to stand for the "bad mother" of second-wave feminism: the mother who lays down the rules and keeps curfew. Conceiving of the conflict between second- and third-wave feminists as merely a daughter's rebellion against her mother, then, is not entirely accurate. For it is not real mothers who seem to be rebelled against but, rather, mother feminism.[30]

As feminist generations proliferate and feminist waves arise, we will need to continue to rethink our understanding of women's relationship to feminism and other women. One of the reasons that the mother-daughter relation is such a powerful trope, both within feminism and in the culture at large, is that we have relatively few models by which to talk about relationships among and between women. The rhetoric of sisterhood that was so common in early second-wave writing—"sisterhood is powerful"—provides us with one model. Yet too frequently, this model seems reliant on similarity and stability at the expense of difference and conflict. (I myself have always found this somewhat odd, since in my experience, sibling rivalry and difference is inherent in sisterhood and should not be read as antithetical to it.) Within both the mother-daughter and sisterhood models, the legacy of women's socialization in dealing with conflict is also apparent. That is, both offer little in terms of how to think about women's anger and jealousy toward other women.

A central problem with the mother-daughter trope is that it forces us to remain within a familial model that lends itself too easily to a psychoanalytic interpretation. Unfortunately, unlike with the father-son relation, classic psychoanalysis has very little to offer us in terms of an understanding of the mother-daughter relation, especially when it comes to conflict. Even within feminist psychoanalytic work, like that of Nancy Chodorow or Jessica Benjamin, for example, very little has been said about the role of conflict and antagonism within this relationship.[31] Part of the problem is that within the psychoanalytic framework there is no equivalent of the Oedipal model for women, leaving us without a means by which to discuss the daughter's desire to "kill the mother." As Erica Duncan argues in her essay "Mothers and Daughters," the story of Electra is often offered as a competing narrative to the Oedipal model; however, "the Electra story, frequently presented as the paler parallel of the Oedipal myth, deals with revenge for the death of the father and not with any autonomous desire to possess what the mother possesses."[32] Duncan's essay stresses the fact that we have no tradition of "the usurper daughter" from which to begin thinking about such conflicts between mothers and daughters; there is a "total absence of competitive daughters in our literature."[33]

This has caused many feminists, I think, to downplay what is a fairly strong expression of hostility in some of these third-wave texts. Susan Faludi, for example, has argued that "The old Oedipal thing of killing one's father is not what this is about."[34] And Gloria Steinem offers:

> Finally, it would help to remember that a feminist revolution rarely resembles a masculine-style one—just as a young woman's most radical act toward her mother (that is, connecting as women in order to help each other get some power) doesn't look much like a young man's most radical act toward his father (that is, breaking the father-son connection in order to separate identities or take over existing power).[35]

In this, I would disagree with Steinem. In fact, many of the young women I have discussed here see their "most radical act" toward mother feminism as "breaking" the mother-daughter "connection" precisely to create "separate identities or take over existing power." It would seem that to create a feminism they can call their own, these third-wave writers must bite the hand that feeds them. What this suggests about the future of feminism has yet to be seen.

NOTES

1. Rose Glickman, *Daughters of Feminists* (New York: St. Martin's, 1993), xiii.

2. Although initially used with skepticism, the term *third wave* seems to have become increasingly accepted and adopted by popular and academic writers alike. See, for example, a recent special issue of *Hypatia: A Journal of Feminist Philosophy* on "Third Wave Feminism" (Summer 1997) and *Third Wave Agenda: Being Feminist, Doing Feminism,* ed. Leslie Haywood and Jennifer Drake (Minneapolis: University of Minnesota Press, 1997).

3. Alice Walker, "Becoming the Third Wave," *Ms.* (January/February, 1992): 41.

4. Rene Denfeld, *The New Victorians: A Young Woman's Challenge to the Old Feminist Order* (New York: Warner, 1995), 2.

5. Katie Roiphe, *The Morning After: Sex, Fear, and Feminism* (Boston: Little, Brown, 1993), 4.

6. Rebecca Walker, "Being Real: An Introduction," in *To Be Real: Telling the Truth and Changing the Face of Feminism,* ed. Rebecca Walker (New York: Anchor Books, 1995), xxx–xxxi. One critic described Roiphe as a woman "who could be said to have imbibed feminism with her mother's milk"; see Carol Iannone, "Sex and the Feminists," *Commentary* 96, no. 3 (September 1993): 51.

7. Barbara Findlen, "Introduction," in *Listen Up: Voices from the Next Feminist Generation,* ed. Barbara Findlen (Seattle: Seal, 1995), xii.

8. Karen Avenoso, "Feminism's Newest Foot Soldiers," *Elle* (March 1993): 114.

9. Roiphe, *The Morning After,* 4.

10. As Rose Glickman has noted, "To be a feminist is one among many options for [women in their twenties and early thirties], because they do not recognize it as a process, as a perspective that informs other choices. They interpret the word as an end in itself" (*Daughters of Feminists,* 5).

11. Findlen, "Introduction," xii. See also Laurie Ouellette, who writes, "I am a member of the first generation of women to benefit from the gains of the 1970s' women's movement without having participated in its struggles" ("Building the Third Wave: Reflections of a Young Feminist," *On the Issues* 14 [Fall 1992]: 10).

12. On the generational difference regarding consciousness-raising, Denfeld writes:

While CR might have been helpful for women raised in eras where women didn't talk about their experiences with sexism—let alone talk about sex—my generation often finds it redundant. Unlike our mothers, we grew up in a world where issues such as sex discrimination, sexual harassment, abortion, birth control, homosexuality, and relationships are openly discussed. My friends and I have the kind of explicit talk about our sex lives and personal experiences that would give Jerry Falwell a heart attack. . . . Yet my mother tells me such a thing would have been unthinkable in her day. (*The New Victorians*, 204–5)

13. Roiphe, *The Morning After*, 3.
14. Gloria Steinem, "Foreword," in *To Be Real*, ed. Walker, xxvi.
15. Rene Denfeld, "Feminism 2000: What Does It Really Mean (to You)?" *Sassy* 9 (May 1996): 60.
16. For example, Denfeld writes:

We are not apathetic, but we are often resistant to organizing. The same rights and freedoms feminism won for us have allowed us to develop into a very diverse generation of women, and we value our individuality. While linked through common concerns, notions of sisterhood seldom appeal to women of my generation. (*The New Victorians*, 263)

17. Naomi Wolf, *Fire with Fire: The New Female Power and How It Will Change the 21st Century* (New York: Random House, 1993), 137.
18. Nancy Chodorow, a feminist psychoanalyst and sociologist, is the main proponent of this theory, otherwise known as object-relations. See, for example, *The Reproduction of Mothering: Psychoanalysis and the Sociology of Gender* (Berkeley: University of California Press, 1978).
19. In comparison to the large body of feminist work that stresses the positive aspects of female gender individuation, relatively little work has focused on the more "negative" aspects of this individuation and the mother-daughter relationship generally. One excellent exception would be Luce Irigaray's "And the One Doesn't Stir without the Other," *Signs* 7, no.1 (1981): 60–67. For an example of someone trying to write the mother-daughter relation in such a way that it is inclusive of both similarity and difference, see Joan Nestle, "Two Women: Regina Nestle, 1910–1978, and Her Daughter, Joan," and "My Mother Liked to Fuck," both in Nestle, *A Restricted Country* (Ithaca, N.Y.: Firebrand, 1987).
20. While the writers who are my focus here clearly see feminism as limiting their individuality—feminism as Big Sister, or more accurately Big Mother—there are other third-wave writers who offer a different understanding of what feminism has to offer them. For these writers, such as several featured in *Listen Up: Voices from the Next Feminist Generation* and *To Be Real: Telling the Truth and Changing the Face of Feminism*, feminism is described as something that enables them to acquire individuality. In other words, feminism is depicted as an empowering force in their lives, allowing them to question society's rules about how they should be in the world. I would argue that this identification with feminism is much more like the descriptions offered by early second-wave writers who describe the process of becoming feminists in positive terms, emphasizing, in Steinem's words, "the joyful freedom" found in coming into feminism. Interestingly, however, even this more positive third-wave understanding of what femi-

nism has to offer seems inextricably linked to the mother-daughter relation. See, for example, Sharon Lennon's "What Is Mine" where she writes:

My mother, who had allowed and encouraged me to be who I was through most of my youth, viewed [my interest in feminism] as a major point of contention between us. . . . In my quest for individuality through feminism, there were a lot of screaming matches between my mother and me. (*Listen Up,* 127)

21. See Jane Gallop, "History Is Like Mother," in *Around 1981: Academic Feminist Literary Theory* (New York: Routledge, 1992), 206–39.
22. Wendy Kaminer, "Feminism's Third Wave: What Do Young Women Want?" *New York Times Book Review* 4 (June 1995), 22.
23. Carroll Smith-Rosenberg, *Disorderly Conduct: Visions of Gender in Victorian America* (New York: Knopf, 1985), 248.
24. Susan Bolotin, "Views from the Postfeminist Generation," *New York Times Magazine* 17 (October 1982): 31.
25. For more on feminist mothers, see Marilyn Webb, "Our Daughters, Ourselves: How Feminists Can Raise Feminists," *Ms.* (November/December 1992): 30–35.
26. Glickman writes:

The daughters speak with one voice about how their parents instilled and nurtured their self-esteem, reminded them of their worth as women, affirmed their equality with men in ability, strength, and rights (at least in principle), and encouraged them to become self-sufficient. This is the strongest common denominator in the daughters' formative years. (*Daughters of Feminists,* 30)

27. Denfeld, for example, thanks her mother "for teaching me what feminism means" in the acknowledgements of *The New Victorians.*
28. Anne Roiphe writes about her daughter's feminism in *Fruitful: A Real Mother in the Modern World* (Boston: Houghton Mifflin, 1996). Of *The Morning After* she writes:

One of my daughters publishes a book. I hold it in my hand. I turn it over. There on the back is a picture of her. Her hair curls, disobedient thick locks, her eyes glare back at the photographer. What do I see? I see sass, energy, womanliness, but not the kind I was taught. I don't see helplessness, pretense, fear. I see clarity, brightness, and sexuality, her own, bold and strong, right there on the cover of her book. I turn pink, so pleased am I. I think my daughter's point of view is bold, humane, and right. My daughter is a critic of the revolution in which I was a foot solider and she was a beneficiary. I agree with her criticism. (231–32)

29. Roiphe, *The Morning After,* 140.
30. In response to the idea that *The Morning After* is just a form of rebellion against her mother, Roiphe has said, "I had plenty of rebellions against my mother, but this isn't one." Quoted in Barbara Presley Noble, "One Daughter's Rebellion or Her Mother's Imprint?" *New York Times,* November 10, 1993, C1.
31. See Nancy Chodorow, *Feminism and Psychoanalytic Theory* (New Haven, Conn.: Yale University Press, 1989); Chodorow, *The Reproduction of Mothering*; Jes-

sica Benjamin, *The Bonds of Love: Psychoanalysis, Feminism, and the Problem of Domination* (New York: Pantheon, 1988).

32. Erica Duncan, "Mothers and Daughters," in *Competition: A Feminist Taboo?* ed. Valerie Miner and Helen E. Longino (New York: Feminist Press, 1987), 133.

33. Duncan, "Mothers and Daughters," 131, 132.

34. Faludi quoted in Avenoso, "Feminism's Newest Foot Soldiers," 114.

35. Gloria Steinem, "Why Young Women Are More Conservative," in *Outrageous Acts and Everyday Rebellions* (New York: Holt, Rinehart & Winston, 1983), 216–17. See also L. A. Winokur's "Interview with Gloria Steinem," *Progressive* (June 1995): 34–37. In this interview, Steinem criticizes the conservative bent of third-wave writers such as Roiphe.

Part IV

Connecting/Disrupting the Motherline

15

Mother of Mothers, Daughter of Daughters: Reflections on the Motherline

Naomi Lowinsky

> Touching what her hand made
> eight hundred years ago
> a woman
> like my mother, like myself
>
> I feel her sitting
> in my bones . . .[1]

There is a worldview that is as old as humankind, a wisdom we have forgotten that we know: the ancient lore of women—the Motherline. Whenever women gather in circles or in pairs, in olden times around the village well, or at the quilting bee, in modern times in support groups, over lunch, or at the children's park, they tell one another stories from the Motherline. These are stories of female experience: physical, psychological, and historical. They are stories about the dramatic changes of a woman's body: developing breasts and pubic hair, bleeding, being sexual, giving birth, suckling, menopause, and growing old. They are stories of the life cycles that link generations of women: mothers who are also daughters; daughters who have become mothers; grandmothers who always remain granddaughters. They are stories that evoke the dead: mother who died while her child was very young; a child who never made it to adulthood. They are stories that show how times have changed and that show that nothing much changes at all. We all know these stories. The voices of our mothers and grandmothers telling stories from the Motherline are

among our earliest memories. They flesh out what we know about what
it means to be human. Yet little of this world view surfaces into print or
into our collective understanding of history. Women lament the lack of
narratives of women's lives, yet women's stories are all around us. We
don't hear them because out perception is shaped by a culture that trivial-
izes "women's talk" and devalues the passing down of female lore and
wisdom.

CARNAL SELF-KNOWLEDGE

It was my fate, unlike that of many of my generation, to become a mother
at a very young age. I have been wondering about our cultural attitudes
toward the mother ever since. I remember myself as an earnest young
woman, newly married, full of longings: to write great poetry, to make a
contribution, to be somebody. I remember how my whole life changed
with the missing of a period.

The physical experience of giving birth changed my universe. I had a
dream, during the pregnancy, of facing a gate through which I had to
pass. There was no choice about it. On the other side of the gate lay darkness. I was afraid. I didn't know whether it was the darkness of birth or
of death I was facing. I learned that it was both. Huge waves of energy,
outside my control, passed through me and opened me up to push an
unknown being out of the darkness of my body into the light of his first
day. This brought me carnal knowledge of my own animal body, my in-
stinctive nature, my connection to all things.

My then very young first husband, present at the birth, was impressed
and moved. This lifted the shame off my naked labor and my blood. My
bodily experience initiated us both into the sacred connection of all
human life to the female body. The universe had moved through me and
he was a witness. We were both a part of everything that was alive. I felt at
once whole and broken, fulfilled and empty, vibrant with life and sorely
wounded. He held his baby son in his arms. It was as if one part of me,
as newly born as my firstborn son, or the daughter that came a few years
later, blinked in the light of a new consciousness: the consciousness of the
primal experience of giving birth. I knew in my own body the story of
where I came from, where my mother came from, where my grandmother came from: how they were born and how they bore; how all the
women all over the world and throughout human time have born and
been born; how their waters have broken; how their bellies have tightened
and their focus been drawn into the absolute power of the contraction;
how they have labored and pushed and breathed and cried out and

sweated and bled and opened up their most vulnerable private secret selves to bring the new life out.

I had been initiated into a great mystery. I had participated in the origin of human life. I was in love with my baby boy. When he woke from his nap, I raced to see his beautiful face, to smell his body, to touch his warm sweet skin.

Another part of me felt totally lost, disoriented, my body given over to the needs of another, my consciousness devoured by crying and feeding and diapering. My husband returned to his studies. But where was the one I used to be? The one who wanted to write poetry? In a daze of exhaustion, a rapture of pleasure, an annihilation of old self and confusion of new selves I felt utterly lost. I had grown up in an academic family. I had been taught to look for books to read when in struggle and turmoil. I could not find books or poems by women about this overwhelming experience I was in; this was the early 1960s. I didn't know that my struggle was the beginning of the thread that would tie me into the pattern of the Motherline, and tug at me until I began to understand it, until I wrote my own book. I did not know I was part of a generation of women that would be finding our own voices, telling our own stories.

CYCLES, THE MOON, AND THE WOMB

But what do I mean by the term *Motherline?* Let me give you some images from my own life to illuminate it. I am walking down a long stretch of beach with my mother and my two daughters. I walk between them, linking generations. It is one of those cool, clear, winter days that bless the northern coast of California. Sea and sky are a vivid blue. There is a light wind, and someone thinks she sees whales out there. I can't remember what we are talking about. But I do remember a surge of feeling that goes beyond words, of overarching connections, of the present moment holding within it the seeds of both past and future, and all of it held in the bodies of these four women of three generations. Walking between my daughters' younger bodies and my mother's older body evokes the feeling of another walk in another time. This time I am the daughter, nine or ten years old. My mother and grandmother walk with me around a lake sparkling in the morning sun. My grandmother's walk is slower. She is older than my mother is now. I am younger than my daughters are now. Time swirls. My grandmother has been dead for many years. How will it feel to become the age she was when I was nine? How will it feel when I am the grandmother, the mother of mothers, as she was, as my mother has become?

Back on the beach, my daughters are giggling, looking at me, then at each other. I realize I must have sunk into that deep place about which they love to tease me. "Oh, oh. Mommy's having one of her archetypal Motherline experiences. Watch out, Grandma—she's going to be talking about cycles, the moon, and the womb!"

THE BRIDGE BETWEEN GENERATIONS

The Motherline is an idea that crept up on me during my years of being a mother and having a mother. I was profoundly moved to see my younger self in my children's development, and to see my older self in my mother's maturation. But I did not fully see the pattern I was in until I did a research project on mothers. I was interested in how women described their own experience as mothers. A woman, whom I'll call Carolyn, told me a story that illuminated the Motherline. She was talking about her daughter's first menstruation:

> I can remember the date, February 14, Valentine's Day! She came in and showed me her underpants and she said, "Have I started menstruating?" And I said yes, and I started to cry. I could just feel, it was an incredible experience, that connection, that sense of being in the middle between my mother and my daughter, and that I was the bridge between generations. She said, "Oh, Mom, what are you crying for?" But I was so moved by it. It confirmed my womanhood, the woman in me. I was seeing the continuum of the women in the family, the pride of being a woman. I think I had a sense both of my mortality and my immortality.

Carolyn was granted a vision of what I came to call the Motherline: the sacred experience of the embodied feminine mysteries. Her daughter begins to menstruate: she has within her the potential to bear a child. Mother and daughter stand outside ordinary time in this moment of recognition: the birth-giving goddess is revealed in a stain on the daughter's underpants.

For women, the Motherline is the living knowledge of ourselves as life vessel. For men it is the connection to woman as life vessel. Women are the carriers of the species, the entry way to life. Although a woman may choose not to have children or be unable to do so, every woman is born of woman. Every woman alive is connected to all the women before her through the roots of her particular family and culture. The Motherline is body knowledge and birth story and family story and myth.

Those of us who have children and those of us who do not are tied by blood to the physical source of our lives, tied by powerful emotions to the woman in whose body our life began. The Motherline ties us to our mortal bodies, our bloody beginnings and endings, our experience of the blood mysteries. Every woman who wishes to be her full, female self needs to know the stories of her Motherline. We all participate in the human drama; our personal Motherlines connect us to universal myths.

The Motherline is not a straight line, for it is not about abstract genealogical diagrams; it is about bodies being born out of bodies. Envision the word *line* as a cord, a thread, as the yarn emerging from the fingers of a woman at the spinning wheel. Imagine cords of connection tied over generations. Like weaving or knitting, each thread is tied to others to create a complex, richly textured cloth connecting the past to the future.

ADULT CHILDREN OF TERRIBLE MOTHERS

To tell the human story from the experience of mothers, to honor the carnal, to speak of how the past becomes the future is to commit a heresy against twentieth-century psychological thought. To include our mothers' stories in telling our stories undercuts a collective fantasy we hold about the perfectibility of childhood. We mothers are seen as all-powerful in psychology, but are personally disempowered. Our subjective experience is unknown and devalued. Yet we suffer the collective wound of being seen as the perpetrators of all suffering.

In my work as a Jungian analyst, I sit with the adult children of terrible mothers day after day. Angry, intrusive mothers who appear as birds of prey in their daughters' dreams, or profoundly depressed mothers who appear half dead in the psychological landscapes their offspring describe. The woman I've called Carolyn told me a story of the working through of a terrible mother-daughter relationship. All through her childhood and early adulthood she lived at the edge of a bitter chasm that severed her from her mother. In her story, the nature of a birth, the first days of life create a Motherline rift that takes most of two lifetimes to untangle. This is what she told me:

> I was born prematurely, two months early. I weighed three pounds. My mother had to leave me in the hospital for six weeks. During that whole time she never touched me. In those days they wouldn't let you. I never understood this until recently: I must have bonded to someone else, a nurse in the hospital. And so when I came home there was this stranger, pretending to be my mother. I think our whole life together has been trying to bridge that gap.

How did they bridge that gap? Many things helped beginning with the birth of Carolyn's first child. Carolyn said:

I remember my mother calling me up after Tommy's birth and saying, "Oh, my baby has had a baby!" I can still see her face the first time she saw him. He had just awakened from a nap and was standing up in his crib. Her whole demeanor was so loving. She gave him some sugar on her finger. Put her finger in his mouth. You have to understand that my mother is a very restrained woman, not warm, not physically affectionate. When I saw her do this, put her finger in Tommy's mouth, it was so sensual. I had never seen that side of her before. It warmed me, touched me deeply.

Carolyn remembered having told a male analyst that she had a memory of being in an incubator. He laughed. She dropped it. She told me that recently, working in therapy with a woman, she was able to understand that the distance between her mother and herself had much to do with her premature birth and lack of bonding. Her mother was her father's second wife. There were children from the first marriage whose mother had died. So she was a stepmother. Carolyn did not begin to understand the complexity of this until she herself became a stepmother. Then she could identify with her mother and appreciate how hard she had worked to hold the family together. And her mother, at age seventy-eight, went into therapy and began to see her own life more psychologically and her daughter less judgmentally.

WRESTLING WITH THE MOTHER

These two women engaged in a long process of what I call mother-daughter wrestling, the struggle at once to identify and differentiate from one another. Mothers and daughters wrestle with bodily, temperamental, stylistic, generational, and usually very emotional differences between them. They also have to wrestle with the power of the feminine mysteries and how little they are honored in our culture.

From the mother's point of view the process of differentiation tugs at the most primal places in her nature. She remembers the child she bore in the very cells of her body. What mother is not wildly subjective about her offspring, driven by a passionate core connection that is the psychological ghost of her pregnancy, her birth-giving, her breastmilk letting down when her baby cried? What mother does not remember being a daughter and the fierce fight to establish her separateness from her mother?

What I learned from Carolyn and other women I interviewed was that looking at stories from the middle of a woman's life, when she can identify both as mother and as daughter and loop back and forth in the generations, gives a rich and complex view of the psychology of women and of the Motherline as an organizing principle. Motherline stories weave pregnancies, births, miscarriages, abortions, deaths, and psychological development into one fabric, not separating body and psyche.

These subjective experiences are not usually recognized in our official version of the world; they are too fearful. Woman as mother is a part of nature. Caught in the awesome jaws of fate in the birth-giving process, her stories clash with our cultural fantasy about mastering the natural world. When she comes to visit we fear the news she brings. We want to believe we can do things better than she did.

THE BALLAD OF MY GRANDMOTHER

For many the grandmother is an easier link to the Motherline than is the mother. Less familiar, less everyday, a grandmother is a woman of another time, telling stories out of long ago; standing closer to death she remembers the dead. She is often the first to tell us the stories of our origins.

I had just one living grandparent when I was growing up. This was my mother's mother, whom my brothers and I called Oma. She was especially important to me when I was a new mother. Once a month as regularly as the waning moon we visited my Oma on Sundays, my first husband, my baby, and I. I was taking classes at the university; my husband was in medical school. Life was arranged around midterms and finals. I was disoriented, as chaotic on the inside as was my living room, with its heaps of unfolded laundry on the couch and Virginia Woolf's *Mrs. Dalloway* lost somewhere under a pile of baby pants.

It was a chorus in my life, a monthly refrain that took us to a sanatorium in the northern California wine country, where Oma lived. Little happened on our visits. We walked around the grounds. We ate a meal together. She held the baby. She told me again and again the central stories of her life. They were the myths of my development. How her mother had died in childbirth when she was very young and she had been raised by a cruel stepmother. How she had gone to Italy as a young woman to study painting. How she had suffered so loudly at the birth of her first child that her husband, who had been pacing the hours of her pain in an adjoining room, came to her after the birth and said, "I'll never put you through that again." There were five more children. Three of them were to die young. Ruth, for whom I was named, died of diabetes when she was ten. Oma told me about the death of her sons. They were young men in their early twenties. They had gone to Austria to ski. There was an avalanche. They never returned. Oma was in her menopause. She told me she went crazy with grief. The only comfort she found was in painting

portraits of those she loved. She was a fine painter, and these portraits
live with me and my brothers and my mother to this day.

SEEING HITLER

Motherline stories have a terrible side, giving us a glimpse of life's horror
our "self-help" culture would like to deny. The death of Oma's sons,
through an unbearable irony, was the avenue of our family's survival.
This part of the story opens simply in a restaurant in Berlin. When Oma
told this part she spoke in a voice of such horror that even now, remembered years after her death, I can feel the fear at the bottom of my spine.
For in that restaurant, in Berlin, she saw Hitler, just a few feet away from
her. He looked straight at her and it pierced her being. She knew that he
knew she was Jewish. I can see him, looking though her to me—old terror. She felt that terror and went home and told my grandfather that they
had to get out of the country, that this man Hitler would destroy them
all.

My grandfather was a successful businessman. Being Jewish was not
an important part of his identity. He was an engineer, the manager of a
company. He always had been treated with respect. He thought my
grandmother was being hysterical. Hitler would pass, just like other difficult political phases passed. After the death of his sons, however, he
agreed to listen to his wife and to leave Germany. That was 1932.

Always, telling this story, Oma would shake her head in wonder at the
workings of fate. "We might all have died in concentration camps. He
would never have agreed to leave with one boy in medical school and the
other studying engineering. If they had not died we might all have been
dead."

That I am here today would not have been possible without my grandmother's terrible losses. I am now about the age she was when she left
Germany. I can't imagine facing the journey she had to make, leaving behind all her familiar world and the graves of three of her children.

GHOST STORIES

Motherline stories are haunted by ghosts. The unredeemed grief and suffering of generations of women haunt us. Those who were stillborn and
those who died in childbirth, those who were orphaned, abandoned,
murdered, and abused live on past their lives in the nightmares of their
descendants. Women whose ties to life and family were disrupted by the

wild tides of history—natural disasters, human cruelty—cast shadows on our souls.

Nobody can choose her Motherline or her fate. We are all born into a lineage, a family, a historical time filled with difficulties over which we have no control. But we can honor our stories, attend to our ghosts, remember our ancestors, tell their stories to our children and grandchildren.

Motherline stories evoke a worldview in which all beings and times are interconnected, and in which the feminine mysteries are honored. They are as common as the repetitive loops made in weaving, crocheting, and knitting. They are as powerful as the memory of touching a grandmother's face or seeing a daughter suckle her newborn child.

NOTE

1. Naomi Ruth Lowinsky, "Anasazi Woman," *Psychological Perspectives* 19, no. 1 (Spring–Summer 1988).

16

Don't Blame Mother: Then and Now

Paula Caplan

This chapter is about the practice of mother blame from the time leading up to my writing *Don't Blame Mother: Mending the Mother-Daughter Relationship,*[1] up to the present. First I shall explain what motivated me to write the book beginning in the mid-1980s, then I shall discuss how much of what was relevant then remains relevant today, and finally I shall describe the way I have attempted to put some themes about mother blame into theatrical form.

I became interested in mother blaming when I was working in a clinic where we were evaluating families, and I noticed that no matter what was wrong, no matter what the reason for the family's coming to the clinic, it turned out that the mother was always assumed to be responsible for the problem. And if, in the assessment interview, she sat right next to the child, my colleagues would say afterward, "Did you see how she sat right next to the child? She is smothering and overcontrolling and too close and enmeshed and symbiotically fused with the child." But if she did not sit right next to the child, she was called cold and rejecting—and, if the child was a boy, castrating.

So my interest in mother blaming began because it seemed that there was nothing that a mother could do that was right, and it was particularly interesting and painful to me because I was a mother.

In 1986, when I received tenure and considered what I most wanted to teach, one of the two courses I created was about mothers. I wasn't aware at the time of any other course about mothers, so I started trying to design the course and talking to people about it. Often, both men and women would laugh and say, "What are you going to talk about for a whole semester?" or just, "Hah! A course about mothers?" You may remember that that was the reaction people had had ten years earlier to "Oh! You're going to have a course about women?"

237

Teaching that course to graduate students at the University of Toronto's Ontario Institute for Studies in Education led to my writing *Don't Blame Mother* in which I describe aspects of girls' and women's socialization that creates or exacerbates problems between mothers and daughters, as well as methods that mothers and daughters have found helpful in repairing rifts between them. (I did not believe and still do not believe that the mother-daughter relationship is more fraught with problems than the mother-son relationship or the relationships between fathers and their children of either sex; but as a feminist I was primarily concerned with the kinds of socially created—and, therefore, hopefully surmountable—barriers between women.) In addressing the question "To what extent is the content of *Don't Blame Mother* applicable today?" I find it depressing that most of the basic principles that concerned me as I wrote the book still apply today. I shall return to this point later.

After my experience in the clinical setting described earlier, I did some research with Ian Hall-McCorquodale,[2] looking at articles in clinical journals written by psychoanalysts, psychiatrists, social workers, psychologists, behavior therapists, and clinicians of all stripes. We found that mothers were blamed for virtually every kind of psychological or emotional problem that ever brought any patient to see a therapist. We were also disappointed to find that the sex of the person who was writing the paper did not determine the presence or absence of mother blaming, and, even more depressingly, that it didn't get better as the years passed after the resurgence of the women's movement during the 1970s. With respect to mother blame, so many therapists still seemed to be buried under their rocks.

When I began to bring up this subject of mother blame I pointed out that there are myths about mothers that allow us to take anything a mother might do and turn it into evidence of something "bad" about her. Important work that a mother does goes largely unnoticed, except when she doesn't do it, as when she is sick and can't make dinner. I would point out that nobody I knew of was likely to say to their mother, "That was a great week's work of dusting you did" or "That was a week of delicious and nourishing meals that you prepared." When I would say this, people would laugh—and still do, in fact.

So we have to ask, "Why does this make us laugh? Would you laugh if I said, 'Dad, the lawn looks great now that you have mown it'?" Nobody laughs at that. Why? Because we laugh at the unexpected. It is so unimaginable to us that anyone would express appreciation for, or a sense of valuing of, the work that mothers do as mothers and housekeepers and cooks and chauffeurs. So I used to talk about that.

As observed in a review of *The Time Bind: When Work Becomes Home and Home Becomes Work*,[3] Arlie Hochschild points out that women increasingly spend time at paid work because they feel appreciated there. She says that even for relatively uninteresting work, such as factory work, women find work to be a greater source of self-esteem than home life. This was something that had concerned me years ago, because it seemed to me that, as in that story about no one thanking you for dusting, even if you work at a really boring, miserable job, every week or two somebody hands you a paycheck. The check might not be much, but it communicates the notion that somebody puts some value on the work that you do. And it's still no better in terms of mothering.

To come to the heart of *Don't Blame Mother*, there are mother myths I call the "Good Mother Myths" and mother myths I call the "Bad Mother Myths." The Good Mother Myths set standards that no human being could ever match, such as that mothers are always, naturally, 100 percent nurturant. We have a double standard. We don't have that kind of expectation of fathers. So when, 1 percent of the time, mothers don't do what we wish they would do, we feel betrayed, because the myth is that they naturally are able to and in fact are desperate to be nurturant all the time. But when our fathers do anything nurturant, we feel that it is wonderful that Daddy did something like that. (Naturally, the answer is not to stop appreciating what fathers do but rather to be ready to give mothers equal credit when they are nurturant.)

The Bad Mother Myths allow us to take mothers' neutral or bad behavior—because mothers are human, so we do some bad things—or even mothers' good behavior, and transform it into further proof that mothers are bad. One example that disturbs me the most is the myth that mother-daughter closeness is sick, that it is a form of psychopathology. When *Don't Blame Mother* was first published and I was doing media interviews, every woman interviewer would confess, with the microphone turned off, that she talked to her mother every day. I would ask her, "How do you feel afterward?" and the woman would reply, "Oh, great. My mother has a great sense of humor, and we are great friends, and we give each other advice." I would then ask her, "Do you have a partner?" "Yes." "Do you talk to them every day?" "Yes." "Does that embarrass you?" "No." And I would ask, "Well, then, why did you confess that you talk to your mother every day?" These women would reply that they worried that the daily talks with their mothers were signs that they hadn't "individuated" or "achieved autonomy" from their mothers, and if they had been in therapy they would say, "I know it means we're enmeshed or symbiotically fused." My point here is that anything associated with mothers becomes devalued and pathologized.

If you look at the myths about mothers, you find that some of them are mutually exclusive.[4] One of the Bad Mother Myths is that mothers are an endless drain on our energy. Just on the basis of strict physics principles, you cannot be constantly putting out force, as in giving nurturance, while constantly taking in force and energy as you are draining it from others. Another set of mutually exclusive myths involves the Good Mother Myth, according to which mothers naturally, perhaps for hormonal reasons, know everything they need to know about mothering, and the Bad Mother Myth, according to which mothers cannot raise emotionally healthy children without the advice of lots of experts.

I believe that these mutually exclusive myths continue to coexist because every society needs scapegoated groups if the people in power want to maintain their power. What happens if I'm in the powerful group and some member of the scapegoated group does something good? Somebody might get the idea that the scapegoated people are not as bad as I portray them to be, and if that's the case, maybe I don't deserve to have all of the power I have. So I have to make sure there is a myth for every occasion, so that no matter what the members of that scapegoated group might do, I can transform it into further proof that they are wrong, bad, or pathological and deserve to continue to have no power and be scapegoated.[5] That is the powerful function that these myths serve, and that is why we need to keep questioning them.

This power hierarchy still exists, and the women's movement hasn't been able to change it yet. I think it hasn't changed partly because we often substitute the word *mother* for *woman*. For instance, people at a party may stop you when you tell a "joke" that is woman-hating, but if you change the word *woman* to *mother*, you can still get away with the comment. You are much less likely to have someone interrupt you to say, "I don't think that's funny, and I don't want you to go on like that."

What the women's movement can do is to make the repeated exposure of mother myths, the placing of them front and center, a priority. Antifeminist backlash makes all feminist efforts more difficult, of course. But until we recognize the need for what we might call "the Norma Rae-ing of mothers' struggles," the need to reveal mothers' oppression and its systemic nature, few women of any ethnic or racialized group or class or sexual orientation (and certainly not women with disabilities or women who don't weigh the "right" amount) will be free. Why? Because we all had mothers, and so we're connected with what is done to, what is said about mothers. Because we have all been subjected as women to strong pressure to prove we are unlike our mothers. You'll often hear women say, "My greatest fear is that I will be like my mother." What I find that these women usually mean if you explore that statement is, "I don't want to be treated the way she has been treated. I don't want to be demeaned and undervalued the way she is." At the same time as we are taught not to want to be like our mothers, we are taught—sometimes subliminally—that we should want to be like our mothers, when they are passive, pliable, and ashamed of themselves. And no one is free until the truths about mothers are highlighted, because all women, and especially as we age,[6] are expected to be motherly, motherlike, as in being self-denying and serving others.

No, it's not getting any better—not socially and not in the research arena. A recent issue of the *American Journal of Orthopsychiatry* includes a longitudinal report on "Preschool Antecedents of Adolescent Assaultive Behavior."[7] The researchers studied children from preschool through adolescence in an attempt to discern the determinants of adolescents' assaultive behavior. How did they look at the alleged determinants? Among other things, they observed what they call early in their article "parental interactions" with the young children. That really meant "mothers' interactions," even though 86 percent of the children in their study had both a male and a female parent in the home. When they looked at how mothers interact with children and then later on looked at which children become assaultive, it is not surprising that they concluded that it was the children's negative interactions with their mothers that led to their assaultive behavior. The methodology you choose can go far to determine the results that you get. I believe that there are at least two major methodological problems evident in this study. One is not looking at the fathers or the society in which the children live and what the determinants of their assaultive behavior might be. The second is a cause-effect problem. People who are assaultive when they are teenagers, for reasons that may have had nothing to do with their mothers, might have been difficult to handle as children, and thus their mothers' interactions with them would have been observed to be relatively "negative." For example, their mothers might have had to do more disciplining of them, more saying "no." That is just one example of the persistence of the practice of mother blame in "scholarly" journals.

Mother blame also persists on a grand scale in the arena of the diagnosis of mental illness. My book *They Say You're Crazy: How the World's Most Powerful Psychiatrists Decide Who's Normal*[8] is an exposé of the *Diagnostic and Statistical Manual of Mental Disorders*[9] (also called the DSM). The DSM is the "Bible" of mental health professionals that lists 374 supposedly different mental disorders. It is marketed as "science," but the way it is put together is far from scientific, and pieces of relevant scientific research are often ignored or distorted. I became involved in learning about the DSM in 1985 because I was concerned about a new category the American Psychiatric Association was proposing to include in the DSM called "Self-Defeating Personality Disorder." This new category might be described as "the Good Wife or Good Mother Syndrome." It included criteria such as not putting other people's needs ahead of one's own, feeling unappreciated, and choosing less desirable options for their lives when clearly

better ones are available. But this is what society still thinks we are supposed to do as a mother and as a "good" woman. Once involved, I was
horrified when I learned about the way that the DSM's authors decide
who is "normal." I ended up calling their process "Diagnosisgate" because of the similarities to Watergate in terms of lies, cover-ups, and dis-
tortions of what the research literature shows.[10]

This "Self-Defeating Personality Disorder" is a real catch-22 for
women. If women act in those ways, they supposedly have this mental
disorder, but if they do not act in those ways, they are rejected and pathologized for not being real women, not being "good" women.[11] Because
there was a virtual blackout of *They Say You're Crazy* by the major media,
and I wanted people to know about the Diagnosisgate issues, I decided
to write a play on the theme of who decides who is normal. The play is
called *Call Me Crazy*,[12] and I shall include here a couple of excerpts from
it. It is a comedy-drama with scenes alternating between relatively serious
ones in a mental-hospital case-conference room and comedic-grotesque,
"campy" ones like a quiz show called "What's My Diagnosis?" Almost
all of the second act takes place in the conference room, and the psychology intern is making it possible for patients to tell their stories. I chose
the stories for the two women and two men patients because they are typical of what happens in the traditional mental health system. For the two
women's stories, this includes the therapists' disbelieving what women
tell them and pathologizing women in general. Here is the story told by
Patient 3:

PATIENT 3: I was a cheerleader in high school—and homecoming queen.
During my second year in college, I married Eugene, my high school sweet-
heart. Then I got pregnant, and as soon as my tummy started to swell, he
started getting drunk and beating up on me, calling me a fat pig, saying it
made him sick to have sex with me. He left me the night our daughter
Tammy was born. It was hard . . . being a single mother, working in a ribbon
factory, trying to get my prepregnancy body shape back. At the factory, I
met Sam. He's a truck driver, and he's gone a lot, but when he's home, he's
wonderful—funny, gentle, a wonderful father to Tammy. I feel so lucky to
have him, and I'm scared to death of losing him. He says he loves me, not
how I look but who I am. I hope that's true, but I get so frightened of putting
on weight. It's weird. Sometimes the only thing that makes me feel better
when I get scared of getting fat and losing him . . . is eating . . . like a whole
chocolate cake or a whole pot of macaroni and cheese at once. And as soon
as I do that, 'course I get scared again right away . . . so . . . I make myself
throw up. My stomach hurts, and my throat gets raw. I went to a psychologist, and she said I made myself throw up because I enjoyed that pain! I told
her I didn't, but she didn't pay any attention. She said now that I didn't have
Eugene around to hit me and call me names, I had to make the suffering

myself! I told her I hate feeling bad, but thinking about losing Sam was even worse than throwing up to try to stay thin so he wouldn't go. She wouldn't listen. And I didn't know it then, but she wrote in my chart that I enjoyed suffering, that I had a mental illness called "Self-Defeating Personality Disorder." I found out because, when Tammy was four, Eugene suddenly showed up and went to court to take her from me. I'd stayed friends with his sister, so Eugene found out that I'd been seeing a psychologist. And they made her bring my chart to court. The judge sent Tammy to live with Eugene because I was mentally ill. I get to see her two hours every second Sunday.

This scenario is typical of what happens to women, often because of the kinds of women and mothers they are trying to be and because of the way that that gets constructed by the mental health system.

Here is one more excerpt from *Call Me Crazy*. No one has ever heard from Freud's mother, and I thought it was time. How many people even know her name? I went to the library, thinking that I wanted her to be a character in my play but that if I could find no interesting information about her, I would make something up. But as I began to read little fragments about her life in the biographies of her son, I found myself gasping, because it seemed pretty clear to me what she probably would have felt about the various things that happened to her. Notice how she wrestles with the question of what is good and normal mothering. In the play, she steps out of history to speak to the audience. The people who are in the case conference are behind her and have been talking about the DSM.

AMALIA: Thank you for coming. I'm Amalia Freud. Amalia Nathanson Freud. I lived to be ninety-five years old. For decades, I wanted people I met to know my son was the great psychoanalyst, winner of the Goethe Prize for literature. But behind their polite smiles I saw the thought, "This is the mother whose son discovered that all little boys want to have sex with their mothers." Discovered. Hah! Guessed. Claimed. Wrote a story.

A man says with aplomb, "This is what happens," and already it's a discovery. A woman says, "This is what happens," and she's exaggerating or manipulating.

And about girls and their mothers what did he "discover"? That our daughters resent us for not having had the courtesy to provide them a penis. That they look down on us because we don't have penises. I had five daughters. How do you think his words made me feel? I love my Sigmund, but this is too much. . . .

Sigmund was a bright boy, brilliant probably. But maybe he had too much.

He told people he felt all his life like a conqueror because he was my "indisputable favorite." Hah! So he thought. The truth is I adored all of my children. How could I not? My husband, he valued me for my son. His first wife had two sons. Sigmund was my first-born, when I was twenty-one and his father was forty-one. I loved my daughters but kept having to have more—five in all—until Jacob got one more son ten years after Sigmund was born. Most of the time Sigmund was growing up, his father and all the other children and I shared three bedrooms, but he had his own. He needed to study. Often, he took his meals alone in there and received his friends there. He was the oldest child, so maybe it was right to give him his own room. He complained that his sister Anna's piano lessons were noisy when he was trying to study. We got rid of the piano. Anna and I were sad but not angry. We understood. Maybe he had too much. And he decided who was normal.

You know, he threw up his hands in despair and said, "What do women want?" He said women were a dark continent to him. (Shakes her head.) What's not to understand? Is it healthy to take a mother's love or a wife's love and make it seem so complicated?

(Shrugs her shoulders.) Normal, shmormal. Oh, I realize some people have to be put away—they can hurt themselves, or someone else. But it's a tough problem. You start putting people away, and somebody's going to decide who gets put away, somebody's going to choose the rules. Is what these guys (indicating the giant DSM) decide any better than what my son decided? Thinking about it makes my head hurt.

But I'll tell you what I have noticed. Who decides is who has the power. And somehow, they seem to decide the people most like them are the normal ones, the good, the healthy, the deserving. It's the others who are derided, called dangerous . . . sent away. My five daughters—one went to New York, three were gassed in Auschwitz, and the last one starved to death in the camp at Theresienstadt.

Thank you for listening.

And then Amalia leaves the stage.

I want to close with what Patient 3, whom you heard from before, says about classifying people on the basis of the forms of their emotional anguish. What she says applies to seeing mothers and all women through the prism of the myths about mothers.

PATIENT 3: When you look up at the night sky, there are lots of stars. There are no real constellations, but people decide how to divide up the stars into groups and give those groups names. And forever afterward they think they see the Big Dipper and Orion. It makes it hard to see, really see, one unique star as itself.

I hope that this sampling of the recent history of mother blame makes it clear that, despite some gains that feminists have made, there are still miles to go before we can relax in the knowledge that mother blame has been eradicated. For this reason, I suggest that we join together in declaring that women don't speak often enough and don't speak up often enough, certainly not in defense of mothers. Let us vow that at every possible opportunity we will protest, we will educate, even interrupt as we would a sexist or a racist "joke" when anyone in any setting utters or implies any of the dangerous myths about mothers.

NOTES

This chapter is the slightly edited text of an address I gave on September 27, 1997, at York University for their International Conference on Mothers and Daughters.

1. Paula Caplan, *Don't Blame Mother: Mending the Mother-Daughter Relationship* (New York: HarperCollins, 1989). The new edition is scheduled for publication on Mother's Day 2000 by Routledge.

2. Paula Caplan and Ian Hall-McCorquodale, "Mother-Blaming in Major Clinical Journals," *American Journal of Orthopsychiatry* 55 (1985): 345–53; Paula Caplan and Ian Hall-McCorquodale, "The Scapegoating of Mothers: A Call for Change," *American Journal of Orthopsychiatry* 55 (1985): 610–13.

3. Arlie Hochschild, "A Review of Sex Role Research," in *Changing Women in a Changing Society*, ed. Joan Huber (Chicago: University of Chicago Press, 1973), 249–67.

4. Caplan, *Don't Blame Mother.*

5. Caplan, *Don't Blame Mother.*

6. Rachel Josefowitz Siegel, "Old Women as Mother Figures," in *Woman-Defined Motherhood*, ed. Jane Price and Ellen Cole (New York: Harrington Park, 1990), 89–97.

7. Roy C. Herrenkohl, Brenda P. Egolf, and Ellen C. Herrenkohl, "Preschool Antecedents of Adolescent Assaultive Behavior: A Longitudinal Study," *American Journal of Orthopsychiatry* 67 (1997): 422–32.

8. Paula Caplan, *They Say You're Crazy: How the World's Most Powerful Psychiatrists Decide Who's Normal* (Reading, Mass.: Addison-Wesley, 1995).

9. American Psychiatric Association, *Diagnostic and Statistical Manual of Mental Disorders IV* (Washington, D.C.: American Psychiatric Association, 1994).

10. Caplan, *They Say You're Crazy.*

11. For apparently political reasons, Self-Defeating Personality Disorder was removed from the most recent edition of the DSM, but that has not kept it from being used.

12. Paula Caplan, *Call Me Crazy* (1996), script copyrighted by and available from author.

17

Motherline Connections across Cultures and Generations

Sharon Abbey and Charlotte Harris

> All of us need access to our biohistorical sense of continuity to be fully, creatively alive, to face our own mortality and to honor life in all its forms.
>
> —Naomi Lowinsky[1]

As two professors of education whose life paths converged at midlife, we discovered that we both shared similar experiences as divorced mothers of young adult daughters and as motherless daughters. In addition, as the family matriarchs, we are the keepers of our collective maternal stories, charged with the responsibility of selecting what will be passed along to our daughters. Together, we questioned just how prepared we were to offer a thoughtful and considered maternal legacy in such a way that our daughters would view their upbringing as empowering and enriching but not superior to that of others. Knowing very little about the history of our foremothers we challenged ourselves to find out more. At midlife, we appreciated our position to measure our lives in both our mothers' and our daughters' terms and the unique viewpoint this offered. We hope that our efforts will encourage others to draw on the lessons from their own Motherlines.

Naomi Lowinsky defines Motherline stories as archetypal experiences of female body and soul that loop women to the universal source of their own lives and to the origin of all matriarchal consciousness. According to Lowinsky:

> the process of finding one's Motherline is idiosyncratic and chaotic. It takes a lifetime [and] cannot be readily taught. Rather it is a potentiality that can

be evoked by shifting the way we listen to women's voices, and the way we see ourselves, our mothers, and our grandmothers.[2]

In Motherline stories, all beings and times are connected and there are no boundaries between generations, life and death, or biological and emotional spheres. In this chapter we use this model of the Motherline as our guide.

At the time of their deaths, our foremothers were probably unaware of the full potential of their agency and power. Indeed, their collective unspoken wisdom remains an essential female tragedy which serves to disconnect women from their matrilineage and from their struggle to find their places and to fulfill their lives. Since our mothers can no longer speak for themselves, we are aware that any text we create can only be written from our viewpoint as daughters, a necessity that continues to silence and objectify them. For the most part, our mothers and foremothers were not willing informants of our work but in no way do we mean to exploit them. As Michelle Fine eloquently suggests, we appreciate and honor these women "who lived the lives they were supposed to live, kept the secrets of their gendered, raced, and classed lives, preserved the 'moral order' at home and on the streets, and paid dearly and, typically, alone."[3] Our daughters, on the other hand, are young women who are all capable of voicing their own opinions but have consented to our limited descriptions of them from our midlife perspective. As the future keepers of the Motherline, we hope they will find meaning in the patterns that repeat.

We agree with Carolyn Heilbrun that oral history is a particularly valuable means of generating new insights about women's experiences of themselves but that we must also search for the choices, the pain, and the conflicts that lie beneath the "constraints of acceptable discussion."[4] According to Kathryn Anderson and Dana Jack, "inadvertently, women often mute their own thoughts and feelings when they try to describe their lives in the familiar and publicly acceptable terms of prevailing concepts and conventions."[5] As motherless daughters, we are also alerted by Hope Edelman[6] to the temptation of sentimentalizing our mothers after death by remembering only their ideal characteristics and overlooking their deficits. We must also be cautious, as Michelle Fine warns, about "a colonizing discourse of the 'Other' "[7] in which we presume to fill in the gaps in order to retell the stories of others in our own voice and, in so doing, enter a space we don't inhabit, and in doing so, annihilate, erase, or reinvent the M/Other.

Since our maternal experiences are situated in different countries and cultures, we have chosen to foreground cultural diversity as the lens through which to probe and construct deeper meanings and understandings about underlying maternal roles, spaces and influences. In this chapter we begin with biographical accounts to personify the women who collectively inform our lives. Next we will consider similarities and differences that emerge from our overlapping stories with reference to three themes in particular: racial dualism, collective pride, and economic independence. Our data were collected over three years from conversations, personal journals, travels to African and Irish homelands, and archival searches as well as from our recent work together in creating readers' theater presentations.

OUR MOTHERLINE STORIES

Sharon's Prologue

My mother died last year, just after her eighty-second birthday. Although I felt as if I had been set adrift without an anchor, I did not cry at her funeral. As her only child, I had spent weeks at her bedside and shed all my tears with my head on her chest and her frail arms hugging me. We had a great deal of time to say good-bye over countless cups of tea, and I am grateful to have known her for over fifty years. As each day passes I think of more conversations we did not have and wonder whether I did enough to comfort her in the end. Last summer, my mother's only sister, Millie, also died. Although we lived a great distance apart and did not see each other often, I cried inconsolably at her funeral. Since she had no daughters and I have no sisters, my daughter and I are left as the only women in our Motherline. It feels strangely comforting to imagine all the mothers who went before me and who held a little part of me in their bodies from the beginning of time.

Charlotte's Prologue

"No relationship affects us more than our relationship with our mother. . . . If that primary relationship with mother is positive . . . we learn how to be good women and good friends at the same time."[8] I feel that my mother, my daughters and myself each have had a relationship that enabled us to become good women and good friends. My daughters and I have established a synergistic bond that is powerful and mutually felt. However, my mother died when I was eighteen, and I never had the opportunity to become that kind of a friend with her. I feel certain that were she still with me in the flesh, as she is still with me in spirit, we would be good friends. Now fifty years old, I have passed into what Gail Sheehy identifies as Second Adulthood and the Age of Mastery.[9] My mother never reached this age, having died when she was only forty-one. I miss not being able to share our life passages with each other as I am now able to do with my daughters.

Charlotte's Foremothers

What I know of my Motherline before my grandmother I learned from my aunt and from a paper my sister had written at college. My great-great-grandmother, Emily Merrit, of African-American and European-American descent, was born and raised in southern Virginia and had seven children. My great-grandmother, Mary Lou Steptoe (1865–1937), called Big Mama, left home in her early teens and worked her way north, doing domestic work. In northern Virginia she met and married my great-grandfather, Henry Elmer Blackwell. Big Mama and Papa moved to Washington, D.C., where her home was always open to family members who followed them. They had four children, three of whom finished high school, an impressive accomplishment in those days. Big Mama also had four children earlier by a white man. These children passed as white and lived in Lynchburg, Virginia.

Sharon's Foremothers

My great-great-grandmother, Catherine McKennedy, was born in 1821 somewhere in Ireland. According to the Parish of Nelson census returns in 1851, she married Patrick Casey, a man twenty years older than she, and gave birth to at least eleven children. Seven of her children were born in West Cork, Ireland, before the family immigrated to Canada sometime between 1845 and 1850. Patrick was listed as a farmer and most likely was attracted to the grants of free land that were issued near Miramichi, New Brunswick. I can only imagine how desperate Catherine must have been during the Great Potato Famine of 1847 "when corpses lay in the hovels and on the streets, their neighbors too weak to remove them for burial . . . half naked and starving, waiting for soup to be distributed among them."[10]

Of Catherine's four daughters, my great-grandmother, Ellen, born in 1854, was the youngest. My mother told me very little about Ellen, her grandmother, although I know she had fond memories of summer visits to Ellen's farm at Barnaby River. From archival records, I also know that Ellen and her husband James had at least eight children and that my grandmother, Hannah, was the youngest of her three daughters.

Celonia—Charlotte's Grandmother

My memory of my Motherline begins in Washington, D.C., with my mother's mother, Celonia Arguene Blackwell Banks (1903–1970). I remember Grandma as a big woman and a strong family force who wore a lot of face powder and spoke loudly. She had long hair that she wore pulled back in a bun. She would say, "Anybody can have short hair; not everybody can have long hair," in response to any mention of cutting our hair. My mother's hair was shoulder length, and my sister and I also had long hair. And Grandma had fair skin, as did my mother and her sister and their offspring. Light skin and good hair were a part of our identity.

Before marriage, Grandma worked in domestic service and as a government worker for a short time. In 1922, when Grandma was only eighteen, she married Henry Thomas Banks, a veteran of World War I who worked for the federal government. They had three children and were pioneer homeowners in the Washington, D.C., area know as Kingman Park. Granddad sometimes worked two or three jobs to support the family so that Grandma could stay home with the children. That was why she did not finish college. My aunt, Celonia Arguene II, was born in 1922 followed closely by her brother in 1923 and my mother, Charlotte LaVerne, in 1924.

Grandma worked as a volunteer for social agencies, division leader of the Community Chest, membership chair of the civic association, delegate to the first conference of churches meeting in D.C., superintendent of the Sunday school, and past president of the American Legion. She also loved to entertain friends, ministers and neighbors and had big parties at Thanksgiving, Christmas, and New Year's. Grandma's scrapbooks give evidence of a close-knit family with strong Christian principles. Aunt Celonia remembers a happy childhood with a mother who "kept [them] busy" and took them "right along with her."

Hannah—Sharon's Grandmother

I hardly remember my grandmother, Hannah Regan Maher (1886–1954). She lived far away and died when I was young. A newspaper account of her Catholic marriage in Chatham, New Brunswick, to Peter Maher on October 12, 1906, describes the bride "prettily dressed in Alice blue" whose "popularity was evidenced by the many useful and pretty presents received."[11] Few educational institutions were available in rural New Brunswick at the turn of the century, and I can only speculate that Hannah, who married at the age of twenty, completed only the required provincial schooling. My grandfather ran a successful livery stable, and Hannah stayed at home as a full-time homemaker with a hired maid.

The family suffered a loss in fortune during the Great Depression when the stable burned and the automobile made the horse and buggy obsolete. At the same time, Hannah suffered a paralyzing stroke when the youngest of her five children was born. I have a vague image of my grandmother banging her cane impatiently on the floor during one of our few visits to her home. However, most of my impressions of my grandmother were shaped by the few stories my mother shared with me, such as the time her mother excluded her from a family holiday because she left the iron plugged in by mistake. And whenever I undertook a creative sewing project or cooking task, my mother would always remark, "You are just like your grandmother." I think Hannah was artistic, strong-willed, and determined to succeed, and I wonder just how fulfilled and satisfied she was.

Charlotte LaVerne—Charlotte's Mother

Mama (1924–1966) married Charles Wilbur Matthews in June 1947 when she was twenty-two and gave birth to two daughters. I was born in 1948 and named after my mother. My sister Pamela followed fourteen months later in 1949. Both my mother and my aunt had worked prior to marriage and continued to work afterward. Fostering independence, Grandma had advised them. "You keep your job; you keep your money separate and let your husband support the family."

Mama and Aunt Celonia had grown up close and always did a lot together. Grandma sewed and dressed them alike as children. Mama did the same with Pam and me. When they first got married my mother and father shared an apartment with Aunt Celonia and her husband. My aunt's two sons were born within two months of my sister and me. Grandma often baby-sat, and the four of us spent our early years together. Today, my sister and I are very close, as are our children.

Mama and her sister were elementary school teachers. They both attended Minor Teachers College in Washington, D.C., where Grandma had also completed three years. Aunt Celonia, graduating cum laude, received a graduate fellowship and went on immediately to get her M.Ed. at Howard University. Both Minor and Howard are historically black institutions. There were a number of secretarial jobs in the federal government during World War II, but Grandma said, "You're not doing that. You're going right on up there to Minor Teachers College." According to Aunt Celonia, "Mother went to school with Charles Drew and a lot of people like that . . . so she was oriented that way because those were her classmates. She could see the success that they had, and she wanted the same success for her children" (October 29, 1991).

This was also a time when teaching was the most highly rewarded profession for black professional women. Education was considered to be the avenue for the social upliftment of American blacks, and this generation of black, educated, middle-class women was very active in civic organizations, including the black sororities. My mother and her sister belonged to Delta Sigma Theta. My mother was very active in the American Legion

Auxiliary, the PTA, and Sunday school. She also taught school for over ten years before her death of pancreatic cancer in 1966. She had taught at the school that my sister and I attended and was always home with us after school and during the summer. There was a sense of regularity in our lives, and she was at the center of it, as a strong disciplinarian.

Helen—Sharon's Mother

My mother, Helen Maher Thomson (1915–1997), was the third genera- tion of Canadian Irish Catholic women in her family. She had one older sister and four younger brothers. One brother was killed in World War II when he was only nineteen, and her youngest brother was born when my mother was fifteen. As a result of her mother's stroke, my mother became responsible for the care of her baby brother. Although she was a very shy, private person, my mother often told me about sneaking home from school to make sure the housekeeper had fed the baby. In spite of being punished by the Catholic nuns for being late for school, she never re- vealed her mission.

My mother was always critical of herself and always seemed to get into trouble as a child. She was not offered the opportunity to attend college like her sister and instead stayed at home to look after the family. She described herself as inferior to others and never believed that she was ca- pable of matching her sister's accomplishments or living up to her moth- er's expectations. In fact, I suspect she and her mother were not very close. However, she had a quiet strength, a zest for life, and, I believe, a great deal of undeveloped athletic ability. Although she would not agree, I think of my mother as a risk taker who knew how to follow her heart and her intuition. Certainly, her 1937 marriage outside the Catholic faith to the handsome and charismatic Earle Howard Thomson took great cour- age and created a tension with her family that was never resolved.

Cut off from family support, my mother worked briefly as a clerical worker at the wartime naval docks in Halifax, Nova Scotia, while my father worked out of town as a salesman. After their two-year-old daugh- ter, Joanne, died of leukemia in 1942, my mother bravely and confidently left home and followed my father to Ontario. After she suffered through five miscarriages, I was born in 1945 and raised as an only child by two devoted parents. As my father's business became more successful and de- manding, my mother centered her identity exclusively on her domestic role as mother, wife, and provider of a secure, dependable home base. Although she volunteered at the church, played golf, and curled, she took a great interest in every stage of my life. I think it was important for her to establish the close relationship with me that she never had with her own mother.

She loyally stood by her husband and his entrepreneurial dreams until his untimely death in 1969 threw her into a very unprepared state of widowhood when she was only fifty-two. In the end, I believe her blindness and cancer were the result of her lack of confidence and dependency. As well, breaking with the Catholic tradition of raising a large family weighed heavily on her as a sign of failure. In retrospect, my mother has taught me to trust in and take care of myself in order to be truly available to others.

Charlotte

Going to college and getting good grades was expected and my parents had saved for our education. My sister majored in physical therapy at Boston University and I in English education at Adelphi University in New York, both predominantly white universities. Like my mother and her sister, and my grandmother before them, I pursued education as a career, teaching high school English in Prince George's County, Maryland, for eleven years before accepting a position in higher education and moving away.

Getting married was also expected. I got married six days after graduation in 1969 at the age of twenty-one and gave birth to two daughters, Michon and Nikki, in 1972 and 1978, respectively. Unlike my foremothers, my babies were not born as soon after marriage or as close together. My sister also got married in the summer following her graduation and gave birth to a daughter, Celine, in the same year that Michon was born, and to two sons over the next seven years.

I separated from my husband when my daughters were eight and two. They have watched me with respect and admiration as I pursued successful educational and career goals. They have been witness to my ability to function effectively and independently as a single mother for over ten years—to purchase two homes, to buy a car, to relocate with them to another region of the country—to provide for their basic needs while at the same time pursuing advanced degrees.

I cannot discuss my Motherline without discussing sisterhood—Grandma and Aunt Bessie, Mama and Aunt Celonia, Pamela and me, Michon and Nikki. So much of who we are and who we are becoming is a function of the fact that we did not grow up as only children but with sisters who shared our experiences. Our views of the world are complementary and must be influenced by how we were raised. We are positive and open in our relations with people—calm and easygoing, nonjudgmental and trusting, caring and compassionate. We practice a relational ethic that Nel Noddings describes as an orientation "characterized in terms of responsibility and response . . . rooted in and dependent on natural caring . . . tied to experience."[12]

We inherited a strong sense of family and of community from our mother and grandmother. Although we were connected to our extended family, our primary living arrangement and interactions were as a nuclear family, and we lived not unlike the families we watched on television in the 1950s and 1960s. The mother of the family provided stability, regularity, and calmness. My sister and I carried these behaviors and expectations into our own marriages. Even though my family life is more disparate—divorced and remarried with elements of estrangement—I believe I also model similar ideals.

Sharon

As an only child, I was given all the financial advantages of schooling and travel that had been denied to my parents. I know that being proud of me was my mother's greatest pleasure, and it was important for me not to let her down. There was no question that I would attain the high marks needed to attend university. Higher education had more to do with filling in time and making myself more marketable to marry a professional who would take care of me than with future career goals. Miriam Johnson refers to this mind-set as the white middle-class woman's game "to find a man who is better than she and to gain a livelihood and status though him."[13] Accordingly, I married a lawyer a month after graduating from university in 1967 when I was twenty-one. Although my husband wanted a stay-at-home wife, I attended teachers' college the next year. After teaching kindergarten for one year, I willingly resigned and soon gave birth to my daughter Hilary in 1969. The universe moved through me that day and changed me forever. I felt more strongly connected to my own mother through our common experience of motherhood.

Just before my daughter was born, my father died suddenly and shortly afterward, my husband left our marriage. Together, my widowed mother and I struggled to balance our lives on our own. While she chose to immerse herself as a grandmother and replicate her familiar caretaking role, I chose to return to graduate school, resume my teaching career, and create a new identity for myself. I blamed myself for failing to be the perfect wife and mother, and I also felt tremendous guilt about leaving my children and neglecting the domestic chores. I could look to no other women in my family who had experienced any of this. Although my mother was willing to take care of my children and was pleased to see me challenged and fulfilled, I sensed her disapproval of my need to pursue a career. I also envied the close bond she and my children had established. In response to these confusing emotions, I blamed my mother for raising a well-educated daughter who was capable of thinking for herself and for modeling such a narrow path.

I became a thirty-something rebel intent on acts of deliberate resistance and accepted an administrative position with a school board some distance away. I also began to turn my attentions to a kind and gentle man who was raising four sons on his own. In deciding on him, almost twenty years later, I have been true to myself and my principles rather than to a value system set in place for me by others. I hope that my "need for self-definition and self-actualization as a single, working mother who continually questions conventions and challenges the status quo"[14] provides a map of encouragement and strength for my daughter to learn from.

Michon and Nikki—Charlotte's Daughters

The tradition of obtaining a college education has been carried on by my daughters. Michon completed a bachelor's degree in finance at Central State University in Wilberforce, Ohio, and a M.Ed. degree at Howard University. Although teaching was not her original goal, one week before receiving her undergraduate degree, she announced that she wanted to be a teacher. Nikki, a senior at Ohio University, is majoring in history. Although teaching is not her career goal, she is planning to teach English in Japan for a year and then join the Peace Corps before pursuing advanced studies in public policy.

Consistent with the model of black womanhood described by Patricia Hill Collins,[15] my daughters have learned independence, self-confidence, self-reliance, resourcefulness, and perseverance from me. But what have I taught them about male-female relationships? There was a time when my daughters felt disconnected from me and complained, justifiably, that I put whatever man was in my life before them. After ten years as a single parent, I married a man they do not like. I struggle with the estrangement that exists between my daughters and my husband. They struggle with the contradictions I offer as a model of womanhood, who at times was unintentionally abusive, weak, or neglectful.

Hilary—Sharon's Daughter

I encouraged my daughter to attend a university far away from home as a deliberate reaction to my mother's need to live vicariously through my life. Perhaps as a result of my influence, she attended university in Montreal and spent time in Quebec and England as an exchange student. Although Hilary often stated that she would never want to be a teacher or work as hard as me, she did become certified and taught elementary school for three years. Feeling somewhat confined and restricted, she has taken a study leave and enrolled in graduate school at the same university where I teach.

Just as I resemble my grandmother, my daughter shares similar traits with her grandmother. Like my mother, Hilary struggles to recognize and claim her self-worth and to move out from the shadow of her sibling. She used an eating disorder to keep her from dealing with the sense of loss and guilt manifested by my divorce from her father. Not surprisingly, her grandmother understood her vulnerability better than anyone and was more sensitive and compassionate than I could ever be. Like my mother before me, I am unable to prevent my daughter from crossing her own perilous terrain, but I learn from watching as she uncovers deep layers of strength, resilience, and compassion and builds herself into the reflective, self-directed, and courageous woman she is becoming. Today she remains single, free-spirited, and open to new directions in her life.

Sharon's Epilogue

I knew my mother into old age, and she knew me from childhood to middle age. Since her death, I look in the mirror and hate the fact that I see an aging face, her face, staring back at me. Although she dealt with her illness quite courageously, I did not like what she became at the end—withdrawn, self-absorbed, and isolated. I regret that I often begrudged her the time and attention that she required in her latter years, that I was not more sensitive to her fierce pride and loss of dignity, and that I was not the patient caregiver that she had always been. However, I am beginning to appreciate the adjustments she was able to make in her life to cope with illness, death, widowhood and divorce just as our foremother Catherine did by leaving centuries of family roots behind in Ireland and bravely embarking on a voyage to a new, unknown world.

Charlotte's Epilogue

I am proud to be a member of a Motherline of strong, independent, resilient, educated black women. Its future now rests with my daughters. At this writing, Michon wants marriage but no children, while Nikki wants children but is not sure about marriage. Yet their appreciation of the mother-daughter relationship we have inspires in them the desire for a similar relationship with daughters of their own. Therefore, the possibility and the anticipation of a continuation of our Motherline exists.

RACIAL IDENTITIES ACROSS MOTHERLINES

Charlotte's Black Culture

We are black. We grew up in a predominantly black world of schools and neighborhoods in D.C., the chocolate city. However, having light skin is a significant variable in our life experiences because it influences how both black and white Americans respond to us as well as how we view ourselves. As light-skinned people with good hair, we have been benefactors of a racist system of privilege that resulted in "social and economic advantages, both within and outside [the black] community," and perpetuated "a social hierarchy based on appearance."[16] My foremothers, by virtue of their appearance, were members of an elite group that had/has discriminated against and segregated itself from darker-skinned black Americans to preserve its "unique status as a buffer class."[17] They were participants in exclusive black social clubs, vacationed at the once restricted Highland Beach on Chesapeake Bay, and attended good schools, such as Dunbar High School and Howard University, that favored light-skinned blacks. Washington, D.C., happened to be one of several urban centers noted for its black elite. Russell, Wilson, and Hall explain this phenomenon:

> In a society that is politically and economically controlled by Whites, those members of minorities with the lightest skin and the most Caucasian-looking features have been allowed the greatest freedom. The unique privileges granted to mulattos under slavery enabled them to advance further.[18]

Although I remind myself that I am privileged by the colorism that exists within and without the black community, and that some might wonder whether I am white or mixed, I was not taught color discrimination at home. My father has light skin and my mother's father had light skin, but several of my relatives have varying shades of darker skin. My first husband has dark skin and my daughters' skin color is in the light brown and midbrown range. In my neighborhood I played with, went to school with, and was friends with black children of all hues, though we were all victims of cruel name-calling based on color. There was minimal race mixing and there were few white teachers at our schools. Although I went to predominantly white Girl Scout camps and we went out to eat and vacationed everywhere, our daily lives were centered in a diverse black community. What was passed on to me by my foremothers was the ability and desire to get along with all people.

It is difficult to separate race and color from class, or socioeconomic status. We were part of the black middle class, due to the legacy of economic and educational advantage we enjoyed as light-skinned black people. There was the tendency among the members of the black middle class "to adopt certain white, middle-class values. . . . A large part of the black community believed that the way to defeat racism was to obey every rule of proper behavior to the letter, to offer no provocation for discrimination."[19] My home culture was very much the same as the dominant American culture with respect to language, dress, foods, behaviors, aspirations, and so on. As a consequence, we probably identified more with middle-class whites than with lower- or working-class blacks.

Sharon's White Culture

In my Ontario community everyone looked like me and I took my physical appearance and racial identity for granted. Apart from the television coverage about school segregation in America or the assassination of Martin Luther King, racial issues did not affect my life and the opportunities to get to know black people simply did not exist.

Alice McIntyre questions the tendency for white researchers to focus on people of color in order to dichotomize and make sense of their own racial identities as either ideal or bad, haves or have nots, and rescuers of others or protectors of their own privilege. [20] She concludes that white people must come to know themselves, not just in relationship to people of color but primarily in relationship to a larger white group. By focusing on my own Motherline, I was able to attend to a particular group of white women, as McIntyre suggests and, by doing so, gain deeper insights about myself. However, in my attempt to understand systemic constructions of whiteness, I found surprisingly few studies that isolate specific characteristics of white mothering[21] as compared to those that attempt to define black mothering.[22] Patricia Hill Collins, for example, describes a distinct African-American experience of mothering that involves a

> collective effort to create and maintain family life in the face of forces that undermine family integrity . . . [and] recognizes that individual survival, empowerment, and identity require group survival empowerment, and identity.[23]

Similar distinctions of white mothering experiences are not as clear.

Perhaps little attention has been paid to the explicit study of whiteness because we do not choose to deconstruct our privilege and critique our roles as oppressors. Most of the Western literature assumes white experience to be the universal norm that continues to advantage the dominant group and supports the notion that difference equals deficiency in the Other. Yolanda Neimann points out that whites are carefully taught to ignore the complexities of race and to deny white privilege at the expense of others as a significant aspect of our social location.[24] As she explains, most white people have internalized institutional racism while believing they have rejected personal racism. Certainly this was true for my mother who saw nothing inappropriate about calling all of her caregivers by name except for a black nurse whom she referred to as "the colored girl."

I believe that the numbing effect of group homogeneity also contributes to the transparency of whiteness in the literature as well as to the difficulties this imposes on defining and politicizing a discourse of whiteness as a self-conscious cultural critique of positionality. According to Joan Griscom, "when Whiteness is atheorized and invisible, it tends to become normative."[25] Only by problematizing the system of whiteness, speaking openly and honestly about our own collusion, and acknowledging ourselves as racial beings can we begin to puncture illusions and dismantle barriers that insulate white people in their own invisibility and disrupt racial practices of privilege and advantage.

DISCUSSION

By comparing our Motherlines, we have identified three common themes in each generation of women as we replicated or resisted what our mothers had modeled: racial dualism, collective pride, and economic independence. The implications of each theme will briefly be addressed.

Racial Dualism

By probing beneath the veneer of polite cross-racial dialogue, we realize how limited our early interactions had been outside our own racial communities and how little we knew about each other's culturally lived experiences. For the most part, our lives in segregated neighborhoods and schools did not offer opportunities to question the institutional racism that informed and reproduced our stereotypical thinking. As privileged members of our respective patriarchal class-based cultures, we inherited and internalized a "unidimensional dualism"[26] that reinforced our ambivalent belief that we belonged to good, caring families who were sensitive to the Other and, not wanting to jeopardize our own advantage, that our social system was fair and just. This belief helped us justify the multiple ways we benefited from racism.

In many ways, including her emphasis on light skin color and nice hair, Charlotte identified more strongly with assimilation into the accepted norms of white culture than she did with inclusion of a black heritage into a rich multicultural structure. However, as McIntyre[27] argues, the recognition of different standards for blacks and whites is a crucial step in beginning to locate racism within the individual and to unpack the systemic structures that advantage one group over another and construct notions of asymmetrical power and privilege. Indeed, by attempting to include themselves in the cultural mainstream, Charlotte's family was privileging the foundations of a system that favored whites and was defending the myth that blacks would do well to follow the example of whites rather than working to reconstruct the system.

Sharon's family, on the other hand, ignored or denied the complex barriers that were built to advantage whiteness, to support entrenched white ideals and their benevolent veneer, and to reward white people as rightful recipients based on their birthright and so-called efforts and work ethic. Furthermore, no one felt the need to justify this social privilege. She agrees with McIntyre that "It's a painful realization for White people to admit that our history is fraught with the destruction of other peoples in the name of democracy, freedom, and equal rights."[28] It is important to challenge these misrepresentations within our own families rather than "abdicating responsibility" or "feeling defensive or powerless"[29] in order to fully examine the conditions under which they were produced.

Collective Pride

We also appreciate the fact that for several generations our foremothers had been part of a tightly insulated community filled with a shared history of strong ethical principles as well as various degrees of colonial hardship. Undoubtedly, the women in our Motherlines shared a collective sense of pride in their identity as an African-American minority group or as Irish Catholic immigrant farming wives. Their ability to overcome insurmountable obstacles such as slavery, famine, perilous transcontinental sea voyages, poverty, illness, death, widowhood, and divorce provided powerful models for their daughters.

In Charlotte's family, pride was associated with physical appearance and education, while Sharon's foremothers placed more value on their Catholic duties to raise large families and remain loyal and dependent on their husbands. There were close intergenerational links between the women in Charlotte's family, and they celebrated and honored their mothers' achievements. In contrast, the female bonds between the generations do not appear to be as strong in Sharon's family, and the women did not seem to place as much value on their accomplishments. As a result, much of their maternal history is lost. In Charlotte's Motherline, a strong sense of community responsibility was manifested through social service and relational occupations and avocations. Her foremothers were teachers and community leaders/activists, participants in women's charity organizations. Such an emphasis on community is a major theme in the legacy of black women in America. Charlotte feels a similar connection to public school education and the preservice teachers she mentors. She seeks the kind of caring relationship with students that she shares with her daughters.

Economic Independence

According to Collins, "African-American women have long integrated their activities as economic providers into their mothering relationship" as "an important and valued dimension of Afrocentric definitions of Black motherhood."[30] As black girls, Collins recalls, we "learn by identifying with our mothers" and

> are raised to expect to work, to strive for an education so that [we] can support [our]selves, and to anticipate carrying heavy responsibilities in [our] families and communities because these skills are essential for [our] own survival as well as for the survival of those for whom [we] will eventually be responsible.[31]

Consistent with this attitude, Charlotte believes that her foremothers modeled self-reliance, assertiveness, and independence, while at the same time relinquishing self in their roles as wives and mothers. Charlotte also relies on other mothers such as her aunt and her sister. Her daughter Nikki shares her views:

> I guess the model of womanhood I identify with is the strong type who can make everything happen, is the glue of the family, has a career, and is a good mother. There are white women who have babies and let their husbands do the breadwinning. Some even have housekeepers. To me, that's not an option. The women I know have historically not had that option. I don't expect male folk to stick around and help out. I want to be prepared to do it on my own in case he cuts out early. At this point, I have decided against marriage for myself. (September 8, 1996)

Although Sharon appreciates the legacy of care, sacrifice and unconditional love that her mother left to her and her children, she identified more with her father as the strong, independent role model in her life. Perhaps, as Johnson explains, middle-class white mothers were often so financially and psychologically dependent on men that they defined men and marriage to their daughters as essential and in doing so, elevated the status of wife while marginalizing that of the mother.[32] Certainly, this was the case for Sharon's mother and probably for her grandmother as well. In contrast, black mothers, according to Johnson, were often less dependent on their husbands' financial support and, as such, were viewed by their daughters as stronger and more powerful. As a result, the role of the black mother was held in higher esteem.

According to Darlene Hine and Kathleen Thompson, "teaching became the vocation most often chosen by young middle-class black women" as it was "an opportunity for service to the race."[33] Consistent with this viewpoint, Charlotte remembers her mother and grandmother urging her to become an educated professional in order to be financially self-sufficient. She recalls that, unlike many blacks in her generation, she was not a first-generation college graduate, and although the professional opportunities available to black women have expanded tremendously, teaching has continued as an occupation of choice for women in her family. Her daughter Michon now teaches fifth grade in the same county where she once taught.

In contrast to several generations of teachers in Charlotte's motherline, Sharon was the first woman in her family to receive a university degree and to work outside the home. However, as a result of her divorce and her need to prove her self-worth and to focus her energies in some meaningful way, Sharon returned to her teaching career and also earned her M.Ed. and Ed.D. degrees. Unlike her foremothers, Sharon now places far less faith in the financial security of marriage and advises her daughter to "develop a career that will allow you to be financially independent and able to take care of yourself!" Based on comments written in a birthday card to her mother in 1995, Hilary seems to admire these independent qualities herself. She wrote, "You have overcome so many impossible obstacles throughout my lifetime. All your difficult struggles represent so much strength and hope for me. You have given me wings to fly."

CONCLUSIONS

Initially, we focused on the commonalties in our maternal experiences such as class privilege, divorce, single parenting, teaching, leaving home, guilt, and mother loss. However, it was not until we attended to our cultural differences that we were able to shift the way we saw and listened to ourselves. For example, Sharon was able to appreciate how her former research perpetuates the invisibility of white norms. In fact, we both came to realize that the exclusive communities in which we grew up emphasized power and privilege and affected our limiting ideals about generic motherhood. According to Joan Griscom, most white feminist psychologists have foregrounded their similarities with black women in an attempt to affirm sisterhood "without first fully recognizing and understanding difference."[34] Perhaps it feels more collaborative to focus on sameness or perhaps dominant groups are less able to assume a standpoint of difference.

As a result of our focus on obvious cultural differences, we came to realize there is more diversity between generations of women in our Motherlines than there is between our cultures. For example, we have not placed the same value on self-sacrifice and inequitable divisions of labor as our foremothers. Likewise, our daughters, as part of the backlash culture, do not seem to be in such a hurry to marry, have children, or settle into careers. Moreover, they do not see equity issues of gender and race to be the serious problems they were in the 1950s and 1960s. The youngest members of our Motherlines are determined not to tie themselves down to responsibilities and obligations to others too soon and are more interested in taking advantage of all their options.

In their turn, each foremother introduced changes to the Motherline, such as moving from her homeland, resisting religious restrictions, acquiring educational degrees, restricting the size of her families, and coping with illness and death. Perhaps we, and our daughters who follow, will leave a legacy of female empowerment, resistance, and broken silences for those who come after us to build upon. By comparing our maternal experiences, we realize how difficult it is to interrupt the tendency to rely on group consensus and to keep the focus on the actions of others in order to ignore biases within ourselves. During each generation, powerful forces emerge causing us to view ourselves as victims and to anesthetize constructive critical dialogue. As a result of sharing our stories with each other, we conclude that to pass on a thoughtful and well-considered Motherline to our daughters, we must first deconstruct dominant ideologies and hegemonic discourses of cross-cultural motherhood ourselves.

NOTES

1. Naomi Lowinsky, *Stories from the Motherline: Reclaiming the Mother-Daughter Bond, Finding Our Feminine Souls* (Los Angeles: Tarcher, 1992), 18.

2. Lowinsky, *Stories from the Motherline*, xii.

3. Michelle Fine, *Disruptive Voices: The Possibilities of Feminist Research* (Ann Arbor: University of Michigan Press, 1992), xi.

4. Carolyn Heilbrun, *Writing a Woman's Life* (New York: Norton, 1988), 30–31.

5. Kathryn Anderson and Dana C. Jack, "Learning to Listen: Interview Techniques and Analyses," in *Women's Words: The Feminist Practice of Oral History*, ed. Sherna Berger Gluck and Daphne Patai (New York: Routledge, 1991), 11.

6. Hope Edelman, *Motherless Daughters: The Legacy of Loss* (New York: Bantam Doubleday, 1994), 253.

7. Michelle Fine, "Working the Hyphens: Reinventing Self and Other in Qualitative Research," in *Handbook of Qualitative Research*, ed. Norman K. Denzin and Yvonna S. Lincoln (Thousand Oaks, Calif.: Sage, 1994), 70.

8. Carmen Berry and Tamara Traeder, *Girlfriends: Invisible Bonds, Enduring Ties* (Berkeley, Calif.: Wildcat Canyon, 1995), 137.

9. Gail Sheehy, *New Passages: Mapping Your Life across Time* (New York: Ballantine, 1995).

10. Joseph A. King, *Ireland to North America: Emigrants from West Cork* (Toronto: Meany, 1994), 32.

11. "Wedding Bells," *North Shore Leader*, Chatham, New Brunswick, October 12, 1906, 1 (17).

12. Nel Noddings, "An Ethic of Caring and Its Implications for Instructional Arrangements," in *The Education Feminism Reader*, ed. Linda Stone (New York: Routledge, 1994), 173–74.

13. Miriam M. Johnson, *Strong Mothers, Weak Wives* (Berkeley: University of California Press, 1988), 40.

14. Sharon M. Abbey, "Mentoring My Daughter: Contradictions and Possibilities," *Canadian Woman Studies* 18, nos. 2 & 3 (Summer/Fall 1998): 22–29.

15. Patricia Hill Collins, "The Meaning of Motherhood in Black Culture and Black Mother-Daughter Relationships," in *Double Stitch: Black Women Write about Mothers and Daughters*, ed. Patricia Bell-Scott et al. (New York: Harper Perennial, 1991).

16. Kathy Russell, Midge Wilson, and Ronald Hall, *The Color Complex: The Politics of Skin Color among African-Americans* (New York: Doubleday, 1992), 4.

17. Russell et al., *The Color Complex*, 16.

18. Russell et al., *The Color Complex*, 34.

19. Darlene Hine and Kathleen Thompson, *A Shining Thread of Hope: The History of Black Women in America* (New York: Broadway, 1998), 182–83.

20. Alice McIntyre, *Making Meaning of Whiteness* (New York: State University of New York Press, 1997), 79.

21. See, for example, McIntyre, *Making Meaning of Whiteness*; Maureen T. Reddy, ed., *Everyday Acts against Racism: Raising Children in a Multiracial World* (Seattle: Seal, 1996).

22. See, for example, Bell-Scott, ed., *Double Stitch*; Elizabeth Brown-Guillory, *Women of Color: Mother-Daughter Relationships in 20th-Century Literature* (Austin: University of Texas, 1996); bell hooks, *Talking Back: Thinking Feminist, Thinking Black* (Boston: South End Press, 1989); Joyce E. King and Carolyn A. Mitchell, *Black Mothers to Sons: Juxtaposing African-American Literature with Social Practice* (New York: Peter Lang, 1995); Audre Lorde, *Sister Outsider: Essays and Speeches* (Trumansburg, N.Y.: Crossing Press, 1984); and Alice Walker, *In Search of Our Mothers' Gardens* (New York: Harcourt Brace, 1983).

23. Patricia Hill Collins, "Shifting the Center: Race, Class, and Feminist Theorizing about Motherhood," in *Mothering: Ideology, Experience, and Agency*, ed. Evelyn Nakano Glenn, Grace Chang, and Linda Rennie Forcey (New York: Routledge, 1994), 47.

24. Yoland Neimann, "Nurturing Antiracism: A Permeation of Life," in *Everyday Acts Against Racism*, ed. Reddy, 35.

25. Joan Griscom, "Women and Power: Definition, Dualism & Difference," *Psychology of Women Quarterly* 16, no. 4 (September 1992): 408.

26. McIntyre, *Making Meaning*, xii.

27. McIntyre, *Making Meaning*, 86.

28. McIntyre, *Making Meaning*, 89.

29. McIntyre, *Making Meaning*, 69, refers to these affective expressions experienced by white people that are related to positions of privilege as "privileged affect" that serve to discount the conditions and feelings of others.

30. Collins, "The Meaning of Motherhood in Black Culture and Black Mother-Daughter Relationships," 48.

31. Collins, "The Meaning of Motherhood in Black Culture and Black Mother-Daughter Relationships," 53.

32. Johnson, *Strong Mothers*, 41.

33. Hine and Thompson, *A Shining Thread of Hope*, 123.

34. Griscom, "Women and Power," 408.

18

Constantly Negotiating: Between My Mother and My Daughter

Joonok Huh

I am a first-generation immigrant. Since I came to this country in 1974, I have spent half of my life in the West, in America, and the earlier half in the East, in Korea. I often feel as if my home is somewhere in between, like over the Pacific Ocean—no roots, but always floating. My relationships with my Korean mother and my American-born daughter seem to share the same diasporic, constantly shifting, floating, just like my identity or home. Marianne Hirsch in her *Mother/Daughter Plot: Narrative, Psychoanalysis, Feminism* says that selfhood

> would have to balance the personal with the political, the subjective experience with the cognitive process of identification with various group identities. It would have to include a consciousness of oppression and political struggle. It would have to be both familial and extra familial.[1]

I often feel that my immigrant status has intensified the nature of personal and political discourses, and my relationships with my mother and my daughter have provided a space for the intersection of "both familial and extra familial" in a more obvious manner.

Both culture and politics create symbols that we try to adapt to our personal use (using *symbol* in the broadest sense—of fitting parts together to make a whole). We try to make connections between what is going on at the individual level and what is going on out there in the larger sense. We construct identity on the basis of what it allows us to do in the world. My constantly shifting, floating identity, the immigrant status, over the Pacific Ocean between my home country and my adopted country, seems to always challenge the meanings of both familial and extrafamilial.

The mother-daughter relationship is no exception. As a first-generation

267

immigrant mother living in the United States, I have often felt ambivalent about my role as mother of my twelve-year-old daughter and as daughter of my seventy-five-year-old mother. Whenever I visit my mother in Korea and need to play the daughter role for her, I wish my mother would let me be my own person instead of insisting that I be a Korean woman. She asks me at least to pretend I am a Korean woman while in Korea. When I resume my mother role upon coming back to the United States, I am confronted by my daughter's question, the same one that I raise to my mother while on the other shore. She is not happy with me for reminding her that she is Asian-American, not American. I sometimes think that to my daughter, I am just like those immigrant mothers portrayed in the work of Jade Snow Wong and Monica Sone; yet to my mother, I am one of those rebellious daughters in Maxine Hong Kingston and Amy Tan.

I locate myself between my American daughter and my Asian mother, and as I shift between the roles of mother and daughter I see that what is most important is not my negotiation with either my mother or my daughter but, rather, our survival together. For the daughter-writers of our century, narratives are a means of rescuing themselves and their mothers through the act of storytelling. As Michel de Certeau would say, these are fragile narratives, "seized on the wing" as it were by people who, until now, were regarded as almost invisible.[2] My conflicts with my daughter and with my mother form trajectories with writings by Asian-American women to reflect a distinct relationship with the dominant culture. This relationship is dialogic: thus, while I move outward from the individual self to the dyad, and from the dyad to the family and the larger society, and thence to nation and culture, I see a simultaneous action inward—from culture back to self.

There is no set theory, no formula in the mother-daughter relationship: there are dyads, dyadic hierarchies, dyadic predicaments, dysfunctional dyads, but no formulas. Perhaps we should go back to the basics: the mother-daughter relationship is grounded in the body, and the physical ground is the source of representation. Daughter is separated from mother at birth, and this fact is the source of a beautiful metaphor that contains the seemingly elemental processes of reining in and breaking free, composing and decomposing, mothering and birthing, holding together and letting go. We glimpse the nature of freedom. Even as the daughter separates herself from her mother's society, as in my case, she carries with her both the capacity to re-create the process and the consciousness that she is both the same as and different from her mother. As both fact and metaphor, the mother-daughter relationship creates a space for creative play. And this space for creative play is the intersubjective space Hirsch alludes to.

It is the same kind of space that exists between history and politics, or between family and culture. When I try to recapture my relationship with my mother and my relationship with my daughter, I see myself breaking free of the ideology on motherhood through the examination of motherhood in Asian and Asian-American cultures. The result of breaking free is a loss of identities, both familial and extrafamilial identities. I locate in a space that is neither Korean nor American but that is both Korean and American. On a personal level, I lose myself and gain my mother, or lose myself and gain my daughter. Identity becomes extremely fragile, and opportunities for self-revelation are "seized on the wing." In short, the mother-daughter relationship represents all of the dynamics of hierarchy, social negotiation, individual modeling, role playing, displacement, accommodation, resistance, and subversion. Narratives are begotten because of and in spite of cultural limitations.

I grew up in a very protected environment in Korea. My mother stayed home and did all those traditional jobs prescribed for women. She was one of many women in my home country who were thankful for her comfortable life and her generous husband. My mother's everyday life was devoted to her family: serving her husband and my brother, and preparing four daughters for the same woman's life course as hers. Most times, she felt happy because she believed she was better off than the average woman in Korea. Yet there were times she seemed uncertain about her prescribed roles as mother and wife. While teaching us girls to be decent future wives, she was very protective of us because of the gender roles awaiting us once we left her nest. My father used to chide my mother for "spoiling the girls." He worried that we were not trained enough to be good homemakers, and thus we would suffer once we married. My father himself spoiled us terribly, but as the man of the family, he was acutely aware of gender hierarchies. My mother's defense against his concern was always the same: "I would like to give them opportunities to enjoy their lives while they can. Once they marry, they can't anymore." The implication was clear: she had to teach the life she herself was ambiguous about. Thus she tried to do her best for us to enjoy life while we could under her roof. I appreciated her tremendously for her own sacrifice for us; nonetheless, it bothered me that she was preparing us for a life she did not care about. At my young age, I made up my mind not to resemble her in my future.

That was why I decided to come to America upon completing my B.A. degree. With the bachelor's degree, we girls were expected to marry, and that would have been my life course as well. When I presented my acceptance letter from Indiana University, my mother felt she was in a bind. For my parents, education was a religion; for a good education, they would have done anything, everything. My father promised to support my higher education in America, but at the same time he asked my mother to arrange a marriage for me before I left. She was of two minds: she was aware that I was planning to go to America partly because I didn't want to follow the prescribed course of a Korean woman's life; at the same time, she was concerned about my going to this "wild" country on my own. One day, she was perfectly understanding of me and was willing to support me; another day, she felt she was failing me. She engaged marriage brokers to please my father and to a certain extent herself. She knew I was simply playing along to buy time until I would leave for the new country. The new life in America was beautiful. It was my first time ever to be on my own. The first night in a dorm room, I was only happy about the open future that was mine. Whenever my mother called me, I had a bit of a guilty conscience about not missing her as much as she missed me. But it is another chapter of my life story, so I'll stop there.

While doing my graduate work, I had this vision of myself becoming an independent woman, the image that I yearned for so much while in Korea. The year I started my graduate program in 1974, Indiana University began their women's studies program. In a sense my American life began with this women's studies program. My second summer in America, my mother visited and spent about a month with me. It was the first chance I had ever had to have that much time with her alone; it was the first chance she had stayed away from my father or family that long. Having spent two years in America as a graduate student in English and women's studies, I felt like a Western-educated liberal. I was rather critical about my mother being an "Asian" mother—not an independent woman. I raised the questions that I would not have dared to if we both had been in Korea. Perhaps in my own mind, it was a chance for me to have a woman-to-woman conversation with my mother. I was daring enough to talk about all kinds of personal questions including a taboo subject, sex. The most impressive thing was that my mother was willing to open up to me; in fact, she was eager to talk about anything and everything with me, including that taboo subject. It was obvious that the environment had made her a different person: she was herself, rather than her role. For the first time in my life, I realized that my mother had been trapped in her prescribed life; for the first time, I learned that she has had her own dreams. Her whole life, she has walked between her desire to live her life and her duty to family and society. Her environment did not present her much choice; in a Confucian society, she had to marry, produce children, and serve her husband and family. Deep down, however, she had her own dreams, knowing that they would remain only dreams. And she told me she was determined to support my dream of going to America for higher education at any cost. Perhaps she wanted to live out the dream that she has had but never dared to dream about living.

Another revelation about my mother was her relationship with her mother. My mother used to think my grandmother was odd or strange mainly because her values were different. Her mother studied Western theology in Japan during the early 1920s, during Japanese colonization in Korea. When she came back to Korea, her "modern" education made my grandmother different from the rest of the townspeople. In addition, she appeared to be proud, distant, liberal, which was not allowed for Korean women at that time. My mother had mixed feelings toward her Western-ized mother—envy, fear, embarrassment. Culturally, in this case, the daughter did not know what to make of her "modern" mother. Anything modern or Western was very much rejected in Korean society in the be-ginning of the twentieth century, so by labeling my grandmother "mod-ern" or "Western," my mother created a comfortable cultural distance. In a sense, my mother was making a political statement of her own: rejecting her mother's values was like rejecting the Japan that was forcing the tradi-tional Korean society to Western modes of life during the Japanese An-nexation. Since my grandmother died when my mother was only twelve years old, I never knew her. But from the stories, "weird" in my mother's eyes when she was growing up, I have always been attracted to this woman who seemed to be born about half a century earlier than she should have. My mother used to say that her mother could not have lived long anyhow because of different values and ideologies about life. I often wonder whether she was one of those unheard/unspoken potential femi-nists who lived much earlier than feminism was introduced to us.

Since that summer, the nature of my story with my mother has been constantly unfolding. I expected that my story with my daughter, in other words, me as a mother someday, would be different from that with my mother. But the crucial understanding of my mother as mother did not come until much later, until I became pregnant myself, almost ten years after that summer. My pregnancy after seven years of marriage turned out to be one of the most critical moments in my life. For the first time since I came to America, I was challenged by the identity questions. On the one hand, I was happy about becoming a mother and building a bond with the child inside me, a biological bond between two human beings. On the other hand, I had a terrible fear about the possibility of having to lose what I had built up and enjoyed in America. All of a sudden, cultural norms and expectations oppressed me. The fetus reminded me of my mother's life, which I decided not to repeat a decade ago. Once that came to my mind, the baby became a symbol of cultural practices of being a mother in Korea. Pregnancy seemed to pull me back to Korea and the norms that I did not care about. I felt forced to think about myself, my past, and my future on both planes, both East and West. Somehow, in my fetus, East and West came together and clashed. Friends and relatives were very happy since they had waited seven years for the news and especially since the baby's dad was the only son from a very traditional, prestigious family in Korea. I felt as if there were a conspiracy to send me back to the Confucian cultural practices. More than anything, however, I was angry at myself for not being able to enjoy the baby and pregnancy because of the cultural expressions of my different identities.

At the fifth month of pregnancy, I found that the sex of my baby was female. Once again, I felt it was a mixed blessing. I myself wanted a girl who could grow up as a wonderful feminist, who could live the life that I felt I had missed, but on the other hand I felt pressure inside coming from a male-preference tradition. I was disappointed seeing myself a product of that tradition. After all that struggle and effort to get away from those cultural practices, they were still present inside me, no matter how minute they might be. My reaction to the sex of my fetus brought back a memory of what my mother used to say about her pregnancy with me. I used to hear about it as an anecdote but was never hit by the story until that point in my life. When she was pregnant with me, she was almost terrified. It was her third pregnancy. Before, she had two daughters. For the third time, there was enormous pressure on her to produce a son. Have a third girl? It was intolerable to my father, who was the only male heir in his own family. It really was not a matter of love between them. It was a cultural expectation, and my father wanted a boy so much. My mother once told me that when she gave birth to me and realized I was another girl, she cried. She felt like a sinner to my father and his family; more than that, however, she was sorry for me having to face the same lot in the future. Because of my own anxiety and resentment about not being able to enjoy my own pregnancy and body as much as I should, I understood what my mother's motherhood was like more clearly than ever.

After my initial reaction to pregnancy—mostly about East and West and gender issues—came another fear. This time, I anticipated racial conflicts between the first-generation parent and the second-generation, American-born children. I began to see anxiety in me about becoming a mother like Maxine Hong Kingston's mother, although in my academic papers I admired what Kingston's mother has done for Kingston. Theoretical, political, cultural questions, concerns, worries dominated me during my pregnancy. In other words, motherhood appeared to be all "role" rather than "relationship." I wanted to be the best mom; I was not aware that I was creating my own role of motherhood in reaction to "the role" from which I desperately liberated myself. Once my child was born, however, I learned that she was real. I had to change her diapers, feed her. She needed me not as an Asian or Asian-American mother but as mother, a biological bond, a connection between us, nothing else.

As a mother interested in this topic, I had the illusion that I was prepared for the problems that we often see portrayed in the mother-daughter relationship because I had studied about it. Once in a while, I was secretly pleased because my feminist ideology about motherhood seemed to be working for me. But that was when Chris was not able to express herself and when she was not fully exposed to social, cultural expectations of her. In everyday life, I constantly face clashes, surprises, and realize that I will never be the "ideal, perfect" mother that I dreamed about becoming. While I try to manipulate the relationship before it unfolds, I realize my daughter is growing up, too suddenly, it seems. She is an individual. Also, we both live in the social framework, not in my academic, theoretical framework.

Four years ago, I had a chance to realize that my relationship with Chris is also a constantly unfolding experience, just like that with my mother. I was visiting my family in Korea with my then eight-year-old daughter. My younger sister and I were trying to catch up with each other's lives and were talking about family—typical sister talk. My sister was describing her conflicts with her teenage daughter. She was having a tough time with her daughter's independence. Chris, who had overheard part of the conversation, surprised me when she blurted out, "But, Auntie, it's just another mother-daughter thing, so why are you making such a big deal out of it?" I was stunned. My reaction was "What have I done to my child?" Her dismissal of my sister's struggle simply as something between any mother and any daughter was not right. Just another mother-daughter thing? It sounded as if the mother-daughter thing was just a phrase, an academic exercise, not worth all that talk because, in the end, everything would be all right. In the years I have been working on this topic, she has grown up with it in her environment (books, movies, tapes, telephone conversations, my computer screen), and she probably formed her opinion that it is academic stuff. Her nonchalant remark shook up my pride about myself as a mother. I realized that my concept of motherhood did not take her feelings into account. More specifically, as long as the child is not able to express herself, the mother may be able to think that the relationship is just fine. Yet there is a point when the daughter begins to think independently and evaluates her mother's presuppositions. For her, what I write about the mother-daughter relationship, it exists in theory alone.

As Chris grows up, her perception of her Asian mother—me—changes. And I am convinced that the changes about me reflect the changes of her own idea of herself, an Asian-American girl. Until she started kindergarten, she was not aware of being different from the rest. It was when she was about five years old. She caught me off guard one day by asking, "Mom, why do I have this black hair? Why not red hair like Little Mermaid or blonde hair like Sleeping Beauty?" That was the initial moment of our ongoing conversation about our being Asian-Americans. Then she began to draw the line between me and herself, me being an Asian and her being an American. My accent, for instance, used to embarrass her in public. In her mind I represented the "foreign" identity she was anxious to deny in herself. However, that separation anxiety from me seems to be over. In the present stage, I even see some sense of pride in Chris toward me.

This past summer, Chris and I were roommates during the six weeks of my National Endowment for the Humanities summer seminar in New York City. It turned out to be one of our greatest times together in spite of our anxiety about spending six weeks in one room away from home. All of a sudden, I felt she became my friend, able to share every experience from cultural to academic. One evening, we were reading together one of the books for the seminar, E. L. Doctorow's *Ragtime*. When I mispronounced a word, Chris was teasing me: "My Ph.D. professor mom, not knowing how to pronounce this word?" What I detected in her joke was her respect and pride of where her mom is in spite of handicaps. She is more accepting of what I represent—from food to cultural values—and, to me, it is a sign of her accepting herself, who she is.

That is the personal story between the two of us. In reality, however, our relationship is constantly being visited by characters in Asian-American literature, characters who are doubly marginalized, not simply because they are women, but because they are ethnic. For my daughter and me, the relationship is more precarious in the political sense than for my mother and me while I was growing up in Korea—my daughter and I need to deal with not only cultural differences but political implications stemming from postcolonial conditions. In Maxine Hong Kingston's *Woman Warrior*,[3] Brave Orchid, her mother, teaches the Chinese woman's virtue of being quiet, silent, almost demure; at the same time, mother pressures daughter to be able to speak up. I see the double role Brave Orchid must play for her daughter, to be Chinese and American at the same time. Through Brave Orchid, Kingston realizes that dual identities are what she is, and further, that they can be transcended. Like Brave Orchid for Maxine, I am the cultural transmitter for my daughter—Asian and American, both and neither. As it was to Kingston, growing up in America is confusing for my daughter. Like Brave Orchid, I am waiting for my daughter to realize why I seem to be confusing, at times even paradoxical.

As a daughter to my mother, I defend individual freedom and values, which my mother believes to be the product of a Western education. On the other hand, as a mother to my daughter, I defend the values of the family and community. Individualistic to my mother, collectivist to my daughter, my bipolar role used to trouble me, but it no longer does. Like my first-generation immigrant status, this bipolar position has enabled me to see the in-between space, between times, between locations, and between values.

Whatever it might be, the truth is that the mother-daughter relationship is another case of unfolding realizations: daughters realize how their mothers have been caught between traditions, and the daughters change when they themselves become mothers. It is a continuing story as the sense of being caught moves from generation, and as each sense of being caught charts the story of political change as well as the story of a culture. Narrative disclosures that unfold on the personal level suggest other, per- haps more complex, relations. Within a mother-daughter relationship, disclosures unfold in multiple ways: from mother to daughter, daughter to mother, and in my examples, and daughter to grandmother. All the while, each generation carries its burden of extrafamilial struggle: in one, the burden of Japanese values, in another, the legacy of a Confucian patri- archy, in yet another (mine), the immigrant experience. The power of the mother-daughter relationship is its ability to amplify complex relations and to define a new kind of middleness—one that is both value-laden and value-free, one that admits limitations yet is able to find liberation within these limitations. We define a middle ground or third space to accommo- date the intersection of life and politics, society and history. It is a lonely space, complex, at times confusing, yet full of possibility. In the most min- imal sense, the mother-daughter relationship presents us the opportunity to claim an identity, to empower ourselves, and invite others to do the same.

NOTES

1. Marianne Hirsch, *The Mother/Daughter Plot: Narrative, Psychoanalysis, Femi- nism* (Bloomington: Indiana University Press, 1989), 194.

2. Michel de Certeau, *The Practice of Everyday Life,* trans. Steven Rendall (Berke- ley: University of California Press, 1989), xix.

3. Maxine Hong Kingston, *Woman Warrior* (New York: Vintage, 1989).

19

Revisioning the Maternal Body: Loving in Difference in Ngozi Onwurah's Film *The Body Beautiful*

Andrea Liss

> To a world that sees only in black and white,
> I was made only in the image of my father.
> Yet . . . she lives inside me and cannot be
> separated. I may not be reflected in her image
> but my mother is mirrored in my soul.
>
> —Ngozi Onwurah

Ngozi Onwurah's remarkably powerful and poignant film, *The Body Beautiful*[1] (1990), makes visible the intense conflicts and deepening love in a British Nigerian daughter's changing and transformative relationship with her white British mother (see figure 19.1). Onwurah's bold and loving merging of visible differences into the intimacies of a particular mother/daughter bond takes place in the face of patriarchal value systems that divide women into those who are desired and those who are scorned. *The Body Beautiful* is life-affirming in its exploration of healing the cruel schisms that have severed the power of women's connections to each other, even as it takes into account the debilitating effects and possibilities of strength that result in confronting generational differences, illness, and racism.[2]

The last stunning passage in this beautifully unfolding and nonlinear story reveals the heart of the two women's intertwined narratives. As the dénouement in a series of deeply interwoven fictionalizations of events and memories, the daughter watches and creates for the viewer a devastatingly powerful and tender fantasy realm in which the mother imagines

277

a young British-African man making love to her, perhaps standing in for her Nigerian husband's absence in the film. This scene takes place at the same time as the daughter, a budding fashion model, is directed to look like she is making love during a photo shoot. Their distinct expressions of pleasure slowly merge on the screen—the daughter's contrived, the mother's tangible—culminating in the daughter's outrage, a cry of protection, perhaps jealously, as she screams out, "Don't touch her!" yet that is also audible as an affirmation and a plea for her mother's sexuality: "Touch her!" The scene resumes a quiet hush as the daughter slowly undresses, enters her mother's bed that now replaces the fantasy one where the lover had been, and the two women embrace. With the daughter's head resting visibly on her mother's breast, the site of her mastectomy, she softly intones:

> to a world that sees only in black and white, I was made only in the image of my father. Yet she has molded me, created the curves and contours of my life, colored the innermost details of my being. . . . She lives inside me and cannot be separated. I may not be reflected in her image but my mother is mirrored in my soul. I am my mother's daughter for the rest of my life.

When I wrote earlier that this film is a healing exploration, I meant it in the deep literal sense of the word *exploration*, "to cry out" or "to weep." In the afterbirth of watching *The Body Beautiful*, I feel my own sorrows and sources of life. I am caught between two bodies: the daughter's fluid, lithe one of young womanhood and the awkward yet calm body of the mother. In actual years I know I am closer to the mother, but my perception of myself does not often match my own changing body—the public presentation of self that my body gives outside of me. And yet the gap closes in ever faster between my body and my mother's; two generations of stories begin to overlap between my mother's life and my own, stories about cancers, mastectomies, and a myriad of other illnesses. "Mother, comfort me," I hear myself say as I rub my mother's hot forehead with a cold washcloth as she lays outstretched in her bed in the intensive care unit. I'm not used to being the tending one, the tender one to you, even though I lavish it on my own child, your grandson. My grandmother's fleshiness, surprisingly cool and fresh, encompasses me as I rail against the movie we've just watched together on TV somewhere around the year 1965. I think it was *One Potato, Two Potato*, starring Sidney Poitier. The film's closing scene shows a girl born of a black father and a white mother being driven away from them as she looks out the back window of the car that with each second divorces her implacably, cruelly, and illogically from her family. Strange that some of my earliest memories of racism and representations of separation merge with more recent dislocations, as

Fig. 19.1   Sian Martin in *The Body Beautiful,* a film by Ngozi Onwurah

Source: Photo courtesy of Women Make Movies.

they are each encoded within the comfort, strength and vulnerability of maternal bodies.

Through the mending force of its interplay between intimate memories, projected desires and cultural history, *The Body Beautiful* fluidly elicited psychic clips from my own life. The enormous power of this poignant film resides in part in its ability to bring the viewer outside of herself and back into a transformed and reflective space within herself. In addition, this "outside of herself" is worlds apart from traditional film narratives that separate the self from itself by directing the spectator's focus into the actions and gazes of a dominating character within the film. In the culmination of *The Body Beautiful*, neither mother nor daughter dominates the other. This subtle and bold film thus pivots around a stunning series of differences—traditional and re-explored expectations of beauty and the dichotomies between age and race—paradoxically played out through the mother's and the daughter's intersubjectivities. Onwurah as daughter and filmmaker guides us through her memories of her child self to young womanhood as she remembers her mother's vulnerabilities, the daughter's embarrassments and the intense love as well as the tensions between her plain-looking white British mother and her own visibly elegant black self. The film moves beyond the daughter's selfishness into a tale of mutual love between the mother and the daughter, their interdependence and poignant intersubjectivities. *The Body Beautiful* eventually leads the viewer to the daughter's realization of her mother's remarkable psychic strength and sense of personhood.

The film's central metaphors of intersubjectivity and revisioning the maternal body are constructed through an ingenious interplay between memory, fantasy and actuality. *The Body Beautiful* merges a creative reworking of the narrative documentary style with a courageous and strategic use of autobiography—the mother is Onwurah's real mother in the film. The doubled truth or verité in this subjective documentary helps bring into representation deep cultural taboos that are brought to bear on the body of the "disfigured" woman, doubly discounted and desexualized if she is a mother. Onwurah's approaches to autobiography and documentary filmmaking are deeply invested in challenging a patriarchal structure of knowing and seeing. In this essay, I explore *The Body Beautiful* in terms of the unique structure Onwurah has created to reach into the rawness of feeling, the ethics of care and the depths of maternal narrative in her remarkable testament to her own real-life mother, Madge Onwurah.

The mother's and the daughter's separate and mutual desires are given rich texture through the representation of voice in the film. *Voice* in this context refers both to the acknowledgment of previous devaluations and the enunciation of uncovered stories, as well as to the literal use of voices—and of silences—in the film. The film's direction and point of view are largely guided through the daughter's retrospective frame, yet she brings in her memories of and desires for her mother through the actuality of Madge's own voice. Interestingly, the two women's voices are rarely spoken through their bodies and are not directed at each other as in the relay of traditional dialogue. Instead, the voice-over is used to stage and reenact memories and fantasies of their transforming relationship. When one of the actors or actresses speaks directly with their own voice, it creates a jolting disruption in their interior musings and critical reflections. Remember the daughter yelling at her mother's imagined lover at the end of the film, enjoining him to touch and not to touch her mother as her words put an end to her mother's fantasy? Another such violent rupture occurs in the film's opening shot, in which the teenage daughter stands rebelliously at the top of a stairwell, dominating her mother's smaller figure below. Her voice cuts through the almost unrelenting, haunting calm of the background music score, wounding her mother through her taunting words: "You titless cow."

Both of these audible dislocations represent the daughter's teenage dependency on and resistance to her mother's authority, framed through her almost unwillfull desire to kill the mother, or at least the mother's spirit. These are scenes in the staging of a particular mother-daughter relation. They do not necessarily signal the typical Freudian scenario, in which the daughter's rejection of the mother and her eventual begrudging acceptance of the mother's supposed passivity to the rule of the father create her own cliché of woman. Onwurah begins her film with the adolescent daughter testing her own and her mother's limits, creating an in-flux frame on which to note the daughter's development and transformations necessary to the connection and transformation of the mother-daughter bond that is the heart of the film.

Like the passages that compose the film's ending, the emotionally frantic opening is transformed into more hushed and slowed down scenes as the movie unfolds into a series of reenacted memories narrated by the now grown-up daughter and her mother. These replays commence with the adult daughter recounting through voice-over her brother's birth, coupled indelibly in her mind with her mother's cancer and the mastectomy immediately following her sibling's birth. As the daughter's voice solemnly remembers, the visual screen shows the young girl, perhaps six or seven years old, visiting her mother in the hospital. We see intensely moving scenes of the two of them silently holding each other, gazing at each other in a timeless and protected space, keeping calm and strong for the other. These are interwoven with scenes of the daughter's and mother's traumatic dislocations as Madge is rushed down a cold and frightening hospital hallway, a vial of blood breaking in her wake. We also hear the mother's voice from within. She is shown in her hospital room, alone, as her voice-over recounts somber stories of desolation and sacrifice: her separation from her husband through the turmoils of Nigeria's civil war, her need to ignore the cancer in her body lest it endanger the delivery of her child, the callousness of the medical institution toward her body and personhood as she remembers the idiotic words of her doctor, ironicized through his voice as she remembers the hurt they caused her. Thus, the figure of the mother begins the film as the emblem of sacrifice, a tripled icon through the birth of her son, her own bodily loss and the absence of the father.

My account of the film might seem to interpret it like a classic case of female victimhood or religious sacrifice, reinforced by its incision on and transposition onto the body of the mother. Indeed, traditional patriarchal stories of the "good" mother figure her through acceptable allegories steeped in her ultimate giving to and sacrifice for her child, from religious tales of the Mother Mary to more modern woes of those "better" mothers who valiantly give up good financial earning power in order to stay at home. Even in our recent stories in philosophy and cultural theory, the paradigm of the mother is often unwittingly coupled with the notion of the "good," even with the general idea of ethics itself. For example, feminist philosopher Elizabeth Grosz interprets philosopher Emmanuel Levinas's idea of ethics as a response to the recognition of the primacy of alterity—the giving up of the self—over one's own identity. As she considers Levinas's ideas, ethics is that field defined by the other's need, the other's calling for a response. Grosz adds that "the paradigm of an ethical relation is that of a mother's response to the needs or requirements of a child."[3]

Onruwah's film admits to this traditional if not impossible notion of motherhood defined through the ethics of the mother's lack of selfhood, insidiously bonded with patriarchal concepts of victimhood. That we know the story is staged and framed by the daughter herself might lead to the conclusion that the mother's redemption, her transformation from victim to active agent or even to sainthood, is possible only through the eyes of her daughter. Or perhaps the mother becomes a superwoman outside of the domestic realm, leading all kinds of social and sexual victories. Onwurah's film does not take either path, both paths of least psychic resistance. She makes no such grandiose assumptions about or demands on her mother or herself. The strength of the film lies in its groundedness in the difficult mundane victories of the everyday and in the daughter's painstakingly realized wins and losses toward maturity. The film's early scenes reveal some of the sources of her mother's sorrows, through the mother's and the daughter's voiced and unvoiced stories. The daughter does not judge or devalue; she enacts a testimony that is brought to recog-

nition through Madge's staged reliving of memories. Through the difficult and tenuous act of remembering, she listens to her mother's stories.
This listening forms a bridge between them, so that the mother's memories can be heard again, recounted and taken into account. The film thus
gives Madge one of the deepest forms of respect: the recognition and
translation of her maternal joys and sacrifices.

Onwurah also recognizes the insidious trap of devaluation in which
her mother is caught and how motherhood for Madge is paradoxically if
not perversely empowering. For example, a scene that follows soon after
the series of hospital shots figures Madge at the playground watching her
children with pride. Yet through her gestures and looks, we are made
stingingly aware that a nearby man who plays with his dog does not notice her, and that this is deeply hurting. We hear her voice-over: "Men
belonged to another life. Children were my shield, protecting me from
rejection and disgust, but most of all, protecting me from pity." These are
her critical reflections on how she both resists and gives in to male-inflected expectations of female beauty. Through the everyday labors of a
strong and loving woman, we are made aware that cultural limits are ex-
ceedingly difficult to cast off. And in one of the film's most wrenching
admissions, Madge says, "Somewhere between the rheumatism and the
mastectomy, I had been muted." However the crucial difference between
inevitable victimhood and moving beyond limits is in the way the mother's stories are told. Hearing Madge's own voice and having her actual
presence in *The Body Beautiful* cuts through generations of encoded devaluation of women's/mothers' supposed passivity and acquiescence. The
film's construction of ruptures in these stereotypical limitations is especially effective in a scene toward the film's ending in which the camera
moves slowly around the walls of what looks like Madge's bedroom or
study, as she takes a journal from the shelf and writes in it. We hear her
voice-over: "But my life, as I had defined it, was full. I had dignity. I lived
my life and my children lived theirs." Madge views herself through an
honest and stark perspective in which both her vulnerabilities and her
independence are expressed with the same solidity and studied care that
her body conveys. Onwurah's tribute to her mother is at once the daughter's story about her mother and Madge's own account of her womanhood. Thus, this tale of alterity is partly about maternal sacrifice yet it
does not rest its case solely on "the mother's lack of selfhood."

Alterity in Levinas's conception of identity is based on the giving up of
the self in order to give to another. Interestingly, he also invests the one
who needs with a position of strength in his/her vulnerability. According
to Levinas, the vulnerable one holds the promise of calling for another's
response. Through what he calls the other's "appeal," a forceful demand
is made on the giver to open the tense and implacable space between self

and other.⁴ In mother-child relations, the child would seem to be the one in need. However, if we take mother-child relations into the realm of other human relationship possibilities, the notion of giving and care can be extended to other crucial interconnections. If we stay within the mother-child bond and reverse the usual expenditure of care and energy from mother to child, a new form of the maternal being might arise. If we envision the mother who is able to relinquish some of her burdens and responsibilities and who can ask to be cared for, a revolutionary notion of love and giving might be born.

A crucial scene in *The Body Beautiful* insinuates such a possibility of the mother's need transformed into the strength of interdependence. Madge's children wash and rinse their mother's hair, a chore turned into a luxury because Madge can no longer endure the pain of undertaking this herself. This is an intensely brave and tender scene, mixed with bitter-sweet humor as the children use too much water and too much force. They are remarkably comfortable together in their naked bodies. A scene of such stark, unsentimentalized, and everyday beauty among a mother and her child(ren) is rare in filmmaking, let alone in the larger realm of visual representation.⁵ Beauty here is not defined by any false notion of objectivity framed by a male-inflected projection of his desires. Beauty in this scene is the metaphor of the mother giving her children the gift of caring for her and the example of caring for others, a form of love that offers a different foundation for relationship other than the phallic, indi-vidualistic humanism that has shaped too many cultural paradigms.

This scene of extraordinary intimacy, naturalness, and ease stands in stark contrast with a closely following one in which Onwurah has staged a tense scenario full of pathos picturing Madge and her daughter in a sauna with several other women of mixed ages. The daughter has repeat-edly tried to convince her mother not to be "a prude" and to partake of the pleasures of a sauna. Madge finally gives in. In close-up scenes of their faces, mother and daughter exchange looks of delight as each of them moves into her own experience. Madge's relaxation and abandon leads to her loosening grip on her towel, exposing her breasts and the site of her mastectomy. The camera stays fixed on Madge's body and face for some time until she awakes and becomes aware of her disclosure, her daugh-ter's concern for her and the discomfort this sight causes the other women as they look and then look away. Depending on our own experiences and those of the women we love, this scene asks the demanding question whether we, too, look away. The daughter's voice-over reinforces this question through her own revelation: "I remember that day in the sauna was the first time I saw my mother as a woman. I was forced to see her as others might." Indeed, the camera's slow, semicircular movement start-ing from Madge and circulating around the enclosed space of the sauna leaves open the suggestion of the film viewer's positionality. Such an open-ended use of the filmic framing refuses any singular or fixed gaze, which opens up the possibility that we, as spectators, not only look at Madge, we might be brought into an enactment of empathy with her and move into our own self-reflection. That we are brought so powerfully into this relay of identifications is all the more remarkable when we remember that this scene is sustained through the tensions between raw yet weathered vulnerability and the filter of acting that Madge brings to it through her own lived experiences. Through this critical perspective, Onwurah's challenging film provokes and proposes new ways of looking, feeling, and knowing.

The sauna scene conveys a strong realism, although it is filtered by the dreamy and haunting music that creates a softness and a harboring for the harshness of this film passage. The following lovemaking scene between Madge and her imagined lover is also a complex combination of realism and fantasy, although its elaborative staging makes it appear to weigh more in the realm of illusion. These two tense scenes are bridged by a moment of release in which mother and daughter are no longer the focus. We follow their gazes as they enjoy a warm drink together and watch a group of young men playing pool. Madge's gaze is met and returned by one of them, and it is through his desiring look that this everyday scene is transformed into the heightened scene of lovemaking. Gauzy curtains and oversized candles make the setting appear melodramatic and baroque. These trite and overplayed symbols of romance seem to be staged as a parallel to what might initially appear as an awkward and unlikely pair of lovers. However, as they embrace each other with passion and tenderness, the scene becomes remarkably believable and normalized. Indeed, as Madge's voice-over recounts her desire, "I wanted him for his very ordinariness, his outrageous normality." As the viewer hears Madge's words, the camera focuses first on her white hand on his dark back, and then on his hand on her back. The contrast of their skin is an encompassing metaphor for the interplay and merging of differences at the core of the film. As the young black man brings her pleasure and caresses her breast, the scene achieves an emotional depth and intimacy that is almost unbearable. This scene's clichéd setting verging on kitsch allows a foil for its intensity, bringing to the surface the taboo of picturing both a woman's mastectomy and the forbidden fantasy of a mother's sexuality.

This critical scene is then interrupted by the daughter's scream/plea that I described at the opening of this essay, a transition that moves the viewer to the final scene of the mother's and daughter's embrace. The camera travels around the couple and slowly shifts to a view from above, then it moves in closer. The filmic structure allows the viewer memories of intimate passages from one's self to another and back to the self, through the sameness of bodies and then through their inevitable distances and visual differences. The film as a whole elaborates the healing force of intersubjectivities; that is, the complex places between one subject and the other. It courageously opens up places of merging and sameness, which in any intimate relation, we know, are often sharply broken by tensions and confusions between where one person's sense of self begins and where it is projected onto and sometimes trampled upon by the other lover or the mother. In the psychic arena where boundaries between mother and children, especially a daughter, always fluctuate between intense intimacy and painful separation as well as the possibilities of compromise, interracial subjectivities dramatize the heightened emotional and political stakes in maternal relations of sameness and difference. Feminist legal scholar Patricia J. Williams uses the mother/child paradigm as a metaphor for imagining new cultural relations of alterity in an image that is strikingly close to Onwurah's in the closing scene of *The Body Beautiful:*

> The image of a white woman suckling a black child; the image of a black child sucking for its life from the bosom of a white woman. The utter interdependence of such an image; the selflessness, the merging it implies; the giving up of boundary; the encompassing of other within the self; the unbounded generosity, the interconnectedness of such an image. Such a picture says that there is no difference.[6]

The Body Beautiful is remarkable for the daughter's ability to face her mother's different body, her mother's redefined self-image as well as her joyous and difficult life experiences. It magnificently articulates a visual representation of how the mother's love is intertwined and transformed into the daughter's giving to her. By strategically displacing traditional concepts of feminine beauty and reembracing maternal qualities of caring, empathy, and sacrifice, the film grants women the gift of what is normally taken for granted. Indeed, *The Body Beautiful* focuses on intersubjectivities that recognize the material realities as well as the intimate desires of the daughter and the mother. The film is so poignant and provocative for its power to construct images that represent the difficult psychic spaces of fear, intimacy, and love between the daughter/filmmaker Ngozi Onwurah and her mother Madge Onwurah. The distances and the intense bonds they share are echoed through the film's eventual merging of their dichotomies between white/black, aging/ripe, and mother/child. *The Body Beautiful* powerfully revisions the maternal body by loving in difference.

NOTES

1. I would like to thank Nancy Braver for first bringing this groundbreaking film to my attention. *The Body Beautiful* is available through Women Make Movies in New York City. Some of the film's contributors include Peter Collis, director of photography; Liz Webber, editor; Richard Gray, sound; Anthony Quigley and Johnathon Hirst, original music score.

2. For Onwurah's different focus on the experience of children of mixed racial heritage and the harassment they face, see her film *Coffee Colored Children* (1988), also available through Women Make Movies.

3. Elizabeth Grosz, *Sexual Subversions: Three French Feminists* (Sydney: Allen & Unwin, 1989), xvii.

4. Among the works of Emmanuel Levinas, see especially *Totality and Infinity: An Essay on Exteriority*, Alphonso Lingis trans. (The Hague: Nijhoff, 1979).

5. Another rare example of a film that gives full range to the spaces of maternal thinking and transformation is Laura Mulvey and Peter Wollen's *The Riddle of the Sphinx* (1976). This complex and lovely film endows the mother with the active stance of looking. The camera's slow, sensuous caressing and often circular trajectories within the domestic and social spaces of the kitchen and the child's room project a different guiding system for the gaze. I am also thinking of the many films by Trinh T. Minh-Ha, which, although they do not focus on the maternal image, redefine tenderness, intersubjectivity, and sentimentality in intriguing and important ways.

6. Patricia J. Williams, "On Being the Object of Property," *Signs* 14, no. 1 (Autumn 1988): 15.

Index

About the Contributors

Sharon M. Abbey, Ed.D., is an assistant professor of education at Brock University, where she teaches courses in social studies and women's studies, as well as a founding member of the Center on Collaborative Research. Previously, she spent twenty years as an elementary school teacher, curriculum consultant, and school principal. She received the FWTAO Ruby Kinkaid Doctoral Studies Award and the University President's Award for coordinating a Speakers' Series on Eating Disorders and Body Image. Currently, Dr. Abbey is the president of the Canadian Association for Studies on Women in Education, the book review editor for *Teaching Education* and a member of the board of directors for the National Foundation for Eating Disorders. She is the coeditor of the recently published book *Redefining Motherhood: Changing Identities and Patterns.*

Christina Baker was born in Gastonia, North Carolina, in 1939. She is a professor of English at University College in Bangor, Maine. She received her B.A. from Furman University in 1961, her MAT from Duke University in 1962, and her Ph.D. in American studies and women's studies from the Union Institute in 1991. Recipient of the 1992 Presidential Outstanding Teacher Award at the University of Maine, she is the author of *In a Generous Spirit: A First-Person Biography of Myra Page* (University of Illinois Press, 1996) and coauthor, with her daughter Christina Baker Kline, of *The Conversation Begins: Mothers and Daughters Talk about Living Feminism* (Bantam, 1996). Mother of four daughters and grandmother of four grandsons, she is currently serving her second term as representative in the Maine State Legislature.

Janet Burstein is professor of English at Drew University where she teaches Victorian literature and women's literature as well as Jewish-American literature. She has published in all three fields. Her most recent publications include essays on Jewish women writers in Joyce Antler's *Taking Back: Images of Jewish Women in American Popular Culture,* in Judith

297

Baskin's *Women of the Word: Jewish Women and Jewish Writing,* and in the new *Jewish Women in America: An Historical Encyclopedia,* edited by Paula Hyman and Deborah Dash Moore (Routledge, 1997). She has also published a book on American Jewish women writers called *Writing Mothers, Writing Daughters: Tracing the Maternal in Stories by American Jewish Women.*

Paula Caplan, Ph.D., is a clinical and research psychologist, actor, and writer of nonfiction books, plays, and screenplays. Her books include *Don't Blame Mother: Mending the Mother-Daughter Relationship; Between Women: Lowering the Barriers; The Myth of Women's Masochism; Lifting a Ton of Feathers: A Woman's Guide to Surviving in the Academic World; You're Smarter Than They Make You Feel: How the Experts Intimidate Us and What We Can Do about It;* and, coauthored with her son, Jeremy B. Caplan, *Thinking Critically about Research on Sex and Gender.* The workshop she most enjoyed teaching was the one she did with her daughter about mother-daughter relationships at the First International Conference on Judaism, Feminism, and Psychology. Her play *Call Me Crazy* won second prize in the 1997 Lewis Playwriting Contest for Women, and two of her plays have been produced Off-Off Broadway at Sage Theatre in New York.

Andrea Doucet is assistant professor in the Department of Sociology and Anthropology at Carleton University. Her publications combine her interests in feminist theory, qualitative research, and caring. Her current research, funded by the Social Sciences and Humanities Research Council of Canada, explores the links between economic restructuring, fatherhood and masculinities. She has three daughters, Vanessa and Hannah and Lilly.

Gillian Dunne is a senior research fellow at the Gender Institute of the London School of Economics and a former senior research associate at the Faculty of Social and Political Sciences, Cambridge University. Her research aims to extend feminist and sociological debates about gender, work, and family life by providing empirically grounded theoretical insights on the experience of nonheterosexual people. For the past three years she has been researching division of labor between lesbian couples with dependant children. She is now studying the different dimensions of gay fatherhood. Gill is the author of *Lesbian Lifestyles: Women's Work and the Politics of Sexuality* (University of Toronto Press, 1997). She can be contacted via electronic mail for further information on research and publications at gdunne@jasmine.u-net.com.

María-José Gámez-Fuentes is a teaching assistant in the Department of Hispanic and Latin American Studies at the University of Nottingham

(U.K.) where she contributes to the undergraduate and postgraduate curriculum on Spanish language, literature, and film studies. She is currently completing her Ph.D. in critical theory and Hispanic studies at the university on the representation of motherhood in post-Franco cinema and women's literature in Spain. Her publications focus on the representation of femininity in contemporary Spanish cinema and in the work of Spanish female writers in the democracy.

Elizabeth Bourque Johnson teaches literature and writing at the University of Minnesota, where she completed her Ph.D., a dissertation on mothers' work. As a poet, she has published in various journals and has won several awards, including an Academy of American Poets Prize. As a nurse, she has written for *Second Opinion,* a journal of medical ethics, and has developed a course in "Writing through Grief." Most of all, she is a mother.

Charlotte Harris, Ed.D., is chair and assistant professor in the Department of Foundations and Secondary Education at Georgia College and State University (GC&SU) in Milledgeville. Formerly a teacher of English in Prince George's County, Maryland, she currently coordinates GC& SU's master of arts in teaching program in secondary education. Her research interests are in the area of black feminist thought, education feminism, teacher education, multicultural education, and narrative inquiry.

Astrid Henry is a Ph.D. candidate in the modern studies concentration of the English Department at the University of Wisconsin–Milwaukee, where she teaches courses in women's studies, gay and lesbian studies, and literature. She is currently completing a dissertation that examines the relationships between various strands of 1990s and 1970s feminisms, including popular feminisms, black feminisms, and queer feminisms.

Joonok Huh is a professor of English and women's studies. She is currently working on a book on mothers and daughters in Asian-American literature. She teaches Asian-American literature, American literature, Asian literature, and women's literature. She is constantly amazed to see her daughter growing up to be her own person.

Andrea Liss is the contemporary-art historian/cultural theorist in the visual and performing arts program at California State University, San Marcos. She recently published *Trespassing through Shadows: Memory, Photography and the Holocaust* (University of Minnesota Press, 1998) and is working on a book about feminist motherhood and contemporary representation.

Naomi Lowinsky, Ph.D., is a Jungian analyst, a member of the San Francisco Jung Institute, a poet, and poetry and fiction editor for *Psychological Perspectives*. Her book, *The Motherline: Every Woman's Journey to Find Her Female Roots*, was published by Putnam in 1992. She has a private practice in Berkeley, California. She has grown children and stepchildren, and grandchildren.

Susan MacCallum-Whitcomb holds a Ph.D. in English from the University of New Brunswick and has been granted awards by the University of Toronto, the University of New Brunswick, and the Social Science and Humanities Research Council of Canada. She teaches American literature at the University of New Brunswick (Saint John). Dr. MacCallum-Whitcomb's special field is contemporary American poetry, and her current area of research is American maternity literature. Her most recent work is *"This Giving Birth, This Glistening Verb": Pregnancy and Childbirth in Women's Literature*, a critical anthology, coedited by Dr. Julie Tharp (Bowling Green State University's Popular Press, 2000). She is a feminist activist and the mother of two young children.

Andrea O'Reilly, Ph.D., is an assistant professor in the School of Women's Studies at York University where she teaches courses on Toni Morrison, motherhood, and mothers and daughters. She has presented her research at numerous international conferences and authored more than a dozen articles and chapters on these topics. She is coeditor of *Redefining Motherhood: Changing Identities and Patterns* (Second Story Press, 1998); *Mothers and Daughters: Connection, Empowerment and Transformation* (Rowman & Littlefield, 1999); and the special twentieth anniversary issue of *Canadian Woman Studies* (Fall 1998) on mothers and daughters. She is the author of *Toni Morrison on Motherhood* (Ohio State University Press, forthcoming). She is currently editing *Mothers and Sons: Feminist Perspectives*. She was coordinator of the first international conferences on "Mothers and Daughters" (1997) and "Mothers and Sons" (1998) sponsored by the Center for Feminist Research at York University. In addition, she was coordinator of the international conference on "Toni Morrison's *Paradise*," February 1999. O'Reilly is founding president of the Association for Research on Mothering (ARM). In 1998 she received the "University Wide" Teaching Award at York University. She has conducted numerous community workshops on motherhood, mothers and daughters, and mothers and sons and has been interviewed widely on these topics. Andrea and her common-law spouse of sixteen years are the parents of a fourteen-year-old son and two daughters, ages nine and twelve.

Deborah Orr is a philosopher with a specialty in Wittgenstein and an interest in issues of epistemology, gender, and ethics. She teaches gender and ethics courses for the Division of Humanities at York University.

Ivy Schweitzer is associate professor of American literature at Dartmouth College, where she also teaches in the women's studies and comparative literature programs. Her first book, *The Work of Self-Representation*, is a feminist analysis of colonial New England poetry. Currently, she is finishing a study of narratives of women's interracial friendships entitled "Milk Sisters" and coediting an anthology of early American literatures for Blackwell. For the past several years, she has been teaching a course titled "The Literature and Psychology of Mothers and Daughters."

Cath Stowers is completing her D.Phil. on the trope of the journey in contemporary women's writing at the Center for Women's Studies, University of York, United Kingdom. Her specialties include feminist literary theory, French feminism, postcolonial women's writing and theory, and lesbian fiction and theory. She also writes fiction. She instigated the York Women's Writing Collective and runs the International Network on Contemporary Women's Writing, and she has taught widely in adult education and university departments. Her publications include "Journeying with Jeanette: Transgressive Travels in Winterson's Fiction," in *(Hetero)-Sexual Politics,* ed. Mary Maynard and June Purvis (Taylor & Francis, 1994); "Detonating the Lesbian Body: 'Written on the Body as Lesbian Text,'" in *"I'm Telling You Stories": Jeanette Winterson and the Politics of Reading,* ed. Helena Grice and Tim Woods (Rodopi, 1998); and "The Seductions of Travel: Problematics and Possibilities in Two Post-Colonial Women's Texts," in *Diegesis: Journal of the Association for Research in Popular Fictions,* ed. Nicola King (1998). She is currently coediting a collection of essays on contemporary women's writing (forthcoming).

Barbara Turnage received both her bachelor's of science in social work (1982) and master's of social work (1987) from the University of Nebraska at Omaha. Ms. Turnage earned her Ph.D. in 1998 in social work at Tulane University's School of Social Work, where she was awarded a four-year Regent's Fellowship. Her dissertation topic addressed adolescent African-American females' self-esteem development. A practitioner and an academician, Ms. Turnage has presented and participated in regional, national, and international conferences. Currently she teaches social work at Arkansas State University. Ms. Turnage plans to direct her future research toward Africans throughout the diaspora. She is currently interested in five areas of research: (1) differentiating cultural determinants of domestic violence, (2) understanding how parenting styles affect spiritual and emotional health, (3) exploring the impact language has on self-esteem development, (4) investigating the relationship between frustration and global self-esteem levels, and (5) identifying ways to redirect self-destructive behaviors.

Jeanne Wiley has a Ph.D. in continental philosophy from the University of Louvain in Belgium. She considers herself a "narrative philosopher" and is keenly interested in how stories reflect, shape, and sometimes distort our lived experience. She currently teaches philosophy, religious studies, and women's studies at the College of Saint Rose in Albany, New York.

Sue Marie Wright completed her Ph.D. in 1994 at the University of Oregon. She currently holds a position as assistant professor in the Department of Sociology at Eastern Washington University where she teaches courses on gender and the family. She also serves on the Women's Studies Curriculum Committee at Eastern Washington University and teaches courses for the women's studies program. Dr. Wright's research, however, focuses primarily on children's issues. Besides cross-cultural analysis of the impact of education on girls' status, she is involved in research with children in a variety of American settings, ranging from feminist families to farm families. Current projects include a textbook, *Children and Youth in Society* (Wadsworth, forthcoming), and organization of a children's studies program at Eastern Washington University. When not involved with children's issues in the academic setting, Dr. Wright spends her time enjoying recreational and educational activities with her husband, Rick, and sons, Chris (twenty) and Oliver (eight).